Muslims and Others in Sacred Space

AAR
AMERICAN ACADEMY OF RELIGION

RELIGION, CULTURE, AND HISTORY

SERIES EDITOR
Jacob N. Kinnard, Iliff School of Theology

A Publication Series of
The American Academy of Religion
and
Oxford University Press

ANTI-JUDAISM IN FEMINIST RELIGIOUS WRITINGS
Katharina von Kellenbach

CROSS-CULTURAL CONVERSATION
(Initiation)
Edited by Anindita Niyogi Balslev

ON DECONSTRUCTING LIFE-WORLDS
Buddhism, Christianity, Culture
Robert Magliola

THE GREAT WHITE FLOOD
Racism in Australia
Anne Pattel-Gray

IMAG(IN)ING OTHERNESS
Filmic Visions of Living Together
Edited by S. Brent Plate and David Jasper

CULTURAL OTHERNESS
Correspondence with Richard Rorty, Second Edition
Anindita Niyogi Balslev

FEMINIST POETICS OF THE SACRED
Creative Suspicions
Edited by Frances Devlin-Glass and Lyn McCredden

PARABLES FOR OUR TIME
Rereading New Testament Scholarship after the Holocaust
Tania Oldenhage

MOSES IN AMERICA
The Cultural Uses of Biblical Narrative
Melanie Jane Wright

INTERSECTING PATHWAYS
Modern Jewish Theologians in Conversation with Christianity
Marc A. Krell

ASCETICISM AND ITS CRITICS
Historical Accounts and Comparative Perspectives
Edited by Oliver Freiberger

VIRTUOUS BODIES
The Physical Dimensions of Morality in Buddhist Ethics
Susanne Mrozik

IMAGINING THE FETUS
The Unborn in Myth, Religion, and Culture
Edited by Vanessa R. Sasson and Jane Marie Law

VICTORIAN REFORMATION
The Fight over Idolatry in the Church of England, 1840–1860
Dominic Janes

SCHLEIERMACHER ON RELIGION AND THE NATURAL ORDER
Andrew C. Dole

MUSLIMS AND OTHERS IN SACRED SPACE
Edited by Margaret Cormack

AAR
AMERICAN ACADEMY OF RELIGION

Muslims and Others in Sacred Space

Edited by

MARGARET CORMACK

OXFORD
UNIVERSITY PRESS

OXFORD
UNIVERSITY PRESS

Oxford University Press is a department of the University of Oxford.
It furthers the University's objective of excellence in research,
scholarship, and education by publishing worldwide

Oxford New York
Auckland Cape Town Dar es Salaam Hong Kong Karachi
Kuala Lumpur Madrid Melbourne Mexico City Nairobi
New Delhi Shanghai Taipei Toronto

With offices in
Argentina Austria Brazil Chile Czech Republic France Greece
Guatemala Hungary Italy Japan Poland Portugal Singapore
South Korea Switzerland Thailand Turkey Ukraine Vietnam

Oxford is a registered trade mark of Oxford University Press
in the UK and certain other countries

Published in the United States of America by
Oxford University Press
198 Madison Avenue, New York, New York 10016

Library of Congress Cataloging-in-Publication Data
Muslims and others in sacred space / edited by Margaret Cormack.
p. cm.—(Religion, culture, and history)
Includes index.

ISBN 978-0-19-992504-9 (hardcover : alk. paper)—ISBN 978-0-19-992506-3 (pbk. : alk. paper)
1. Islam—Relations. 2. Islamic shrines. 3. Sacred space. I. Cormack, Margaret.
BP171.M867 2013 297.3'5—dc23
2012006849

1 3 5 7 9 8 6 4 2

Printed in the United States of America
on acid-free paper

Thomas Sizgorich was the inspiration for this volume. A paper of his delivered at the 2006 meeting of the Medieval Academy of America sparked the idea for the conference on shared sacred space held in 2007 from which these essays derive. He was a valued participant at that conference and a cheerful contributor to the volume; his chapter was singled out for unqualified praise by Oxford University Press's readers. His untimely death in January 2011 came as a shock to us all. It was a tragic loss to scholarship, as well as to his family, to whom we express our sympathy. He will be sorely missed. We dedicate this volume to his memory.

Contents

List of Maps and Illustrations

Preface and Acknowledgments

THIS VOLUME ORIGINATED in a conference on "Muslims and Others in Sacred Space" held at the College of Charleston in March 2007 in conjunction with a course on Islam. The object of the conference was to highlight peaceful interactions between Muslims and members of other religious communities at a time when the national news featured only violent ones. The obvious place to look for such interaction is at locations whose perceived power (or that of entities associated with them) could override religious identity. The papers that follow discuss the meaning a variety of sacred times and spaces—graves, caves, churches, festivals, mosques, and monasteries—had for Muslims and members of other communities in the past and present. The authors contributing to the volume bring to this question backgrounds in history, religious studies, Islamic studies, Jewish studies, art history, geography, and medical anthropology. Gross, Ross, and Laird base their papers on fieldwork in Tajikistan, Senegal, and the Occupied West Bank, Palestine. Damrel and Laird describe devotional practices in South Asia and Palestine, respectively. Damrel's article discusses criticisms of such practices; the voice of "authority" also appears—only to be ignored—in Laird's and Cuffel's essays. Wolper and Gross illustrate the development of foundational legends that give legitimacy to sacred spaces in Anatolia and Badakhshān, while Ross describes the process of formation of such spaces, and the uses to which they are put, on Senegal's Cape Vert peninsula. The multivalent figure of Khiḍr / Khaḍr discussed in Wolper's essay gives his name to al-Khaḍr, the village visited by Laird. Gender is an issue for the Muslim scholars studied by both Cuffel and Damrel. Our lamented colleague Thomas Sizgorich provided a brilliant analysis of the ways in which monastic space provided the setting for Christian and Muslim literary fantasies about the relationship between the two religions. Peter Gottschalk has contributed a theoretical introduction that considers the nature of sacrality and the many ways it appears in the material examined.

I thank all who contributed to the success of the original conference: Elise Jorgens, Provost of the College of Charleston, for financial support; the Jewish Studies Program for allowing us to use the best lecture space on campus; Juliann Fowler for helping with the technology; Mrs. Zinn for her wonderful baklava; and the readers of Oxford University Press whose comments improved the volume. The authors have all contributed much more than a chapter, helping me in various ways to craft a volume dealing with areas outside my field of expertise. This has truly been a communal project. Eric Ross, in particular, not only created the maps for the volume but also read the entire text several times.

We hope the resultant essays will be as interesting and thought-provoking to other students and readers as they were to us and to the original audience.

Margaret Cormack

Contributors

Margaret Cormack is Professor of Religious Studies at the College of Charleston, SC. Her area of expertise is medieval Scandinavia, but she has a wide-ranging interest in the cult of saints. She is author of *The Saints in Iceland: Their Veneration from the Conversion to* 1400 (1994) and has edited *Sacrificing the Self: Perspectives on Martyrdom and Religion* (2002) and *Saints and Their Cults Around the Atlantic* (2007). She is working on an interactive on-line database of saints' cults.

Alexandra Cuffel is Professor of Jewish Studies at the Centrum für Religionswissenschaftliche Studien at Ruhr Universität, Bochum. She is completing a monograph, *Shared Saints and Festivals among Jews, Christians, and Muslims in the Medieval Mediterranean* (forthcoming), is the author of *Gendering Disgust in Medieval Religious Polemic* (2007) and coeditor of *Religion, Gender, and Culture in the Pre-modern World* (2007).

David Damrel is Associate Professor of Religion at the University of South Carolina Upstate. A specialist in Islamic mysticism in South Asia, he is also a research associate connected with the Oxford Centre for Islamic Studies project, *An Atlas of the Social and Intellectual History of Muslims in India*. A Fulbright scholar in Indonesia in 2008, his current research addresses sacred space in east Java as well as Latino/Latina conversion to Islam in the United States.

Peter Gottschalk is Professor of Religion at Wesleyan University. He is the author of *Beyond Hindu and Muslim: Multiple Identities in Narratives from Village India* (2000) and *Religion, Science, and Empire: Classifying British India* (2012), coauthor of *Islamophobia: Making Muslims the Enemy* (2007), and coeditor of *Engaging South Asian Religions: Boundaries, Appropriations and Resistances* (2011). Peter has also codesigned the interactive website "A Virtual Village" (virtualvillage.wesleyan.edu).

Jo-Ann Gross is Professor of Middle Eastern and Central Eurasian History at The College of New Jersey. Her research focuses on early modern Iran and Central Asia, with an emphasis on the social history of Sufism, Islamic shrines, and hagiographic narrative traditions. She has published widely on aspects of Sufism in Central Asia and the role of the Naqshbandi Sufi order. Her publications include *The Letters of Khwaja 'Ubayd Allah Ahrar and His Associates*, co-authored with Asom Urunbaev (2002), and her edited book, *Muslims in Central Asia: Expressions of Identity and Change* (1992). Recent publications include her guest-edited volume of the *Journal of Persianate Studies* on "The Pamir," and she is currently writing a monograph entitled *Muslim Shrines and Spiritual Culture in the Perso-Islamic World*, under contract with I.B. Taurus, International Library of Iranian Studies.

Lance Laird, Th.D., is Assistant Professor of Family Medicine and Assistant Director of the Master's Program in Medical Anthropology and Cross-Cultural Practice at Boston University School of Medicine. He has published articles on Palestinian biblical interpretation, religion and public health, the healthcare and chaplaincy needs of Muslim patients, as well as the role of charity clinics and Muslim physicians in elaborating American Muslim identities. Laird is also Assistant Director of the Boston Healing Landscape Project, an institute for the study of religions, cultures, medicines, and healing (www.bu.edu/bhlp).

Eric Ross is a cultural and urban geographer. He is Associate Professor of geography at Al Akhawayn University in Ifrane, Morocco. Ross has conducted research on the role of Sufi orders in contemporary urbanization in Senegal, published as *Sufi City: Urban Design and Archetypes in Touba* (2006). He also studies cultural heritage, tourism, and urban planning in Morocco, and contributed to a multidisciplinary study of the impacts of tourism in the historic port city of Essaouira (*Assessing Tourism in Essaouira*, 2002).

Thomas Sizgorich was Associate Professor of History at UC Irvine. He had published numerous articles on Islam in Late Antiquity, as well as the *Violence and Belief in Late Antiquity: Militant Devotion in Christianity and Islam* (2008). A valued teacher and colleague, his career was cut short by his untimely death in January 2011. His wife and colleagues are working on publication of a monograph treating early Islamic ideas of empire and holy war that he had nearly finished at the time of his death. We thank his wife Nancy McLoughlin for permitting publication of his contribution to this volume.

Ethel Sara Wolper is Associate Professor of History at the University of New Hampshire. She is the author of *Cities and Saints: Sufism and the Transformation of Urban Space in Medieval Anatolia* (2003). She wrote the entry on "Islamic Art" in *The Art Museum* (2011) and has published a series of articles on the legendary Muslim saint Khiḍr.

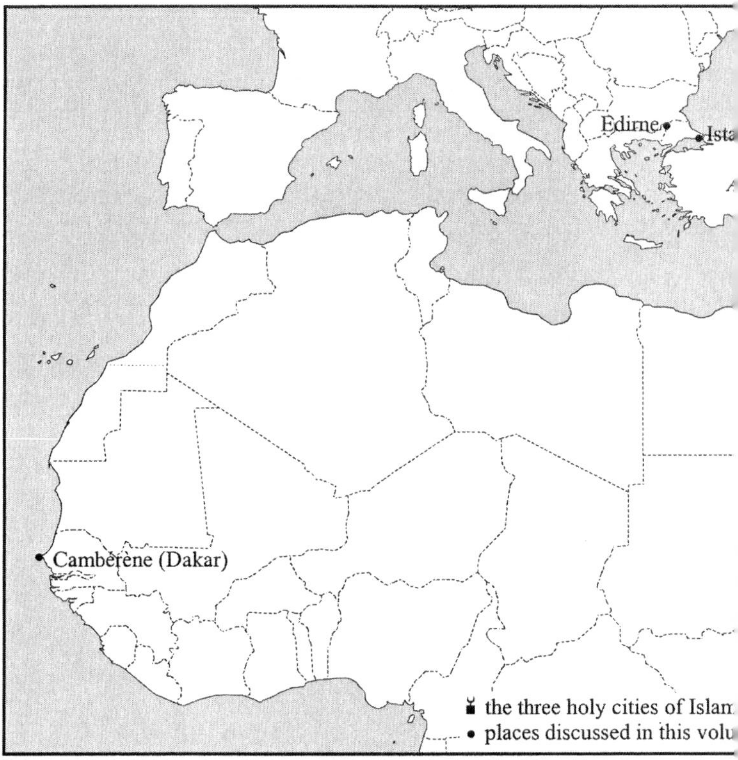
Edirne
Ista
Cambérène (Dakar)
the three holy cities of Islam
places discussed in this volu

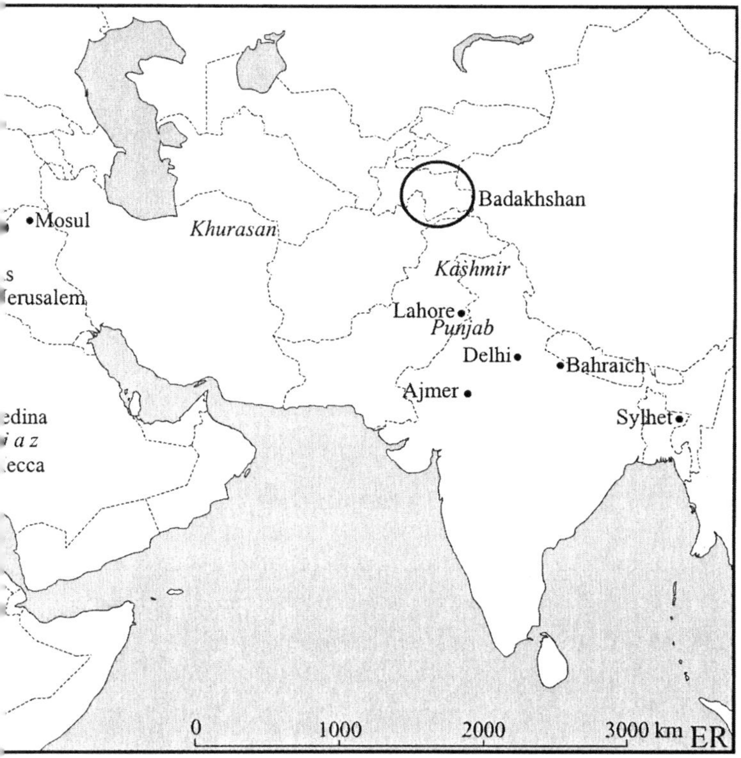
Badakhshan
Mosul
Khurasan
Kashmir
Lahore
Punjab
Delhi
Bahraich
Ajmer
Sylhet
0
1000
2000
3000 km
ER

Muslims and Others in Sacred Space

Introduction

Peter Gottschalk

THIS IMPORTANT COLLECTION of essays offers a broad set of examples that demonstrate how significantly Islamic practices and beliefs vary among Muslim communities and how convergent they can be with Christian and Hindu ones. Comparison of these compelling cases suggests important thematic threads, none so important perhaps as the notion of sacrality. Both its centrality here and the scholarly debate regarding its usefulness suggests that we should unpack this term somewhat and explore its use in the following chapters. This analysis borrows in part from the work of Jonathan Z. Smith, a historian of religion who has critiqued and built on previous understandings of "the sacred" in the context of his scholarship on ritual. My approach borrows Smith's portrayal of sacrality as a socially determined condition that, for purposes of ritual, often finds expression in specific places, which might also be imbricated with economic and political networks of exchange and power. I will endeavor to complement Smith's approach by emphasizing more than he does the importance of narrative, the role of multiple identities, and the difference between sacrality associated with power and sacrality associated with reverence.

Many of the collection's authors have figured the sacred into their declared effort to "map" the contours of the cultural, social, and/or political landscapes on which the religious phenomena in which they are interested become manifest; some even include maps illustrating the localities involved. Since the Renaissance, Westerners (among others) have tended to see cartography as the most empirical and trustworthy of sciences. Maps popularly seem to be transparent representations of reality upon which many daily rely, whether navigating a mass transit system, using their car-mounted GPS, or following online directions to a friend's home. But maps, like all representations, condense and abstract reality, reducing people's perceptions of it to a familiar set of symbols and categories that help us order our worlds. As Smith has refashioned Alfred Korzybski's words, "Maps are not territory, but maps are all we have."[1]

Among the intellectual maps upon which scholars of religion have relied, the category of "the sacred" features fairly prominently. It serves to describe objects, people, places, and superhuman agents charged with a power, a quality, or an essence set apart from its opposite, "the profane." Not surprisingly—given the history of the nonsectarian study of religion—the term derives from Western religious history. A Latin term, it originally referred to the space within an ancient Roman temple that stood apart from the facing forecourt, in which things became *profanum* once they had been "brought out" of the *sanctum*.[2] By the time the term "sacred" entered English, it first referred adjectively to the Eucharist of the Roman Catholic Church. The word did not become a noun—that is, it did not refer to a substantive object—until quite late in its history, the seventeenth century.[3] Smith argues against sociologist Émile Durkheim and historian of religion Mircea Eliade, who described "the sacred" as though it was a substantive object. Instead, he emphasizes the relational quality of sacrality, denoting how uses of the term occur as a transitive category in relation to the profane: "They serve as maps and labels, not substances; they are distinctions of office, indices of difference."[4]

The following essays demonstrate just how broad and complicated a category "the sacred" can be. "Sacred place" might refer to a site associated either with a revered person, a miraculous event, or superhuman power. Similarly, "saint" for an Anglophone is a category that may include a *wali* (friend of god), *pir* (master), or Sufi among Muslims, as well as a virtuous person associated with miracles among Christians or any number of exemplary figures among Hindus. To add to the complexity, the English terms "sacred" and "saint" also have various antonyms. These range from terms denoting their opposite (e.g., "desecrated" and "sinner") to those communicating a normative absence of the quality that defines them (e.g., "profane" and "common"). By detailing some of these comparative distinctions in light of the examples provided by the volume's authors, this introduction attempts to offer a complement to their fascinating descriptions. In doing so, I hope to demonstrate how these essays challenge straightforward binaries like "sacred and profane," teasing out the multiple dimensions of these terms as they find historical expression in particular cultural, religious, political, and economic circumstances.

The challenges of translating indigenous terms into concepts familiar to a nonindigenous audience is readily apparent when considering an Arabic

Islamic term that would first appear nearly identical to "sacred." The association of *haram* with both the religious and the forbidden would seem similar to certain associations Anglophones make with sacrality. So, for instance, many Muslims refer to the Ka'ba as *masjid al-haram* ("the sacred mosque") and the mosque atop the Temple Mount in Jerusalem as *al-haram al-sharif* ("the noble sanctuary"). Indeed, many Muslims consider part of every mosque *haram*, a place in which certain everyday practices are forbidden (e.g., the wearing of shoes and baring of heads).[5] But the binary comprised of *haram* and its opposite *halal* ("released") cuts in a different direction than that of "sacred and profane." When an animal is sacrificed for one of the major festivals, the slaughter must be done in a manner that makes the sacrificial meal *halal*. To complicate matters further, *haram* as an adjective exists within this binary yet also stands in a fivefold juridical distinction between actions that are obligatory, preferred, neutral, discouraged, and forbidden. Of course, not all Muslims rely on these terms, but their tempting equivalency—yet inexact match with "sacred" and "profane"—demonstrates the obvious challenges in translation. To make matters worse, there is also the vast linguistic divergence among Muslim communities to consider even in reference to the same term. Indeed, when they say *mazar*, north Indian Muslims refer to any tomb, while South African Muslims mean only a Sufi's tomb.[6]

Yet translate we must, if only *because* of the diversity of terms used among Muslims. But crafting larger categories such as "sacred" becomes even more important when endeavoring to compare different religious traditions, a condition particularly obvious in these collected essays. Hindu temples; Christian churches, monasteries, and gravesites; and Muslim mosques, tombs, shrines, and *dhikr* (devotional remembrance) grounds all figure into the religious, social, and political topographies depicted here along with imperial capitals, new-founded villages, national territories, houses, and vineyards. Some of these become sacred, some lose their sacrality, some are more sacred in some people's eyes than others, and some never attain any such status. Some locations have zones more sacred than others (witness the concentric areas of the ancient Jewish Jerusalem temple with its increasingly exclusive zones leading to the "holy of holies," YHWH's earthly throne). Examples persistently demonstrate Smith's argument that sacrality never escapes its temporalized status as the difference that difference makes, despite claims to the contrary made by some devotees and practitioners. Those who assert that the sacred necessarily and entirely removes an object, place, or person from the profane fail to understand how its recognition as sacred relies on a juxtaposition with the nonsacred.

But while acknowledging this indigenous recognition of specialness, we need to avoid any simple equivalencies that might suggest that "the sacred" is a one-size-fits-all kind of category. The manner in which a mosque is *haram* for Muslims is unlikely to be exactly the same as the *shuddh* quality of a temple for Hindus. Differences become manifest in the most unfortunate manner when knowledgeable antagonists in one community seek to desecrate (i.e., forcefully desacralize) a site, person, or object in another. Hence Hindus and Muslims have flung dead pigs and cows, respectively, into the mosques and temples of their opponents with calculated aggression, while leftists exhumed and displayed the corpses of nuns, priests, and saints during the Spanish Civil War.[7] What might upset one community might barely ruffle another, while what might desecrate one site might be considered harmless in another.

Perhaps one way to nuance the notion of sacred among the sites described in this volume is by differentiating between "energized" and "nonenergized" places. As opposed to the sacrality associated with the latter because they serve as sites of devotion to a superhuman agent, we can perhaps describe a place as energized when devotees recognize it as emitting a self-actualized power, either because of the location itself or some object present there. Muslims often speak of *baraka*, a divine blessing commonly associated with the tombs of Sufis and figures such as Khiḍr/Khaḍr. For instance, as David Damrel notes in his discussion of South Asian Sufi shrines, devotees of Shaykh Nizam al-din Awliya visit his tomb in Delhi to access the emitted *baraka* and ask for his intervention or *shifa'a*. In my own research in the region, I have noted how Muslims will as likely describe this power as *shakti*—a Sanskrit-derived term associated with divine energies—as Hindus will say *baraka*. In a particularly startling example of the power a figure embedded in (a) place broadcasts, Jo-Ann Gross in her essay on Central Eurasian shrines and the Isma'ili imamate describes how Muhammad spoke from his Medina grave to Shah Khamosh. This, in turn, triggered this Isma'ili pilgrim's encounter with the long-dead Sufi Junayd al-Baghdadi as he circumambulated the Ka'ba. As this demonstrates, certain energized places are understood to manifest their powers through miracles occurring either spontaneously or through ritual.

Smith concisely explains, "Ritual is, first and foremost, a mode of paying attention. It is a process for marking interest."[8] The rituals that occur at energized places mark the devotee's interest in obtaining some result, usually by tapping into the power being discharged. In the economy of such sites, this attention (complemented perhaps by donations of money, food, or other items) is exchanged for objects that through their proximity to the source of the power absorb some residual energy that can be borne away. These objects—including dust, wash water, and oil—serve as media that allow the power to be transferred to either the devotee or someone else. As attested by examples from Bangladesh and Palestine, some devotees make vows at such places, offering the collateral of future sacrifice to secure a contemporary outcome.

In contrast with these energized sites are nonenergized places that attain a degree of sanctity through what might best be described as reverence. Many of the authors describe various mosques, among other sites, as sacred to the communities they study without the suggestion that these places are perceived to radiate power. Smith's observation that "place directs attention" is perhaps all that makes nonenergized places sacred: They primarily serve the individual and community's efforts to direct attention toward a superhuman agent. The design of mosques that allows lines of Muslims to pray side-by-side while oriented toward the Kaʿba intends to uniformly direct the attention of the *umma* (community of all Muslims) to Allah. In contrast with this transnational unidirectionality (or, rather, monopolarity), shrines built around energized sites are usually constructed so as to lead visitors to a proximate encounter with some relic (e.g., a Sufi's physical remains or personal items) associated with whoever or whatever provides the connection to power. This differentiation between energized and nonenergized sites does not attempt a universal distinction: Undoubtedly some Sufi tombs have no power associated with them while some mosques might. Instead, it endeavors to offer a way of recognizing the different perceptions by which people understand sites and which shape their engagement of them.

The difference between energized and nonenergized places helps explain the suspicion and protestation of some Muslims regarding the former. In contrast with the Quran- and Hadith-prescribed practice of praying to Allah in mosques, accessing power through alternative sites suggests one needs an intermediary to reach god (a forbidden notion in most Islamic theologies) or, far more troubling for many Muslims, that other agents offer divine power (which smacks of *shirk*, associating someone else with god, the worst of sins in the view of many). The juxtaposition between energized and nonenergized sacred places becomes starkest perhaps in the example given by Ethel Sara Wolper of a column in an Anatolian mosque—associated with the prophet-saint Khiḍr—that some approach for remedies to their children's illnesses. Of course, for the *ʿulama* who may profit from their status as orthoprax and orthodox authorities, any realignment of power that circumvents their policed avenues of religiosity represents a threat to their status. Certainly the Wahhabis had such concerns, among others, when they destroyed Arabia's tombs that memorialized Sufis and Muhammad's companions, although grave visitation (*ziyara*) had long been recognized as conducive for reflection and unmediated prayer to Allah. However, it would be simplistic to reduce all such reform-minded efforts by Salafi, Deobandi, and Tablighi activists to politically driven motivations: Many reflect, in part, a tension found throughout Islam and Christianity between theological ideals of a transcendent, universal deity and popular desires for immanent, local agency.

Perhaps another manifestation of the difference between energized and nonenergized locations can be found in divergent understandings of purity. These are suggested by Eric Ross's description of various places associated with the Layenne order in Senegal. In terms of the establishment of the original settlement by the group's founder in the nineteenth century—a site still considered sacred today despite the group's resettlement elsewhere—Ross notes how its location miraculously appeared after the cleansing of the founder's house by an unusually high tide. In contrast, the Friday mosque and *dhikr* recitation space in the community's new settlement do not appear to have any original or self-generating purity, and their sacred status relies on conditions of ritual cleaning and shoe removal. Similarly, Wolper notes that Sultan Mehmet, after conquering Constantinople, had the Hagia Sophia ritually cleaned before allowing Islamic prayers to be performed there.[9]

Among his critiques of older scholarly models for sacrality, Smith notes how scholars often fixated on the notion of "the center," seeking sacred mountains and holy cities as *axis mundi* around which cosmogonic sacrality revolves. However, as the above discussion suggests, many sites may be considered in some manner sacred without the conceit of centrality. While the two Layenne settlements described by Ross physically center on mosques, such is hardly the rule for all Muslim-majority cities and villages. Alexandra Cuffel describes how Mediterranean Muslims might have joined Christian processions that moved through, from, or to important urban Christian centers (e.g., the Church of the Resurrection in Jerusalem), but these sites were not necessarily central for participating Muslims. In other instances, Muslim rulers orchestrated Jewish and Christian participation in processions they organized to traverse their capitals.

Smith anticipates this political inflection as he argues that when ritual does involve centers, it is often associated with a ruler's legitimation and the reassertion of social hierarchy. Among urban cultures, some cities serve as ceremonial centers with ritual displays that model exemplary civil space.[10] Cuffel's research reflects this, especially in the responses to moments of crisis she describes. During calamities such as plague and drought, Muslim rulers often directed processions and prayers involving their capitals' entire population and, thus, temporally suspended the hierarchical subjugation of *dhimmis* (non-Muslims) relative to Muslims. The sultan's appropriation of a Sufi robe for one ceremony also collapsed the distinction between temporal power and spiritual status that Sufis often promoted, if only ideally. However, this conflation of political power and religious status in an urban center did not always have such sanguine consequences for the prevailing social order. Repeatedly, conquering groups sought to portray their new political order as the natural successor of the old by appropriating the religious centers associated with the vanquished. Wolper's essay focuses on how this dynamic occurred among the sites associated with Khiḍr throughout Anatolia. Even (and most poignantly) Hagia Sophia—the imperial church that Byzantine emperor Justinian had built on the site of Constantine's church—would be assumed under Khiḍr's powers. Similarly, Wolper notes how Damascus Christians built a cathedral dedicated to John the Baptist atop a site previously dedicated to Jupiter. Later, an Umayyad caliph replaced the cathedral with a mosque while carefully keeping in place the purported relic of John's head.

Whether in an urban or rural setting, the violent, political appropriation of religious space represents an important additional theme in regard to sacrality. Earlier scholarship on South Asia gave particular emphasis to this theme given its preoccupation with Hindu and Muslim antagonisms. Yet, even Aurangzeb's desecrations of Hindu temples have become occasions for challenging simple conclusions. The policies of this, the most intolerant of Mughal emperors, ironically reflect the continuities between Hindu and Muslim rulership by demonstrating two significant qualities of rule, religion, and sacred place in the subcontinent. First, the patronage of principal sacred places had long served as the qualification of a legitimate ruler, no matter what his religious identity. Hence, Aurangzeb could hardly afford to destroy what the subjugated—but always potentially rebellious—population expected him to maintain. Many of the examples of iconoclasm that the emperor's chronicles record have been proven to be spurious, and the occasional construction of mosques atop the devastated temples of conquered Hindu foes (such as in Benares) represent exceptions to his normal policies, which included funding many other temples. Second, far from being an idiosyncratic practice of Muslim leaders, the appropriation and rededication of sacred sites through which the previous ruler had legitimated his rule represents a commonplace Indic articulation of conquest, change, and continuity that Hindu monarchs had practiced against one another for centuries.

Notably, however, Muslim victors appear to have been unwilling to destroy the mosques associated with a Muslim predecessor's reign, thus reflecting a divergence in how Hindu and Muslim leaders expressed their legitimacy through sacred place. Whereas Hindus often legitimated their rule through their dedication to a specific deity whose propitiated presence in an appropriately lavish temple protected the royal dynasty, no specific mosque—even the massive *jama' masjid* (Friday mosque) projects—would serve as the primary expression of the ruler's divine legitimacy.[11] That legitimacy relied instead on founding an Islamic civil and legal order. Although endeavors to do so might include the establishment of religious institutions, overall legitimacy would not be manifest in any particular one. In other words, although both royal temples and imperial mosques may have served as politically associated sacred places, the appropriation or destruction of a temple might represent a dynasty's annihilation and victor's succession in a way a mosque could not. Whereas the royal temple represented a spatially particular, energized site sanctified by a deity's appearance, the imperial mosque usually provided only a nonenergized place of reverent prayer located according to temporal, not divine considerations. While the expansion of a Muslim presence might bring *both* Muslim desecration *and* patronage for Hindu temples as heads of state attempted to meet the expectations of a *dharmic* ruler found among their Hindu subjects, it also fostered the development of new energized sites in South Asia. Sufi *dargahs* (tomb shrines) often accumulated devotees drawn to their purported *shakti* or *baraka*. Indeed, the instances when imperial states established mosques in relation to energized sites occurred when they built them to accompany important *dargahs*.

Returning to the issue of state uses of urban, sacred centers, the volume's essays repeatedly demonstrate how Mecca and Medina—if not Arabia in general—persistently served as sites of pilgrimage and political legitimation. Hence, among the narratives that Gross relates, one attempts to sanction the Isma'ili imamate in Central Eurasia with a narrative oriented around the two cities: Following Muhammad's order from the grave, Shah Khamosh travels to Mecca where the Sufi master Junayd then imparts his wisdom as they circumambulate the Ka'ba. This narrative navigation of the sacred precincts of Mecca and Medina portrays Shah Khamosh as under the direction of the prophet (to whom he claims genealogical lineage) and under the tutelage of the Sufi (from whom he declares spiritual descent). In other instances, Muslims attempt to create localized versions of the Arabian sites via claims of equivalent sacrality. For instance, as Damrel shows through reference to a tract criticizing such practices, South Asian devotees have equated water used to wash Sufi tombs with the Zamzam water which hajjis routinely share with family and friends upon their return home. As Ross describes in the case of Senegal's Layenne order, its founder—who patterned his life on Muhammad's —homologized his movement's locales with those of the Hijaz. When the founder, Seydina Limamou, established a colony for those of his followers excluded from the movement's main settlement and named it Cambérène, a reference to Medina, he valorized the excluded members of his movement by associating them with the "helpers" of Medina who did not share the Meccan origins of the first Muslims yet who proved essential for the founding of the first Islamic society. In so doing, Limamou spatially mapped the Hijaz onto his own region, even as he narratively superimposed Muhammad's biography onto his own. By creating a Senegalese Medina and Mecca, the founder invited devotees to live the intertwined narratives of his and the prophet's biographies through their local experience.

These examples almost all demonstrate the importance of narratives in efforts to craft connections between geographically disparate sacred places. If, as Smith suggests, architecture differentiates a place from surrounding spaces so that it can serve as a "focusing lens" in which ritual directs the attention of practitioners, then narratives can be used to create a temporal architecture that molds causal associations among specific events in order to connect people, places, and occurrences. Despite the centrality of Mecca and Medina as places of Islamic history, veneration, pilgrimage, and learning, they do not figure into all narrative efforts of association. Hence, the biographies of Shah Khamosh and other missionaries not only connect Central Eurasia to the Hijaz, but also narratively interrelate various regional shrines. This became so successful that some South Asian reformers criticized Sufi shrine cultures when they appeared to undermine the Hijaz as a prescribed locus of religiosity.

Complementing these narratives that establish associations between places, other accounts provided by the volume's essays demonstrate how stories can be deployed to forge a shared veneration toward one location among members of different communities. This is a second thematic expression of my point about how narratives can act as temporal architecture. Examples can be found in Anatolia among histories of former Christian sites converted for Muslim use. Some relied on narratives of the prophet-saint Khiḍr to promote the Islamic qualities of these places, without obfuscating the Christian associations and practices there. Simultaneously, Khiḍr accounts provided a narrative thread that helped the Ottomans embed various Umayyad martyr and Christian saint shrines into a new, *Turkish* landscape. Meanwhile, in the

Palestinian village of al-Khaḍr, Lance D. Laird finds Muslims and Christians appropriating divergent narratives about Khaḍr (Khiḍr, by another name) from their respective religious traditions, yet uniting in rituals that celebrate and propitiate him. These stories not only create a shared moral community, but also promote a sense of Palestinian identity. This theme of narratives facilitating communal conjunction in shared sacred places can be manifest even in imagined locations, as demonstrated by the "monastery narratives" related by Thomas Sizgorich. The tensions and affirmations expressed between pious Muslims and ascetic Christians at monastic locations seem to have mattered far more than the actual location or existence of the monastic settings. They served as rhetorical spaces, as stages for anticipated dramas between love-stricken men and women as well as dutiful anchorites and formidable elites that reflected the negotiations occurring between the once dominant Christian ecclesiastic order and the now hegemonic Muslim social order.

The complexities involved in such examples reflect how participating individuals and communities engage in multifaceted negotiations through practice and discourse. Perhaps the most valuable contribution offered by these essays is how well their portrayals of specific places help make apparent the complicated multiple identities too often simplified by essentialized formulations of "Muslim," "Christian," "Jewish," and "Hindu" communities. The importance of this issue cannot be understated. Scholarship on the Middle East and South Asia too often has depicted societies there as characterized by mutually exclusive, often antagonistic religious identities. Too many scholars have overlooked how individuals may associate with one religious community, yet seldom belong to only one social group. Most individuals manage multiple affiliations, some of which may be shared by members of other religions, some of which may bridge differences between religions, and some of which may even appear contradictory to the individual's religious convictions. In other words, most people do not live in a single communal circle or even in a perfectly congruent set of circles. A better model would be of a three-dimensional Venn diagram of multiple social circles intersecting in an individual. Thus, Christian and Muslim Palestinians rely on divergent sources for contextualizing Khaḍr, but their shared faith in him leads not only to ritual "boundary crossing" (e.g., Muslim baptisms) but, as already noted, his appropriation into their shared Palestinian identity. These examples suggest a local religious cohesion that undermines obvious divergences and occasionally evidences a shared regional identity. If such convergences undermine assumptions of perennially antagonistic and mutually exclusive religious communities, then the internal debates *within* these traditions shatter any essentialized caricature of their uniformity, as denoted for example by Deobandi, Salafi, and Tablighi criticisms of tomb devotions.

Many of the examples offered in this collection of essays reinforce how contextual such alignments are. As we would expect, although individuals may have multiple social affiliations, particular circumstances prompt particular identities to become more prominent at particular times. Hence, shared processions and festivals in the eleventh-century Mediterranean might blur religious boundaries during times of health crisis yet sharpen them in times of political upheaval. While the Crusades and Reconquista led to less tolerant policies toward non-Muslims in Islamicate courts, plague and famine prompted hierarchy-collapsing ceremonies intending to demonstrate the cohesion of society. The possibility of such variations hinted at the existence of shared identifications beyond the boundaries policed by religious chauvinists. Centuries later, the Ottoman appropriation of Anatolian sites concurrently allowed for a continuity of Christian devotions, a new Khiḍr-aided association with Muslims, and a forced discontinuity with Byzantine rule. As Sizgorich so insightfully notes, fences simultaneously conjoin and separate, offering opportunities for distinction and exchange. In the internal world of personal identity, people often experience that their home exists in multiple, complexly related neighborhoods whose dynamics shift according to context.

In conclusion, this volume offers a necessary balance both within each contribution and among them all. This balance recognizes the fluidity of the integrating and disaggregating processes at work within both religious communities and a broader society, while also acknowledging the shifting contexts in which certain places achieve, maintain, and lose sacred status among some, but seldom all, observers. While demonstrating the divergent applications of the concept of "sacred space," the authors have shown the complex negotiations of practice, belief, and identity that have occurred at such sites, right to the present day. The dynamic nature of the examples described inherently trouble any easy distinction between sacred and profane. Cautious as we necessarily must be with the use of a binary so often and unreflectively applied universally, these essays provide the social, political, economic, and historical specificity that must accompany every attempt at cultural translation.

Notes

1. Jonathan Z. Smith, *Map Is Not Territory*. Chicago: University of Chicago Press, 1978. p. 309.

2. Carsten Colpe. "The Sacred and the Profane" in *The Encyclopedia of Religion*, ed. Lindsay Jones. Vol. 12. 2nd ed. Detroit: Macmillan Reference USA, 2005. p. 7964. [pp. 7964–78.]
3. Smith states that Durkheim first used "the sacred" as a substantive term in the singular.
4. Jonathan Z. Smith. *To Take Place: Toward a Theory in Ritual.* Chicago: University of Chicago Press, 1987. p. 105.
5. See, for instance, Alejandro Lapunzina, *Architecture of Spain.* Westport, Conn.: Greenwood, 2005. p. 81.
6. I owe the observation about the South African case to Abdulkader Tayob.
7. Bruce Lincoln, *Discourse and the Construction of Society: Comparative Studies of Myth, Ritual, and Classification.* 2nd ed. New York: Oxford University Press, 1992. pp. 106–109.
8. Smith 1987, p. 103.
9. For a superb deliberation on Muslim sensibilities regarding purity and the individual's cleansing before prayers as evidenced by Islamic legal traditions, see A. Kevin Reinhart, "Impurity/No Danger" in *History of Religions*, Vol. 30, No. 1, The Body (August 1990). pp. 1–24.
10. Smith 1987, pp. 51–54, 72.
11. See Richard M. Eaton, "Temple Destruction and Indo-Muslim States" in *Beyond Turk and Hindu: Rethinking Religious Identities in Islamicate South Asia*, ed. David Gilmartin and Bruce B. Lawrence. Gainesville: University Press of Florida, 2000. pp. 246–81.

1

Baraka *Besieged*

ISLAMISM, NEOFUNDAMENTALISM, AND SHARED SACRED SPACE IN SOUTH ASIA

David Damrel

Introduction

THE IDEA OF "sacred space" occupies an ambiguous and increasingly important position in contemporary Muslim religious and political thought.[1] A project to identify, categorize and plot this religious space—that is, those places where Muslim rituals are performed—must engage both the traditions of Islamic religious authority that authenticate place and ritual as well as the extraordinary diversity of contemporary Muslim place-related practices. Any modern map of Muslim sacred space must simultaneously map current understandings of religious authority, ritual life, and cultural practice within Islam.

The observation that Muslim understandings of religious authority in the twentieth and twenty-first centuries have continually been revisited, challenged, and rewritten in a painful and divisive discourse is a virtual axiom of our time. This conflict is characterized by many as a "crisis of authority within Islam," with debate arising only as to the acuity of the crisis. In this broadly held assumption, authenticity within modern Islam is being contested by rival Muslim authorities who are described with a prolific and imprecise variety of terms such as "moderate," "extremist," "activist," "conservative," "reformist," "puritan," "Jihadi," "fundamentalist," "neofundamentalist," "quietist," "modernist," "Islamist," and others. This crisis over religious leadership within the *ummah*, seen as unprecedented in scale and intensity, is thought by some to signal a striking and historic moment of transmutation for Muslim communities worldwide.[2] As Khaled Abou El Fadl has declared, "Islam is at the current time passing through a transformative moment no less dramatic than the Reformation movements that swept through Europe," adding the sobering note that the European reformations precipitated "long and bloody religious wars."[3] For him, the contemporary transformation is driven by the struggle between two sets of clashing religious authorities, "reformed moderates" on the one hand and Muslim "puritans" on the other, with nothing less than the consensus and near-total commitment of the Muslim *ummah* at stake. Whichever orientation wins out, he warns that it will "possess the formidable power of definition—the power to define Islam for what might turn out to be a considerably long time."[4]

Both this searching reconsideration of authenticity in Islam and the urgent reformulation of religious authority have deep implications for the question of modern Muslim sacred space. At the core of the question, to follow Abou El Fadl, is the power to define—specifically, who has the power to define Muslim sacred spaces and the ritual life within them? This is not an exclusively modern question, as Muslim communities worldwide and across time have consistently struggled to define and redefine local authorities, practices, and spaces within distinctive regional contexts and circumstances. What makes the contemporary situation so striking is a shrill and explicit globalization project among some Muslims that is intended to replace long-established local traditions—including regional understandings of ritual and space—with a monolithic and, in Abou El Fadl's view, authoritarian vision of Islamic religious life.

While all Muslim sacred spaces have been touched in some ways by this contestation, the most prominent and universal sites have so far remained largely above the struggle for authenticity. The general and enforced consensus governing ritual life at foundational centers such as the twin sanctuaries at Mecca and Medina and, for the Shi'a, the major shrines such as those at Najaf, Karbala, and Samarra among others, have proven resistant to most significant modern challenges and efforts at reinscription.[5] However, outside of these well-known transnational pilgrimage centers and their attendant text-bound ritual prescriptions, a larger clash over local sacred space and ritual looms. It is regional sacred space—more particularly the extensive networks of local shrines, tombs, and graves that comprise local religious terrains throughout much of the Muslim world—that has emerged as one of the crucial battlegrounds, literally and figuratively, in the contest over modern religious authority within Islam.

The experience of local Muslim sacred spaces in South Asia offers a vivid illustration of these tensions in practice. In just over the last two decades a number of bombings, grenade attacks, and brutal assaults—all laid at the feet of a range of different "Islamist" and neofundamentalist organizations—have murdered and injured scores of visitors at several major Muslim shrines and cemeteries in India, Pakistan, and Bangladesh.[6] These shrines are typically connected with Islamic mysticism, known generally as Sufism, and are important centers of what some have described as mediatory or miracle-based "folk" or "popular" Islam. Such regional sacred spaces are, as has long been noted in a substantial body of scholarly literature, frequent locations of significant Muslim (both Sunni and Shi'a) and Hindu interaction.[7] In fact, many historical models intended to explain Hindu conversion to Islam and the process of "Islamization" in South Asia assign these sites of religious encounter critical roles in the process.[8] At another level these and similar shrines have been decried as local expressions of "*mazar* culture," a coded expression signifying that the *mazar*s (shrines), their attendant festivals, and their surrounding neighborhoods are scenes of un-Islamic behaviors and moral degeneracy that may include prostitution and drug abuse.[9] These characteristics of South Asian sacred space—their identification with the superstitions of "popular" Islam, the interactions of Muslims and non-Muslims within them, and their connections with undesirable social behavior—figure in the early modern discourse against them.

This paper begins with an overview of the features, history, and functions of Sufi shrine complexes in South Asia, paying special attention to the interactions of Muslims and non-Muslim others within these shared ritual arenas. The investigation then turns to the role of ritual space within traditionalist and Islamist thought in British India and highlights attitudes toward shrine rituals and non-Muslims within these discourses. It concludes with an assessment of the impact of modern neofundamentalist thought on Muslim sacred space in South Asia.

Space, the Word and the Grave

The grave is the preeminent sacred space for the approximately 395 million Muslims who reside in modern South Asia. These Muslims, perhaps one-third of the entire global Muslim population, live in physical, ethnic, linguistic, and spiritual landscapes of extraordinary diversity and richness. For nearly a millennium, these communities, whether operating now as significant minorities in India and Sri Lanka or as majorities in Bangladesh and Pakistan, have created, visited, guarded, and shared a revered landscape that is composed of hundreds if not thousands of grave-centered sacred spaces.

Graves of course are not the only category of religious spaces for Muslims in South Asia. Just as everywhere else, South Asian Muslims routinely created and create necessary ritual spaces such as mosques for communal prayers, cemeteries for interring the dead, *imambargahs* for observing 'Ashura and other spaces as required for religious purposes. The varied and underappreciated processes by which Muslims create formal and informal ritual spaces have recently begun to receive scholarly attention, notably in the context of diaspora communities.[10] Much of this scholarship highlights the critical role of scripture and scripture-based tradition in the creation and demarcation of Muslim ritual space. Regula B. Qureshi suggests that the single most important and near universal marker of these ritual spaces is the presence of the Qur'an, whether heard in a recited verse, painted or carved in a line of Arabic calligraphy, or invoked in a nuanced array of architectural, visual, and aural signs.[11] On a cosmological scale, Seyyed Hossein Nasr has declared, "the Muslim lives in a space defined by the sound of the *Qur'an*,"[12] while for Barbara Daly Metcalf it is the presence of the "Word"—the Qur'an—and Word-centered ritual and practice that indicate Muslim space.[13] It is the Word—whether recited from the Qur'an, offered in prayer, reverberating in devotional poetry dedicated to Muhammad, or sung at annual festivals (*'urs*) at the grave—that marks the tomb as a Muslim space.

The imprint of the Word remained on the shrines of the Sufi "saints" in South Asia even as the tombs became centers of new varieties of popular religious activity. Qur'an-centered practice took a place among other practices and performances that reflected powerful local influences, customs, and concerns. The prominence of local religious practices, attitudes, and sensibilities at ostensibly Muslim shrines has meant that they are easily shared with non-Muslims, local visitors who use "Muslim" sacred spaces in ways sometimes incongruous to a Muslim understanding of the significance of the same place.[14]

Visiting the Friends of God

Our focus here is on the shrines and tombs of thousands of powerful *walis*, the miracle-working "friends of God" (*awliya' Allah*), that plot a sprawling sacred network of national, regional, local, village, and sometimes even neighborhood sanctuaries across South Asia.[15] A typology of these *mazars* and tombs reveals a broad continuum, represented at one end by prominent shrine institutions such as those of Shaykh Mu'in al-din Chishti (d. 1236) at Ajmer, Data Ganj Bakhsh (d. 1071) at Lahore, and Hazrat Shah Jalal Mujarrad (d. 1346) at Sylhet. All three are well-known and well-visited *dargahs*, governed by elaborate ritual protocol and beneficiaries of long-term imperial and state patronage.[16] Muslim, Hindu, and European authorities all recognized the political advantages that public association with shrines could provide, and successive generations of Muslim rulers, including many of the Mughal emperors, found personal and political benefit in visiting *dargah*s, contributing to their maintenance, and, on occasion, intervening in shrine management.[17] In the same way, Hindu Kallar rulers in eighteenth-century South India took pains to patronize and visit the major Muslim *dargah*s in their domain, and later some of these same Hindu-supported Muslim shrines attracted the patronage of other regional non-Muslim powers, including Christian Dutch trading communities.[18] The major tombs across South Asia represented fluid if enduring symbols of rule and society that various political dynasties, regardless of religious orientation, competed to acquire as emblems of legitimacy and power.

Hundreds of smaller complexes—typified by the three more modern shrines in northern India studied in detail by Claudia Liebskind—form a second tier of regional pilgrimage centers.[19] These smaller shrines exhibit their own distinctive ritual practices and, since they rely on local patrons and serve regional visitors, characteristically privilege provincial customs and traditions. These middle-size *dargah*s, though lacking the institutional scale and resources of the larger saintly concerns, frequently support caretakers who have inherited their positions and host annual fairs (*mela*s) and festivals (*'urs*) associated with the interred *wali*.

At the other end of the continuum from the major and second-level shrines are the thousands of simple, locally notable graves distributed throughout the villages and the countryside of rural India, Pakistan, and Bangladesh. These modest village shrines lack the ritual apparatus associated with the larger *dargah*s and form a ubiquitous feature of rural society, particularly in the Punjab and Bengal.[20] The sites, sometimes indicated simply by headstones, a verse from the Qur'an painted on a wall, or even by a pile of stones topped with a green flag, invite individualized ritual behavior.[21] Lukas Werth has suggested that these sites are significant because they provide villages, neighborhoods, or rural social groups with distinctive, localized connections to the divine, and at the same time reinforce a specific collective identity that distinguishes and separates particular groups and particular villages from another.[22]

Today in South Asia, government-instituted management schemes oversee the operations of the major and second-tier shrines. The state, with some important exceptions, has virtually eliminated the powers and duties of the shrine attendants, has appropriated the *waqf* properties that formerly supported the shrines, and monitors and collects the donations of cash and property that visitors make to the shrines.[23] The vast majority of village, regional, and rural shrines has remained largely unregulated, though they are subject to diverse municipal authorities and pressures.[24] The South Asian choice to regulate the shrines, as Katherine Ewing has observed, has allowed the states to promote styles of religious practice that are compatible with government-set goals and aspirations.[25] This approach is in dramatic contrast to the policies of other governments, notably Turkey, Iran, and Saudi Arabia, which have sought to more strictly suppress or curtail public expressions of mysticism.[26] The long-term social and cultural ramifications of how state control over these shrine networks will affect Muslim life remain to be explored another day.[27]

The central attractions of these shrines for Muslims and non-Muslims alike are the pious dead who reside in the tombs. They are the "invisible friends," the saintly men and women whose unique qualities have privileged them with a special closeness to Allah. Shrine visitation (*ziyarat*) can be understood as an audience with these elite dead, a dynamic interaction between the visitor and the visited inhabitant of the grave.[28] Shrines themselves are frequently called *darbar*s, a term whose meanings include "royal court," with the striking result that at many tombs the protocol of proper behavior before the illustrious dead follows the same courtly standards that dictated conduct before Muslim and sometimes Hindu rulers.[29]

The intimacy of the contact between the living and the dead at these shrines is vividly illustrated in an account narrated by the Chishti Shaykh Nizam al-din Awliya (d. 1325). At a visit to the tomb of his teacher, he wondered to himself if his deceased master was aware of his presence. He was answered instantly—in verse—by a voice from the grave.

> Think of me as living like yourself;
> I will come in spirit if you come in body.
> Do not think me lacking in companionship,
> For I see you even if you don't see me.[30]

Even a small sampling of the "historical lives" of the entombed friends reflects tremendous diversity, ranging from chaste "lovers of God" to warriors (*ghazi*s) and martyrs (*shahid*s), from important public figures in well-connected institutionalized brotherhoods to reclusive poets, scholars, and princesses, from mendicants to very wealthy men, from pious wives to madness-tinged husbands, all of these and many more elevated after death to the status of mediator with Allah. Despite the overwhelming mulitformity of these saintly lives,

South Asian hagiographical literature grew to reflect a near consensus on the essential themes and elements a *wali*'s life should ideally possess. A standard index of virtues might include exemplary piety, scrupulous adherence to shari'ah, cautious but pointed displays of miraculous power paired with disdain for worldly achievement, the humility and force of personality to draw non-Muslims to Islam, genealogical descent from a well-born Muslim family, and a number of other noteworthy qualities.[31] The written lives of these God-pleasing men and women, replete with their conversations, mystical teachings, and personalities, were prepared and constantly extended by generations of their families and mystical followers, many of whom had a stake in the promotion of their celebrated predecessors.[32] Such literature, augmented by popular legends, songs, and poetry, helped produce powerful and dynamic reputations for deceased saints that grow with each posthumous miracle attributed to them.

There are two powerful inducements for *ziyarat* to the graves of these powerful dead—the possibility for the visitor to plead for the *wali*'s intercession (*shifa'a*) with Allah, and the chance to experience the divine grace, called *baraka*, which flows from the grave and infuses those present with potent spiritual blessings.[33] These graves then stand as both mediation sites and reservoirs of blessing that draw a local, regional, national, and sometimes international clientele that can include Sunnis, Shi'a, Hindus, and members of other religious communities.[34]

Graveside rites that involve requests for intercession, along with many other rituals often performed at cemeteries, are popular, widespread, and seriously contested in many Muslim communities.[35] As an intercessor, the *wali* is considered sympathetic and potent, an advocate who can present a petitioner's case or, as expressed by a visitor at the shrine of Bari Imam in Pakistan, "the saint submits my application to God."[36] Visitors appeal for mediation on a surprising range of concerns, as noted in Desiderio Pinto's 1980s study of the requests articulated at the Delhi shrine of the Chishti Shaykh Nizam al-din Awliya. There the saint was invoked for such matters as to help find money for dowries, to resolve family disputes, to exorcise spirits, to return prisoners of war, to secure work, to insure the fidelity of errant spouses, to help with the proper burial of loved ones, and so on.[37] Visitors to the tombs expect results as a matter of course. This view of saintly intercession as a virtual entitlement is captured in the *wali* Sultan al-'Arifin's guarantee to his visitors: "Needy people should visit my grave for three days, and if their desires are not fulfilled, then they may demolish my grave on the fourth."[38]

In India, Hindus and Hindu religious practices may also take part in these tableaux of intercessory performances. It is a common practice for individual Hindus to visit and make requests at certain shrines, such as at the *dargah* of Nizam al-din Awliya in Delhi or the tomb of the legendary eleventh-century Sayyid Salar Mas'ud Ghazi, buried in Bahraich near Lucknow. There are also famous traditions of Hindu communities participating in public shrine-based festivals, such as at Bahraich and in the annual *nerccas* (from Malayalam for "to make a vow") ceremonies celebrated by Mappila Muslims in Kerala.[39] In these performances, elaborate communal processions to the shrines of local *walis* and martyrs end as representatives of particular groups (both Muslim and Hindu, divided according to guild, caste, and occupation) present offerings and make requests for prosperity and protection in the coming year. The rituals resonate with Hindu practice, and the *nerccas* demonstrate the complex set of religious, social, economic, and political factors that shrines and their rituals negotiate.[40]

Along with intercession, the opportunity to acquire *baraka* is another major force that attracts pilgrims to graves.[41] Shrine visitation gives petitioners access to the divine blessing which radiates invisibly from the *walis* and their tombs and permeates the immediate vicinity of their graves. This blessing is consumed, captured, transported, or transferred, all according to well-established folk practices and traditions in a process that Richard Kurin describes as "the manipulation of blessedness," or by using objects that Samuel Landell Mills calls the "hardware of sanctity."[42] The benefits of *baraka* manifest themselves in numerous physical ways, including healing the sick, helping those who hope to have children, exorcising both *jinns* and *bhuts* (ghosts), as well as in a variety of more modest forms.[43] Visitors bring or purchase objects to use as offerings, and leave them in prescribed areas within the shrine. These offerings are typically flower garlands, *chadars* (thin cloths that are draped over the tomb), sweets, incense, food, and other items. The offerings absorb the *pir's baraka* before visitors take away the now-blessed artifacts for domestic use. In this way, the commodified *baraka* of the saint flows to individuals and their households. *Baraka* also produces more subtle changes in the recipient besides the physical benefits—merely being present in a *baraka*-infused environment can be soothing, comforting, and produce desirable spiritual changes.[44] The emotional states of troubled, excited, and even spirit-possessed visitors are typically understood as "hot" or "burning," and—according to both Hindu and Muslim folk cosmologies—the cool nature of a saint's *baraka* provides natural and consoling relief for such distress.[45]

Baraka figures too in the major rituals that distinguish the public life of *dargahs*, particularly in the annual *'urs* observed on the *wali*'s death anniversary and in *langar*, the regular communal distribution of food to visitors. Some of the larger *'urs* celebrations attract thousands of pilgrims who are present for *baraka*-distributing rituals such as public processions, the display of relics, cleaning the graves, special recitations of the Qur'an and other localized customs, such as bathing the tombs in sandalwood paste.[46] These gatherings affect local economies significantly, even as some *'urs* celebrations have acquired reputations as settings for unseemly activities. Shrine-affiliated *langar-khanas* (soup kitchens) serve meals weekly and sometimes daily at the shrines, distributing foods blessed at the shrine as part of an important tradition of commensality in South Asian society. While the *langar* have long been valued as an important public service to provide relief to the poor, recent anthropological research has focused on the deep structure of the *langar* and the participation of the individual pilgrims.[47]

The overwhelming diversity, the expansive mystical histories, and the profoundly complex social settings of the graves of the powerful dead in Muslim South Asia should not obscure their essential unprocessed appeal: they are public religious spaces where individuals may seek private satisfaction through personal rituals and communal performance. In short, these centers of healing and consolation operate with equal force for a Muslim and non-Muslim clientele, marking out a unique, original and ambiguous Muslim religious territory that is for some increasingly intolerable.

Indigenous Shrine Criticism through the Twentieth Century

Despite their ubiquitous presence in South Asia, Muslim shrines, tombs, graves, and their attendant rituals have sparked controversy and criticism almost from their earliest appearance in the region. These criticisms and defenses of shrine life reflect a tremendous variety of contexts, circumstances and perspectives, and defy easy generalization. Early shari'ah-minded scholars, for instance, mounted many early critiques of shrine activities, but other critiques came from within some of the Sufi orders themselves. Fifteenth- and sixteenth-century mystics such as the Chishti Shaykh 'Abd al-Quddus Gangohi (d. 1537) and the Naqshbandi master Shaykh Ahmad Sirhindi (d. 1624) both voiced stern objections to particular *mazar*-related practices, but, in the end, turned to legal arguments to vigorously defend most shrine-based rituals.[48] The scholar-mystics connected with this phenomenon of shari'ah-minded Sufism in the Mughal Empire (1526–1857) defended the permissibility of certain Sufi practices even as they sought to discourage or prohibit others.

Many of these indigenous early Mughal complaints about Sufi-based shrine practices resonated among Muslim thinkers throughout the period of formal British rule in India (1857–1947) and among Muslim communities in post-partition India, Pakistan, and Bangladesh. In the nineteenth century, new religious education centers such as the Dar al-Ulum madrasa in Deoband contributed to the rise of an anti-shrine discourse that continued into the early twentieth century and bears many similarities with the contemporary critical discourse of shrines, ritual, and sacred space.[49] It is beyond this study to detail the development and contours of these considerable and widespread critical discourses beyond indicating certain shared elements. First, these discourses all charge shrine-centered rituals with deviating from normative practice—the authentic standards of shari'ah—in unacceptable ways. These unlawful innovations corrupt otherwise permissible visits to *walis*' tombs, to Shi'i shrines, and family visits to graveyards. These critiques also condemn various rituals devoted to living *pirs* as violating proper practice and defying Muslim consensus. Second, these objectionable practices reflect not just negligence or lack of knowledge of proper behavior, but the inclusion and intrusion of unacceptable local customs and practices drawn explicitly from non-Muslim—in this case Hindu—religious life. Finally, the deviant rituals and practices are often part of a ceremonial ensemble of innovative behaviors neither specifically Muslim nor Hindu in origin but that embody local styles of ignorance and superstition and, as one critic characterized it, "customs that are wrongly required."[50]

Broad questions regarding the lawfulness and uninformed nature of South Asian grave-centered rites and Sufism in general formed an important and complex theme in late Mughal and British India. These questions were taken up by a range of Muslim scholar-mystics, and reappeared in different forms in the thought and practice championed by particular social reform movements. Then, as now, establishing the authenticity of both the practices and the deciding authorities was part of a larger and contested process driven at least in part by political, social, and religious change. The Naqshbandi order in particular promoted a pronounced insistence on shari'ah as a pillar of mystical practice, an explicit connection that was expressed first in the teachings of Shaykh Ahmad Sirhindi (d. 1624) before it became a mainstay of Naqshbandi praxis in the eighteenth and nineteenth centuries. Some of leading intellectual figures and religious authorities of the late eighteenth and early nineteenth centuries belonged to the Naqshbandi order, among others, and their attitudes toward shrine practice reflected the order's sober yet enthusiastic appreciation of graveside rites. Two prominent Naqshbandis, the celebrated reform-minded scholar and mystic Shah Waliullah Dehlawi (d. 1762) and his son Shah 'Abd al-'Aziz Dehlawi (d. 1824) maintained a reconciliatory position that secured the legal position of *ziyarat* and yet censured many practices and ceremonies associated with the annual fairs. At the same time, the two major militant social movements of the first half of the nineteenth century—the Fara'idiyya in Bengal and the Mujahidin movement of Sayyid Ahmad Shahid (d. 1831)—both acted vigorously against local Sufi shrines and graves on occasion as part of their wider programs of religious reform.[51] These competing visions of reform and the nuanced debates over Muslim devotional life involving shrines and *pir*s remained leading themes in nineteenth-century South Asian Muslim intellectual life and contributed in real ways to the general climate of reform and dissent just before and after the Indian "Mutiny" against British rule in 1857.[52]

What, if anything, changed in the South Asian discourse over shrines in tombs after 1857, when new British colonial policies forced the reconfiguration of Muslim society and religious authority in India? Barbara Daly Metcalf describes the rise of what she calls "traditionalist" Islamic activism in the second half of the nineteenth century, epitomized by the madrasa-based Deoband movement and other similar organizations.[53] Activist in the sense that they encouraged fresh personal commitment to shari'ah-based worship, dress, and behavior, and traditionalist because of their continued acknowledgement of the ulama and madrasas, these new movements had at best limited tolerance for many shrine-oriented practices. In this same post-1857 milieu, Marc Gaborieau notes a new emphasis on establishing cultural distance between Hindu and Muslim societies, summed up as the effort "to increase, religiously as well as socially, the gap between Hindus and Muslims," and to "exacerbate the sense of Muslim identity and, by reaction, of Hindu identity."[54] Proper management of ritual life at the shrines was essential in this new climate in order to minimize Hindu and Muslim association within them and to help satisfy this fresh need for cultural and communal distance.

Representative of such efforts at self-definition is the treatise *Al-Balagh al-Mubin*, identified by Gaborieau as a post-1857 tract probably composed by an adherent of the Indian Wahhabi tradition.[55] Opening with the express intent to "dispel the schism (*fitna*) which has spread among the Muslim masses because of their association with the Hindu polytheists," the author elaborates that:

> This schism is the worship of tombs (*gor-parasti*). These tomb-worshippers are also called saint worshippers (*pir-parast*). These tomb-worshippers consider their abominable cult as better than obligatory or commendable ritual acts (*'ibadat*); they think that they can replace all obligatory rituals; reversely they do not think that any obligatory ritual can replace the worship of tombs.[56]

The tract next recites a long list of objectionable practices, such as kissing and circumambulating the tombs, lighting lamps and burning incense at them, keeping the water used to wash shrines as holy water "comparable to the water of the Zamzam well," incorporating musical instruments in worship, and so on. It pointedly concludes about Indian Muslims: "They thus do thousands of such acts in the same way as the Hindu polytheists do for their idols (*asnam*)."[57] The treatise then, in what Gaborieau describes as the core of the book, demonstrates practice by practice how Indian Muslims mimic the objectionable features of Hindu idol-worship in their own graveside rituals. The unknown Wahhabi author contrasts such Muslim customs as dressing the tomb, making offerings at the shrines, carrying standards in processions to the tombs, accepting intoxicants distributed by the caretakers of the tombs, and many other practices with similar—and similarly condemned—Hindu practices. Along with detailing condemnable Sufi practices, the text also includes a strong critique of Shi'i devotional rites. The section ends by citing the cautionary *hadith* well known in India, "The one who imitates a people becomes one of them."[58]

This mid-nineteenth-century work combined elements of a growing pan-Islamic discourse against *pirs* and "*pir*-worship" that continued, albeit with significant change, into early twentieth-century South Asia. Some of these same themes recur in the well-known manual, *Bihishti Zewar*, published by the Deobandi reformer Maulana Ashraf 'Ali Thanawi (d. 1943) in the early twentieth century. The *maulana*, taking on the general task of educating Muslim women in the "science of religion," prepared an influential and wide-ranging guide to comportment that contained everything from synopses of the lives of holy women to discussions of marriage customs and offered practical advice on mailing letters, raising children, and even on the preparation of meals. As part of its goal to reconstruct Indian Muslim women, the *Bihishti Zewar* also undertook a general categorization of unacceptable South Asian Muslim ritual practices and particularly warned against the sins, false beliefs, and bad customs connected with visiting graves, shrines, and tombs.[59] According to the *maulana*, for example, it is an act of infidelity (*kufr*) and polytheism (*shirk*) to "respect and venerate any place as equal to the *ka'ba*," or to circumambulate a grave or a building. Excessive respect for *pir*s is among the most grievous sins, with explicit warnings against such practices as calling on *pir*s with requests for livelihood and offspring, venerating their pictures, or believing that they are aware of actions from afar, repeating their name as part of a daily discipline, fasting in their name or prostrating before them. Improper comportment at graves is part of a second echelon of "reprehensible innovations," and Thanawi's extensive treatment forbids Muslims:

> 1. To hold fairs with great to-do at graves; to light lamps at graves; for women to go to graves; to offer shawls to cover the grave; to build a permanent monument at a grave: to revere graves excessively in order to please elders; to kiss or lick *ta'ziya*s or graves; to rub their dust on your face; to circumambulate them; to prostrate yourself; to perform the ritual prayer in the direction of graves; to make offerings of candies, pudding (*halwa*) and sweetmeats and so forth; to keep *ta'ziya*s and flags and salute them or offer them halwa and cake.[60]

He goes on to condemn Muslim participation in Holi and Diwali, and emphasizes that Muslims should not "perform the customs of the Hindus," adding also, as a less grievous offense, that Muslims should not grow "to like the customs of the unbelievers."[61] It should be noted that this discourse, though clearly aimed at "popular" Hindu-Muslim relations, would also apply to a South Asian Muslim community subject at the time to an aggressive and persistent Protestant Christian missionary presence.

While both texts—the *Al-Balagh al-Mubin* and the *Bihishti Zewar*—are keen to correct ritual and devotional practices in South Asia, it is important also to underscore that both texts recognize the validity of certain specific forms of religious activity connected with graves and *pir*s. The *Al-Balagh al-Mubin*, for instance, while excoriating Indian Muslims for their deviant practices and resemblances to Hindus, also explains the correct way for Muslims to seek the mediation (*wasila*) of the saints.[62] In the same way, Maulana Thanawi's condemnations and prohibitions against certain behaviors are offset by his positive descriptions of the virtues of following a *pir* and his detailed account of the correct and lawful way of reciting the *fatiha* to transfer the rewards of good deeds to the dead.[63]

Islamism, Neofundamentalism, and Space

This complicated if conflicted local South Asian discourse on the propriety of shrine-centered ritual has produced an astonishingly diverse set of social and religious relationships at shrines in the twentieth century. As just one example, Peter van der Veer, in a contemporary ethnographic study of an *'urs* in modern Surat, examined the complex interactions first between Hindu and Muslim devotees at a Rifa'i shrine and then between the Muslim devotees and their local Muslim critics, the Tablighi Jama'at.[64] He concluded that the greater tensions were within the two competing Muslim communities, with Hindu participation and presence in the ceremonies being largely a non-issue. Restated, the controversy reflected an internal Muslim debate over proper *Muslim* ritual behavior, and not over the presence of non-Muslims.

Such opposition to "extravagant" ritual practice at Muslim shrines in South Asia carried over from Deoband and Deobandi-influenced groups in the nineteenth century and resurfaced in the portfolios of numerous twentieth-century Islamist organizations. Islamist, as used here, follows Ahmad S. Moussalli's usage of the term to refer to a diverse range of global groups and discourses that seek to refute (*jahiliya*) practices and achieve virtuous Islamic societies governed by Islamic law.[65] In South Asia, Islamist groups and thinkers such as the Jama'at-i Islami of Sayyid Abul A'la Maududi (d. 1979) widened the cultural and religious spaces between various communities by producing taut new definitions of Islamic identity, partly in reaction to growing Hindu nationalism but just as much in response to the flourishing diversity of the Muslim community itself. Maududi's shari'ah-oriented and in many ways antinationalist rhetoric in South Asia had distinct parallels and connections with other like-minded Muslim organizations in the early twentieth century, including the Ikhwan al-Muslimun, the "Muslim Brotherhood," founded in 1928 in Egypt by Hassan al-Banna' (d. 1949). For Sunni Islamist groups in South Asia, reforming unacceptable individual Muslim behaviors—specifically including shrine-based practices but also Shi'i and Ahmadi ritual life—was a requisite step in their larger project of creating a holistic and homogenous Islamic society and state.[66] The Jama'at-i Islami, founded officially in 1941, was able to harness the impulse toward individual regeneration central to "traditional" South Asian Islamic activism and make it part of their long-term project of social rehabilitation, culminating in the establishment and institution of Islamic polity.[67] From the middle of the twentieth century onward, these internal and seemingly eternal contestations over *dargahs* and ritual, imprinted both with Deobandi and then Islamist markings, remained a constant theme in the complex, fluid, and richly textured world of Sunni Muslim thought, movements, and political organizations in contemporary South Asia.

The tone of the religious discourse sharpened in the last quarter of the twentieth century, coincident with shifted political realities and the rise of the phenomenon that Olivier Roy has labeled "neofundamentalism." In this period, the persistent and tense South Asian Muslim discourse over shrines and shrine rituals intertwined with the emergent demands of supranational Sunni thought in the 1980s and early 1990s. Roy insists that neofundamentalism appeared following the failure of Islamism, the "political Islam" that sought to institute shari'ah-compliant nation-states. The impossibility of achieving such an Islamist agenda, he argues, prompted the rise of a new, "globalized" Islam, meaning a stateless, denationalized, and deterritorialized *ummah* that is more compatible with the pressures and configurations of contemporary global communities. These post-Islamists are the "neofundamentalists," a term for those diverse groups, which, while sharing the same general goal of building a modern globalized state-free *ummah* unimpeded by the nation-state, approach the task with extremely divergent perspectives and strategies. One nonviolent manifestation of this neofundamentalist impulse operates in an apolitical and proselytizing mode, constructing the twenty-first-century *ummah* one Muslim at a time through a global campaign of missionary activity (*dawa*). The Tablighi Jama'at is the preeminent example of such an orientation. At the same time, Roy also insists that a range of "Jihadi" and "Salafi-Jihadist" groups share this same neofundamentalist conceptual model, seeking to replace the current global arrangement of nation-states with an unbordered and expansive *ummah* governed under the model of the Caliphate.[68] Simply put, one group seeks to build a global, revitalized, and homogenous *ummah* that is compatible with the present world order, while the other, at the extreme, strives to remake the world to suit a uniform and re-dedicated *ummah*.

Both modes operate in "imaginary worlds" that devalue locality and emphasize instead the connected nature of global societies. As an example, Roy cites missionizing revivalist groups such as the Tablighi Jama'at as imagining and striving to create an *ummah* of committed individual Muslims living as stateless global citizens. Local societies and local spaces, whether in Durban, Peshawar, or Vancouver, are not important in this emerging sense of religious community. Roy suggests the Hizb al-Tahrir as an example of a jihad-oriented group, for whom the envisioned future is an *ummah* existing beneath the aegis of a new Caliphate that supersedes the limits of modern political boundaries.[69] It is the legal status of territory—whether or not it is *Dar al-Harb* or *Dar al-Islam*—that matters in this model, and not local sacred and ritual spaces.

The irrelevance of place is an important theme for neofundamentalists. Roy suggests that those active in modern neofundamentalist missionary work behave in the same way "whatever the cultural and sociological environment, as if they were on an isolated planet," while those who elect neofundamentalist jihad "always ignore the sociocultural context of the people they want to help" and disregard local cultures, national interests, and politics.[70] Regula B. Qureshi characterizes this style of modern Sunni Islam as being marked by "its commitment to universality, its resources of portability, its focus on a single center, and its singularly verbal message."[71] The universality and portability of Muslim ritual life are essential features in neofundamentalism, as is the primacy of the "single center" of the Ka'ba in Mecca as the sole ritually prescribed sacred space.

It is clear that a transcendent, deterritorialized, and unbounded neofundamentalist Islam can cede little room to regional or sectarian Muslim practices, cultures, holy people, or sacred terrains. Homogeneity is the expectation in practice and space and otherness, whether expressed in the ritual life of the Shi'a or by visitors to shrines, is not an acceptable option. In such an understanding of the world, modern national boundaries become arbitrary, inauthentic, irrelevant, and eradicable. In the same way, local Muslim sacred landscapes—the shrines, graves, and tombs that chart local "other" Islam—are also subject to erasure. This emergent perspective disallows even the cautious, regulated shrine-based observances of earlier periods, promoting instead a starkly redrawn Islam with Mecca—and, to a lesser extent, Medina and Jerusalem—as the only legitimate sacred locations. The overwhelming majority of spaces related to shrines and tombs become, in this view, architectural monuments to the need to reclaim Islam. Given the comprehensive remapping of Muslim space inherent in this worldview, the question must arise: what is the future of the ritual spaces associated with saints and their tombs in South Asia, particularly as neofundamentalist sentiments, attitudes, and parties strengthen in Bangladesh, India, and Pakistan?[72]

Conclusion

The violent contemporary dispute over authenticity in Islam must inevitably leave any mapmaking of Muslim sacred space unresolved. The long-term viability of South Asian Muslim shrines and the ritual life that they engender is linked to the fortunes of varied intellectual and social movements, including those we have seen labeled as "traditionalist," Islamist, and neofundamentalist. When certain of these South Asian neofundamentalist movements have elected violent struggle, regional Muslim shrines, their visitors, and their rituals have become natural settings for vicious displays of indiscriminate violence. The *mazar*s and *dargah*s come to embody everything that these post-Islamist global sentiments insist Islam should *not* be—places where Islam is corrupted by idolatry, polluted by Hindu practice, shamed by immoral *'urs* behaviors, and profaned by Shi'i ritual abominations. In short, the local shrines are the repositories of "local" Islam, an unacceptable anomaly and impossibility in the neofundamentalist pursuit of a stateless, eternal Islam.

The persistent rise in the number of violent attacks over the last two decades on shrines in South Asia, including attacks by Muslims against Bari Imam in Pakistan, Nand Rishi in Indian Kashmir, and Hazrat Shah Jalal in Sylhet, Bangladesh, hint at this new dynamic at work. All three shrines have long-standing traditions of Hindu-Muslim interaction, just as they all share both a Shi'i and Sunni clientele and reputations for hosting *'urs* festivals fringed with illicit activities. The motives behind these individual attacks and many others in Baluchistan, Kashmir, northeastern Bangladesh, Gujarat, and Uttar Pradesh spring from a complex set of causes that typically include local feuds, tensions resulting from social and economic dislocation and various other factors. However, also contributing within these immediate contexts of potential violence is the unmistakable rhetoric of a supranational exclusivist Sunni ideology at work.[73]

It remains to be seen how the characteristic spaces of "local" Islam fare in globalized society, even without the opposition of Roy's neofundamentalists. The facts of contemporary international communications and travel may make local shrines less attractive to pilgrims who now have access to a larger selection of celebrated and, presumably, more potent sources of *baraka*. In addition, while immigration and the depopulation of communities have unquestionably weakened some local shrines and Sufi brotherhoods in South Asia, the reverse can also be true. As Pnina Werbner has noted, certain communities of Muslim Pakistanis living in Great Britain reenact certain South Asian rites and practices in their new environments. Rather than the diverse mechanisms of globalization working to erase the "local," in these cases the local takes on a global context.[74]

New styles and modes of authority may well undermine traditional shrine life in ways that are as yet unclear. If, for instance, Muslim societies worldwide are indeed convulsing in a "reformation" that ultimately "disenchants" the world and shrines, we must also ask about the long-term future of a second locus of "local" Islam, namely the scores of shrines across South Asia that house relics associated with the Prophet Muhammad. It is an audacious project for neofundamentalists and others to assail regional sites connected with provincial "friends of God," but an even bolder initiative to besiege shrines honoring the Prophet's relics in South Asia. As an example, the unfiltered spiritual and political power of a prophetic relic such as Muhammad's cloak became dramatically clear when, in 1996, Mullah Umar, the leading political figure of the Taliban in Afghanistan, seized the mantle and wore it over his own shoulders on a rooftop in Kandahar.[75] It seems clear that emotional displays of affection related to the Prophet are still judged differently from similar examples of veneration centered on the *wali*s.

The demarcation of sacred space in South Asia depends ultimately on how the crises of authority within contemporary Muslim communities are resolved. It is a feature of the interconnected world of the late twentieth and early twenty-first centuries that local Muslim debates over the "cult of the saints" in South Asia reverberate and resonate in real time as part of a global discourse that may or may not be subject to resolution. That is to say, the quandary of multivocality and competing Muslim authority may be an issue that contemporary Muslims must simply learn to manage better rather than attempt to decide. In the same way, any mapping of Muslim ritual space must be provisional, impermanent, and not necessarily subject to resolution. We may wish to borrow the precise ambiguity of the mapmaker's term "Line of Control," which both establishes and disestablishes the borders of India and Pakistan in Kashmir, to capture as well the ever-shifting and conditional nature of Muslim space and authority in modern South Asia.

Notes

1. For a general introduction to sacred space as a category of academic inquiry, see David Chidester and Edward T. Linenthal, eds., *American Sacred Space* (Bloomington: Indiana University Press, 1995), pp. 1–42 passim. Their identification of sacred space as ritual space, meaning "a location for formalized, repeatable symbolic performances," is particularly useful; see p. 9.
2. Richard W. Bulliet, *The Case for Islamo-Christian Civilization* (New York: Columbia University Press, 2004), p. 135, flatly asserts, "Islam is immersed in a crisis of authority." In a provocative exercise of speculative periodization, he foresees the centuries from 1800–2200 as an era of the destruction of "various Muslim syntheses" in the encounter with the West, followed by the "creation of new socioreligious syntheses appropriate to the modern world" (p. 137).

3. Khaled Abou El Fadl, *The Great Theft: Wrestling Islam from the Extremists* (New York: HarperCollins, 2007), pp. 5–6.
4. Ibid., p. 7.
5. Despite minor differences and preferences in ritual behavior, there is remarkable overall historical continuity in Sunni and Shi'i ritual practices involving *hajj* (pilgrimage) and *ziyarat* (visitation). Guides, guidebooks, and manuals all help visitors adhere to well-established text-based ritual traditions and long-standing local practices that are little changed in spite of variable political and social environments in the shrine cities. Barbara Daly Metcalf highlights the uniformity and "normative program" of the *hajj* experience in her study of the *hajj* accounts of South Asian pilgrims; see "The Pilgrimage Remembered: South Asian Accounts of the *Hajj*," in Dale F. Eickelman and James Piscatori, eds., *Muslim Travellers: Pilgrimage, Migration and the Religious Imagination* (Berkeley: University of California Press, 1990), pp. 100–1. See also William C. Young, "The Kaba, Gender, and the Rites of Pilgrimage," *International Journal of Middle Eastern Studies* 25:2 (May 1993): 285–300, for notice and analysis of change in gender-related *hajj* rites.
6. The term "Islamist" is used here in preference to the even less exact term "Islamic Fundamentalist." Ahmad S. Moussalli characterizes the term to include both a range of political movements as well as diverse critical discourses that typically share an insistence on privileging divine governance (*hakimiyya*) over human authority along with "refuting paganism (*jahiliya*)." The goal is to achieve just and virtuous societies—so-called "*shari'ah* utopias"—that conform to Islamic law. See Moussalli, "Islamic Democracy and Pluralism," in Omid Safi, ed., *Progressive Muslims on Justice, Gender and Pluralism* (Oxford: Oneworld, 2003), p. 304, n. 2. Compare this with Olivier Roy's preference for the term "neo-fundamentalism," meaning a closed, scripturalist, and conservative view of Islam that rejects "national and statist" dimensions of the faith in favor of a universal *ummah* governed by shari'ah. See Olivier Roy, *Globalized Islam: The Search for a New Ummah* (New York: Columbia University Press, 2004), p. 1.
7. For a sampling of the extensive literature related to South Asian Muslim shrines, see Christian Troll, ed., *Muslim Shrines in India: Their Character, History and Significance* (Oxford: Oxford University Press, 1989); Katherine Ewing, *Arguing Sainthood: Modernity, Psychoanalysis and Islam*, (Durham, N.C.: Duke University Press, 1997); Claudia Liebskind, *Piety on Its Knees: Three Sufi Traditions in South Asia in Modern Times* (Oxford: Oxford University Press, 1998); Carl Ernst, *Eternal Garden: Mysticism, History, and Politics at a South Asian Sufi Center* (Albany: State University of New York Press, 1992); Carl Ernst and Bruce Lawrence, *Sufi Martyrs of Love: The Chishti Order in South Asia and Beyond* (New York: Palgrave Macmillan, 2002); Pnina Werbner and Helene Basu, eds., *Embodying Charisma: Modernity, Locality and the Performance of Emotion in Sufi Cults* (New York: Routledge, 1998); Pnina Werbner, *The Anthropology of a Global Sufi Cult* (Oxford: Oxford University Press, 2005).

8. Richard Eaton describes these theories in *The Rise of Islam and the Bengal Frontier, 1204–1760* (Berkeley: University of California Press, 1993), pp. 113–34. See also his "Approaches to the Study of Conversion to Islam in India," in Richard C. Martin, ed., *Approaches to Islam in Religious Studies* (Tucson: University of Arizona Press, 1985), pp. 106–23.
9. *Mazar*, used for a shrine or tomb complex, is sometimes substituted by *dargah*. For a brief overview of "*mazar* culture," see Katherine Ewing, "A *Majzub* and His Mother: the Place of Sainthood in a Family's Emotional Memory," in Werbner and Basu, eds., *Embodying Charisma*, pp. 160–83, here pp. 160–63. A similar complaint about *mazar*s from approximately a century earlier is found in the tract *Al-Balagh al-Mubin*; see Marc Gaborieau, "A Nineteenth Century Indian 'Wahhabi' Tract Against the Cult of Muslim Saints: *Al-Balagh al-Mubin*," in Troll, ed., *Muslim Shrines in India*, pp. 198–239, here p. 211.
10. The collection of essays assembled and edited by Barbara Daly Metcalf marks an important early effort to address this issue. See her *Making Muslim Space in North America and Europe* (Berkeley: University of California Press, 1996). See also Pnina Werbner, "Stamping the Earth with the Name of Allah: Zikr and the Sacralizing of Space among British Muslims," *Cultural Anthropology* 11:3 (1996): 309–38.
11. Regula Burckhardt Qureshi portrays the connection between the Qur'an and Muslim spaces vividly in her "Transcending Space: Recitation and Community among South Asian Muslims in Canada," in Barbara Daly Metcalf, ed., *Making Muslim Space in North America and Europe* (Berkeley: University of California Press, 1996): 46–64.
12. See the introduction by Seyyed Hossein Nasr to the volume he edited, *Islamic Spirituality: Foundations*, vol. 1 (New York: Crossroads Press, 1987), p. 4.
13. Metcalf, *Making Muslim Space*, pp. 4–6.
14. While the presence of Hindus at Muslim shrines in South Asia is often noted in scholarship on the *dargah*s and tombs, little research has been done on those Muslims who visit and use traditionally "non-Muslim" sacred space. The latter phenomenon challenges the construction of too strict a definition of Muslim and non-Muslim in certain contexts. Dominique-Sila Khan has shown the fluidity of identity and self-definition within both Muslim and Hindu Indian communities, with some attention to shrines and rituals, in *Conversions and Shifting Identities: Ramdev Pir and the Ismailis in Rajasthan* (New Delhi: Manohar Publishing, 1997), particularly pp. 17–37 and 267–72.
15. Muslims in South Asia, as elsewhere, regularly visit the graves of family members to perform particular rituals. Maulana Ashraf 'Ali Thanawi (d. 1943) notes many of these practices with disapproval in his *Bihishti Zewar* under the heading "reprehensible innovations, bad customs and bad deeds." See Barbara Daly Metcalf, *Perfecting Women: Maulana Ashraf 'Ali Thanawi's Bihishti Zewar, A Partial Translation with Commentary* (Berkeley: University of California Press, 1992), pp. 74–75.

16. For these shrines, see P. M. Currie, *The Shrine and Cult of Mu'in al-din Chishti of Ajmer* (Delhi: Oxford University Press, 1989); Eaton, *Rise of Islam and the Bengal Frontier*, pp. 73–76, and Katherine Ewing, "The Politics of Sufism: Redefining the Saints of Pakistan," *Journal of Asian Studies* 42:2 (1983): 251–68.
17. Currie, *Shrine and Cult*, p. 112.
18. Susan Bayly, *Saints, Goddesses and Kings: Muslims and Christians in South Indian Society, 1700–1900* (Cambridge: Cambridge University Press, 1989), p. 218.
19. Liebskind, *Piety on Its Knees*, pp. 4–6.
20. Lukas Werth, "'The Saint Who Disappeared': Saints of the Wilderness in Pakistani Village Shrines," in Werbner and Basu, eds., *Embodying Charisma*, pp. 77–91, here pp. 77–79.
21. These small-scale centers of *baraka* are usually unvisited except by locals and serve exclusively local functions. The graves are not at the center of major annual celebrations and are not supported by any full-time attendants or teachers or anyone to collect offerings. Local residents typically tend the graves themselves, cleaning them, repainting them, and sometimes draping them in fresh *chadar*s (cloth coverings) once a year. Often on Thursday evenings women light small lamps at the graves and may make requests but, in general, the shrines are recognized as only limited sources of blessing. For substantial requests or major vows, these same villagers will often perform *ziyarat* to more famous regional or even international shrines.
22. Werth, "'Saint Who Disappeared,'" pp. 88–89.
23. Some Pakistani shrines have retained their autonomy from the government Auqaf Department; see Harald Einzmann, *Ziarat und Pir-E-Muridi: Golra Sharif, Nurpur Shahan und Pir Baba: Drei Muslimische Wallfahrtstatten in Nordpakistan* (Stuttgart: Steiner Verlag Weisbaden, 1988).
24. As an example, the city of Mumbai undertook a campaign to demolish "illegal" shrines on city property, destroying over four hundred unlicensed Hindu, Muslim and Christian shrines in 2003. See Syed Firdaus Ashraf, "'If a Shrine Is Illegal, It Has To Be Demolished,'" *Indian Express* (Mumbai), 11 November 2003, online at: http://in.rediff.com/cms/print.jsp?docpath=news/2003/nov/11inter.htm, accessed 18 July 2012.
25. Ewing, "Politics of Sufism," p. 251.
26. Ibid. Matthijs Van Den Bos addresses the present status of institutionalized Sufism in Iran in *Mystic Regimes: Sufism and the State in Iran, from the Late Qajar Era to the Islamic Republic* (Leiden: E.J. Brill, 2002).
27. See Ewing, "Politics of Sufism," and Einzmann, *Ziarat und Pir-E-Muridi* and Arthur F. Buehler, *Sufi Heirs of the Prophet: The Indian Naqshbandiyya and the Rise of the Mediating Sufi Shaykh* (Columbia: University of South Carolina Press, 1998), for suggestive analyses of the questions involved.
28. Carl Ernst, "An Indo-Persian Guide to Sufi Shrine Pilgrimage," in Grace Martin Smith and Carl Ernst, editors, *Manifestations of Sainthood in Islam* (Istanbul: The

Isis Press, 1993), pp. 43–67, here pp. 52–53. His translation of the eighteenth-century scholarly Persian guidebook *Makhzan-i a'ras* ("Treasury of Death Anniversaries") by Muhammad Najib Qadiri Nagawri Ajmeri (d. 1742–43) is an important contribution to understanding the role and place of Sufi pilgrimage in South Asia.

29. Both Richard M. Eaton, "Court of Men, Court of God: Local Perceptions of the Shrine of Baba Farid, Pakpattan, Punjab," *Contributions to Asian Studies* 17 (1982): 44–46 and David Gilmartin, "Shrines, Succession and Sources of Moral Authority" in Barbara Daly Metcalf, ed., *Moral Conduct and Authority: The Place of* Adab *in South Asian Islam* (Berkeley: University of California Press, 1984), p. 221–40, remark on the similarities between royal audiences and mystical ones in a Muslim setting; see S.A.A. Saheb, "A 'Festival of Flags': Hindu-Muslim Devotion and the Sacralizing of Localism at the Shrine of Nagore-i-Sharif in Tamil Nadu," in Werbner and Basu, eds., *Embodying Charisma*, pp. 55–76, for similar comments in regard to Maratha royal displays.
30. See Ernst, "Indo-Persian Guide," p. 61.
31. Bruce Lawrence, "The Earliest Chishtiya and Shaykh Nizam ud-Din Awliya," in R.E. Frykenberg, ed., *Delhi Through the Ages: Essays in Urban History, Culture and Society* (Delhi: Oxford University Press, 1986), pp. 108–11, provides important insight into the standard formulation and creation of a saint's posthumous reputation.
32. Although male "friends of God" predominate in South Asian hagiographic materials, women are also noted in a number of primary and secondary sources. See Shemeem Burney Abbas, *The Female Voice in Sufi Ritual: Devotional Practices of Pakistan and India* (Austin: University of Texas Press, 2002); Netty Bonouvrie, "Female Sufi Saints on the Indian Subcontinent," in Ria Kloppenborg and Wouter Hanegraaff, eds., *Female Stereotypes in Religious Traditions* (Leiden: E.J. Brill, 1995), pp. 109–22; Annemarie Schimmel, *My Soul Is A Woman: The Feminine in Islam* (New York: Continuum, 1997).
33. For a clear description and analysis of the process of blessing transfer in South Asia, see Richard Kurin, "The Structure of Blessedness at a Muslim Shrine in Pakistan," *Middle Eastern Studies* 19:3 (1983): 312–25.
34. Desiderio Pinto notes the diversity of the visitors to the Delhi shrine of Shaykh Nizam al-din Awliya in his "The Mystery of the Nizamuddin Dargah," in Troll, ed., *Muslim Shrines in India*, pp. 114–20. For a more recent study of a modern South Asian shrine complex with a vital clientele that is both local and transnational, see Werbner, *Anthropology of a Global Sufi Cult*.
35. For a careful general study of Muslim practices of shrine visitation, see Christopher S. Taylor, *In the Vicinity of the Righteous: Ziyara and the Veneration of Muslim Saints in Medieval Egypt* (Leiden: E.J. Brill, 1998). The rituals and attitudes he describes for fourteenth-century Egypt are recognizable throughout much of the Muslim world today.
36. See Hafeez-Ur-Rehman Chaudhry, "Traditional and State Organizations of the Shrine of Bari Imam," *Al-Mushir* 36:iii (1994): 89.

37. Pinto, "Mystery of the Nizamuddin Dargah," pp. 114–20.
38. Saheb, "Festival of Flags," p. 60.
39. See Stephen Dale and M. Gangadhara Menon, "Nerccas: Saint-Martyr Worship among the Muslims of Kerala," *Bulletin of the School of Oriental and African Studies* 40: 3 (1978): 523–38.
40. See A. R. Saiyed, "Saints and Dargahs in the Indian Subcontinent: A Review," in Troll, ed., *Muslim Shrines in India*, pp. 240–56.
41. *Hajj* rituals comprise an implicit model of visitation operating beneath the surface of much Muslim spiritually motivated travel. As John Renard has observed, shrine visitation is a "popular devotional parallel to the ritual practice of pilgrimage," and appropriate ritual conduct at the shrines may mimic special rituals connected with the *hajj*; see Renard, *Seven Doors to Islam: Spirituality and the Religious Life of Muslims* (Berkeley: University of California Press, 1996), p. 60. Note too al-Jawzi's thirteenth-century account of Muslim ritual practices in Jerusalem at the Dome of the Rock: "They used to stand by the Rock and circumambulate it as they used to circumambulate the Ka'ba, and slaughter beasts on the day of the feast [i.e., 'Id al-Adha]," cited in Amikam Elad, *Medieval Jerusalem and Islamic Worship: Holy Places, Ceremonies, Pilgrimage* (Leiden: E.J. Brill, 1995), p. 53. See also 'Ali bin Uthman al-Hujwiri, trans. Reynold A. Nicholson, *The Kashf al-Mahjub: The Oldest Persian Treatise on Sufism* (Lahore: Islamic Book Foundation, 1980), pp. 326–29, for a mystical interpretation of the significance of the *hajj* that concludes that the spiritual equivalent of the *hajj* can be performed anywhere.
42. Kurin, "Structure of Blessedness," and Samuel Landell Mills, "The Hardware of Sanctity: Anthropomorphic Objects in Bangladeshi Sufism," in Werbner and Basu, eds., *Embodying Charisma*, pp. 31–54.
43. The *dargah* of Mira Data near Ahmadabad in Gujarat lodges a population of *bhut*-afflicted residents, individuals maintained there by their families in the hope that the steady flow of the saint's *baraka* will soothe or expel the disruptive spirits. See Beatrix Pfleiderer, "Mira Data Dargah: The Psychiatry of a Muslim Shrine," in Imtiaz Ahmad, editor, *Ritual and Religion among Muslims in India* (New Delhi: Manohar, 1984): 195–233. The Karachi shrine of Abdullah Shah Ghazi is another site famous for exorcism; there, *qawwali* music performed at the shrine and infused with *baraka* comforts the *jinn*-possessed listeners, causing the demons within them to flee. See Kurin, "Structure of Blessedness," pp. 319–20.
44. Pinto, "Mystery of the Nizamuddin Dargah," p. 117. Pinto suggests that these sorts of visitors—those who make no explicit requests at the shrine but simply find it comforting to visit or return often—may actually form the majority of visitors.
45. Kurin, "Muslim Shrine," p. 321. This sense of the shrine as a source of solace comes through in what a businessman at Shaykh Nizam al-din Awliya's tomb in Delhi reported: "I do not ask for anything, because the saint knows and sees all of my needs. When I come here I feel a sense of peace and quiet and I forget the world with all its meanness and problems." See Pinto, "Mystery of the Nizamuddin Dargah," p. 118.

46. Liebskind, *Piety on Its Knees*, pp. 150–56, describes how the modern Khanqah Karimiya in Salon (in Uttar Pradesh in northern India) celebrates the *'urs* of its founder, Shah Pir Muhammad Saloni (d. 1687).
47. Currie, *Shrine and Cult*, pp. 122–23. Pnina Werbner explores the expectations of the participants at the 1990 *'urs* of Baba Qasim celebrated in Ghamkol Sharif, in northwestern Pakistan. See Werbner, "*Langar*: Pilgrimage, Sacred Exchange and Perpetual Sacrifice in a Sufi Saint's Lodge," in Werbner and Basu, eds., *Embodying Charisma: Modernity, Locality and the Performance of Emotion in Sufi Cults*, pp. 95–116.
48. See David W. Damrel, "The 'Naqshbandi Reaction' Reconsidered," in David Gilmartin and Bruce Lawrence, eds., *Beyond Turk and Hindu: Rethinking Religious Identities in Islamicate South Asia* (Gainesville: University Press of Florida, 2000), pp. 176–98, for a brief account of the relationship between shari'ah and Sufism in Mughal India.
49. Barbara Metcalf summarizes Deoband and Deobandi-modeled movements in " 'Traditionalist' Islamic Activism: Deoband, Tablighis and Talibs," an essay for the *Social Science Research Council After September 11* series, available at the Social Science Research council website: http://www.ssrc.org/sept11/essays/ accessed May 2, 2012. For the idea of neofundamentalism, see Roy, *Globalized Islam*, p. 1.
50. The quotation is from Maulana Ashraf 'Ali Thanawi. See Barbara Daly Metcalf's landmark work, *Perfecting Women*, p. 132.
51. Gaborieau, "Nineteenth-Century Indian 'Wahhabi,' " pp. 206–7.
52. Barbara Daly Metcalf, "Travelers' Tales in the Tablighi Jama'at," *Annals of the American Academy of Political and Social Science*, 588 (2003): 136–48, here p. 137.
53. See Metcalf, " 'Traditionalist' Islamic Activism."
54. Gaborieau, "Nineteenth-Century Indian 'Wahhabi,' " p. 234.
55. Ibid., pp. 230–31.
56. Ibid., p. 209.
57. Ibid., p. 211.
58. Ibid., pp. 225–28.
59. Metcalf, *Perfecting Women*, pp. 73–77.
60. Ibid., p. 74.
61. Ibid., p. 77.
62. Gaborieau, "Nineteenth Century-Indian 'Wahhabi,' " p. 210.
63. Metcalf, *Perfecting Women*, p. 145.
64. Peter van der Veer, "Playing or Praying: A Sufi Saint's Day in Surat," *Journal of Asian Studies* 51:3 (1992): 545–64, here pp. 545–46. Barbara Metcalf, in " 'Traditionalist' Islamic Activism," places the Tablighi Jama'at within the family of Deoband-inspired South Asian activist groups.
65. Moussalli, "Islamic Democracy and Pluralism," p. 304, n. 2.
66. Ibid.

67. See Charles J. Adams, "Mawdudi and the Islamic State," in John L. Esposito, ed., *Voices of Resurgent Islam* (New York: Oxford University Press, 1983), pp. 99–133.
68. Roy, *Globalized Islam*, pp. 234–35.
69. Ibid., p. 287.
70. Ibid., pp. 287–88.
71. Qureshi, "Transcending Space," p. 48.
72. See S. V. R. Nasr, "The Rise of Sunni Militancy in Pakistan: the Changing Role of Islamism and the Ulama in Society and Politics," *Modern Asian Studies* 34:1 (2000): 139–80, for a discussion of the various Islamist groups in modern Pakistan.
73. The question of attacks on shrines and mosques in modern South Asia is complicated by two other critical considerations. First, there is what some have described as a decades-long "low-grade civil war" between Sunni and Shi'i political groups in Pakistan, which includes attacks on mosques and sometimes shrines. Part of this conflict is detailed by S. V. R. Nasr in his "Rise of Sunni Militancy in Pakistan," pp. 139–40. Second, Hindu-Muslim communal violence involving religious sites, as epitomized in the Babri Masjid affair in Ayodhya, introduces yet another set of concerns that can make South Asian Muslim shrines the targets of both Hindu and Muslim assailants.
74. See Werbner, *Anthropology of a Global Sufi Cult* and Werbner, "Stamping the Earth," pp. 309–38 for notice of how particular, often regional devotional practices common in Pakistan have emerged in Great Britain.
75. See Ahmed Rashid, *Taliban: Militant Islam, Oil and Fundamentalism in Central Asia*, (New Haven, Conn.: Yale University Press, 2001) for an account of some of the religious symbolism employed by the Taliban.

2

Boundaries and Baraka

CHRISTIANS, MUSLIMS, AND A PALESTINIAN SAINT

Lance D. Laird

Introduction

TAUFIK CANAAN NOTES that Jews, Christians, and Muslims often shared pilgrimage sites in early twentieth-century Palestine, venerating Elijah, Mar Jiryis (St. George), and Khaḍr (*Khiḍr*) as one shared saint.[1] In the century since he wrote, religious reform, military conflicts, and the politics of occupation have severed Mar Elyas and his Jewish devotees from the common feast.

The Interim Agreement on the West Bank and the Gaza Strip (also called Oslo 2, signed on September 28, 1995) gave Palestinians self-rule in the major population centers of Bethlehem, Hebron, Jenin, Nablus, Qalqilya, Ramallah, and Tulkarm. In the spring of 1996, many Palestinians were still hopeful that the Accords were a step toward statehood and the end of the military occupation. The West Bank (the area between the Jordanian border and Israel's 1967 "Green Line" border), however, was divided by the Oslo 2 Agreement into three different areas of control, each separated by military or police checkpoints: Area A, the central urban areas, where the Palestinian National Authority (PNA) assumed civil and security control; Area B, where the PNA assumed civil control but shared security control with the Israeli military; and Area C, where Israel maintained both civil and security control (see figs. 2.1, 2.2).

In mid-1990s Bethlehem, the church of Mar Elyas (St. Elijah) stood on the Jerusalem side of an Israeli military checkpoint, and Bethlehem-district Christians and Muslims had to apply for a permit to visit; this is still the case today. In a land where lines on the map mark separate spheres of control, where walls of separation mean security to some and exclusion to others, boundary crossing between religious communities assumes social and political significance.

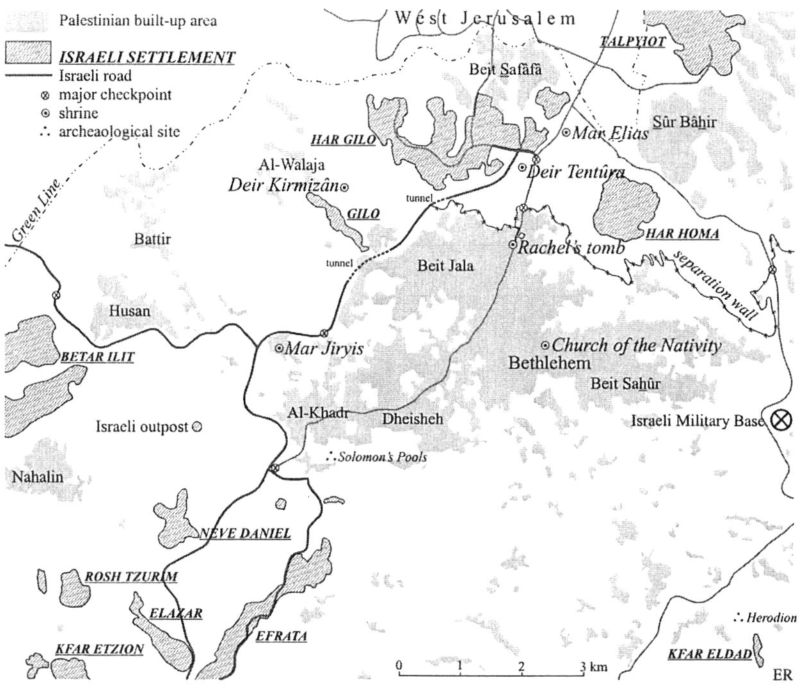

FIGURE 2.1 Map of Bethlehem District in southern West Bank, including al-Khaḍr village. Israeli settlements, roads and checkpoints are firm boundaries for Palestinian towns and villages. © Eric Ross.

In the Muslim village of al-Khaḍr, just west of Bethlehem in the Israeli-occupied West Bank, stands a small Greek Orthodox church that plays a significant role in the confluence of everyday Muslim and Christian devotion in the West Bank. During ethnographic fieldwork on lived religion that I conducted in Bethlehem between 1995 and 1996, informants routinely invoked the curious story of St. George—known to Christians as Mar Jiryis and to Muslims as Khaḍr (classical Arabic, "Khiḍr")—when I inquired about Muslim-Christian relations in the Occupied Territories. A Muslim neighbor recommended that I go to the village named for him, "Al-Khaḍr... There are always Muslims and Christians there!" while a Christian neighbor confirmed, "The Muslims believe in al-Khaḍr just as much as we do!" For centuries, Muslims and Christians in the region have sought protection, healing, and blessings from Mar Jiryis/Khaḍr for matters large and small, and they make common pilgrimages to his local shrines.[2] Yet the stories of saints are never linear nor simply given; and they are frequently refracted through local political and religious conditions. Samantha Riches' recent study of St. George as

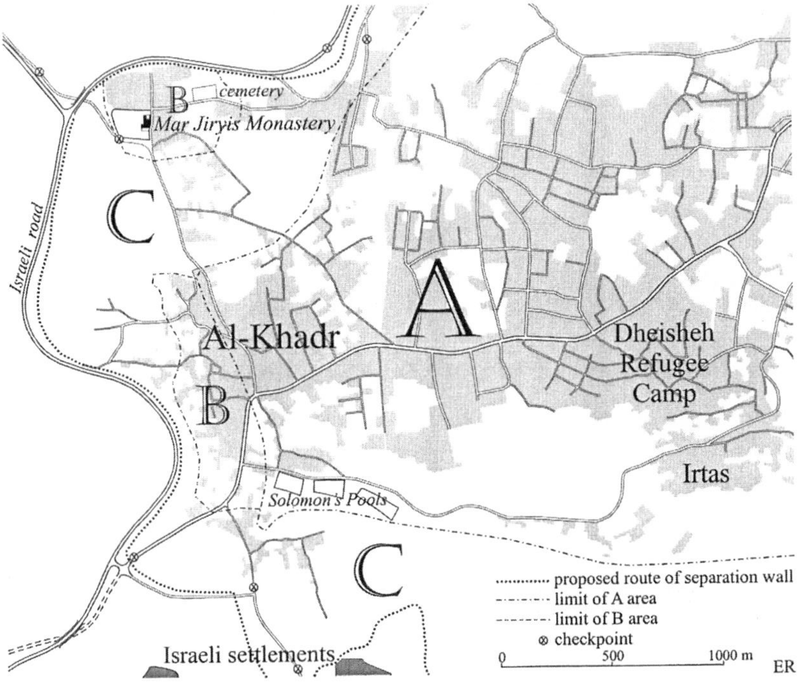

FIGURE 2.2 Map of al-Khaḍr village, showing location of Mar Jiryis church complex. © Eric Ross.

the many-faced patron saint of towns and nations throughout eastern and western Europe and the Levant demonstrates how the saint absorbs popular legends in interaction with diverse political and cultural environments. The most prominent example is his rescue of a Libyan princess from a water-dwelling dragon, which he subdues and kills in exchange for the conversion of the village to Christianity. From this medieval legend comes the standard icon of a young knight on a white horse piercing a dragon's mouth.[3] We need, therefore, to examine more closely the ways in which Palestinian Muslims and Christians (whether Greek Orthodox, Roman or Greek Catholic, or Protestant) use Mar Jiryis/Khaḍr to produce a contextual understanding of Muslim-Christian relations through specific—but often contested and ambiguous—discourses and practices.

Much as Orsi portrays the Virgin Mary, Mar Jiryis/Khaḍr enters into a particular culture's web of relationships between heaven and earth, between individuals, and between communities. Saints make and sustain "culture," even as they are made and sustained by it, "in dynamic exchanges with [their] devout."[4] In Taylor's study of late medieval Egypt, he demonstrates how the nexus of saints, *ziyāra* (visitation) to the shrines of saints, and the stories of the saints related at these shrines reflect the social construction of "moral imagination."[5] Benedict Anderson's notion of nationalism as the social construction of "imagined communities"[6] points us toward the political dimensions of this moral imagination—in other words, the ways a community generates and transmits collective sensibilities of moral order,[7] the boundaries between right and wrong, insider and outsider. Hertz contends that "the holy place speaks for and of a community,"[8] and Brown relates the rise of the cult of saints in late antiquity to hopes for protection and justice in a world whose power structures were rapidly changing,[9] a world not unlike the Palestinian occupied territories. In the holy places where the relics and symbols of saints can be touched and *baraka* received by both Muslims and Christians, we may encounter a contested, ambiguous cultural-religious vessel for healing from personal suffering, for Palestinian national aspirations of security and justice, and for the construction and crossing of boundaries.

The Cult of the Saint(s)

Orsi argues that "the modern world has assiduously and systematically disciplined the senses not to experience sacred presence; the imaginations of moderns are trained toward sacred absence."[10] And yet, for many people the world over, such "presence" of the divine in holy places, objects, and persons is integral to their way of being in the contemporary world. When Muslims and scholars of religion discuss practices of *ziyāra* to shrines of the *awliyā'* (sg., *walī,* one near to God, a friend of God; often translated "saint"), they employ the term *baraka*. The term means "blessing" and connotes a power that is present in holy people and objects. Taylor explains that it is roughly homologous to the Christian concept of *praesentia* or "presence of the holy."[11]

Throughout Palestine, several hundred churches are dedicated to Mar Jiryis, but he is present throughout the "secular" environment as well. The dragon-slaying soldier mounted on a white horse appears in concrete reliefs above the doorway of new houses or office buildings, often accompanied by the pious Muslim phrase, "This is from the grace of God." Needlework portraits of the saint adorn the salon walls of many homes in Bethlehem. In Christian homes, his image often shares wall space with icons of the Virgin and Child and possibly a crucifix or an icon of Christ as Pantocrator. In a Muslim home in Beit Jala hangs a framed black cloth embossed in gold with the Āyat al-Kursī or "throne verse" from the Qur'an, declaring the sovereignty of God. On an adjoining wall hangs an image of the saint, Khaḍr, astride a white horse.

Why is the image of Mar Jiryis everywhere you look, I asked? The simplest answer was: "because he protects the people. I don't know why, but we all believe he protects us." Amina explained her Muslim parents' icon: "Some people believe Khaḍr has the power to protect the house from evil things." These devotional images or "media of presence" mark ways in which Palestinian Muslims and Christians act upon their world.[12] Muslim taxi drivers hang Khaḍr's image and the throne verse from rear-view mirrors to invoke the divine protective power mediated by both saint and Qur'an. Similarly, Christian drivers often place an image of the Virgin Mary, usually a Madonna and child, on the dashboard of their taxi or private automobile "for protection." An image of Mar Jiryis frequently appears beside the Virgin. More common for Christians, however, is a saint pendant on a gold necklace. Mikhail, a Catholic hairdresser, explains, "Mar Jiryis is important to Palestinians because he is a protector." Showing me the small gold image of Mar Jiryis on his neck chain, next to the cross, he said, "He protects me so that nothing will happen to me. Like he protected the girl from the dragon.... Mar Jiryis and the other saints are special people, because God has come to them and given them power over certain things." Mar Jiryis' primary role in everyday life in Bethlehem, then, is protection from evil and harm.

The Story of the Church

I first ventured to al-Khaḍr to meet with the Greek Orthodox priest, Abuna (Father) Theophilos, on a sunny spring afternoon. The taxi headed southwest from Bethlehem to Dheisheh refugee camp, then turned west off the main artery through the archway that marks the village entrance. We drove down the main street of the relatively quiet village, with its flat-topped stone and cement-block houses climbing the northern slope up to the Christian town of Beit Jala, and level fields extending behind houses to the south. Crossing through "Area C" before arriving at the church involved inspection by armed Israeli soldiers at two checkpoints. In the northwestern quarter of the village, in jointly patrolled Area B, stands the Greek Orthodox monastery of Mar Jiryis. An orchard and open fields extend from the main road to an Israeli "ring road" for the exclusive use of Jewish settlers. For months during the years 1995 and 1996, the women in al-Khaḍr confronted Israeli soldiers and bulldozers to protest confiscation of their lands for a "security zone" around the road (see fig. 2.2). Fragmentation of agriculture, trade, social and religious life is an everyday experience.

The monastery in al-Khaḍr is a high-walled complex of three main buildings, with two large courtyards between them. The small church stands between a now-defunct sanatorium and the cloister. The large two-story dormitory, arranged in a horseshoe around the courtyard, houses the Greek monk and priest, Abuna Theophilos from the island of Corfu.

Abuna Theophilos invites me for coffee on his balcony. Ahmad, a twenty-year-old Muslim from the village who lives in the dormitory and takes care of the monastery, joins our conversation. As we enjoy the pleasant breeze, the bearded priest recounts the story of the church:

> Four hundred years ago, just about, there was a priest in Bethlehem, and he had a lot of money. This is the tradition, anyway. Well, one night while he was sleeping, a figure appeared to him and said, "You must build a church for me, in my name." He woke up and remembered the vision, but he didn't think anything of it and tried to forget about it. But then the next night the figure appeared again in his dream and he said, "You must build me a church, in my name." The third night it happened again, and the priest asked, "But who are you?" And the man replied, "I am Mar Jiryis."
>
> When the priest got up that morning, he decided he had to take the dream seriously. So he went out to Beit Sahour [historically a Christian town] to look for some land to buy for the church. A *fellāḥ* [peasant farmer] came up to him and asked what he was looking for, and the priest told him he wanted to buy some land in order to build a church for Mar Jiryis. The *fellāḥ* laughed at him and said, "Why do you want to buy land here in Beit Sahour, when we have no more land? I know a place not far away, though, where there is land that belonged to the mother of Mar Jiryis. This is the place you should build the church."
>
> So they went together from Beit Sahour to al-Khaḍr... When they got here, the villagers told the priest about the tradition that the land here belonged to Imm Jiryis. She was from Palestine, you know. Her family was from Lid [Lydda, near Tel Aviv]... Anyway, the tradition among the Muslims in the village was always that this land belonged to the mother of Jiryis. She had a house here and lands. All this land that you see belongs to the Orthodox Church [pointing out over the expanse of grass beyond the sanatorium]. The people showed this priest from Bethlehem where the ruins of the house were. He decided that this was definitely a sign from God that he should build a church here.

In this story of the church's origin, the saint engages the priest in ways that cross the boundaries between heaven and earth, urban and rural, elite and popular, Muslim and Christian. And yet everyone, including Abuna Theophilos, knows that these boundaries exist, and that the stories of the saints invoked at his church are different, divergent, even contradictory.

The Stories of the Saints

According to a Greek Orthodox Church pamphlet, Mar Jiryis was born in the year 275 CE in Cappadocia. After his father's martyrdom for faith in Christ, his mother fled to her native Palestine, to the city of Lydda (Ar. *Al-Ludd*, Heb. *Lōd*), near modern Tel Aviv. Young Jiryis enlisted in the Roman army, and after valiant service against the Persians, commanded Emperor Diocletian's guard.

Beginning in 303 CE, Diocletian ordered the destruction of churches and the persecution of Christians. After mourning his mother's death and distributing his inheritance to the Christian martyrs' widows and orphans in Asia Minor, Jiryis returned and announced publicly that he was a Christian. Persuasion failing to produce a recantation, Diocletian ordered a series of horrific tortures and attempted executions. Each time Jiryis would reappear before the emperor unscathed. Such miracles provoked conversions among the guards and the court, including the Empress Alexandra, and Diocletian executed all the new converts. Jiryis raised some martyrs from the dead, which only angered the emperor more. Under pretense of recanting, Jiryis entered a crowded temple, forced the god Apollo to confess Jesus Christ as the only true God, and then cast demons out of the temple. Finally the emperor had the willing Jiryis beheaded, and he became a martyr.[13]

In the Orthodox Church, Mar Jiryis is the model soldier and avenger of women.[14] The popular story of his rescuing a young virgin from a dragon is a medieval addition, although the iconography in both Catholic and Orthodox churches, and in Bethlehem's Muslim and Christian homes, adopt the dragon-slayer motif.[15] The shrine over his tomb in Lydda is an important pilgrimage site throughout the Levant region.

The village name al-Khaḍr, however, bears the name of a Muslim, not a Christian, figure.[16] According to Muslim tradition, Khaḍr (*Khiḍr*) is the name of the mysterious figure Moses encounters in Surah 18:60–82 of the Qur'an. Moses and an attendant go searching for "a servant of Allah" to teach Moses the "secret knowledge" of God. Finding him, Moses asks to be his student. Khaḍr tells Moses he lacks the patience to bear the lessons, but Moses promises not to question. The teacher then sinks a boat, slays a young man, and rebuilds a wall in a town that showed him no hospitality. Moses protests Khaḍr's violations of divine law and justice. The teacher explains that his apparent cruelties were actually merciful fulfillment of God's will to prevent further harm, and that his rebuilding of the wall was a way of redressing the unjust treatment of orphans. Then Khaḍr, the immortal one, disappears from the scene.

Muslim commentators debate whether Khaḍr should be considered a prophet (*nabī*) or merely a "close companion" (*walī*). He plays a significant role in the Sufi tradition as a figure who meets traveling dervishes, who inspires them or answers questions, who rescues them from danger, and who sometimes performs a mystical initiation. He is the mysterious and immortal mystical guide.[17] It is worthy of note that "Khaḍr" in Arabic also connotes the color green, leading many non-Muslim scholars to associate this Muslim immortal with a pre-Christian Middle Eastern god of vegetation.

On the feast days of Mar Jiryis, Christians and Muslims converge on the Greek Orthodox church in al-Khaḍr village to venerate both Mar Jiryis and Khaḍr as a single saint. This shared local custom offends many orthodox representatives of these traditions. Local Islamic and Christian officials sought to reject the "popular" practice in terms of ignorance, confusion, and illogical thinking. One Islamic *waqf* official in Bethlehem explained to me:

> Al-Khaḍr is very different than Mar Jiryis. Mar Jiryis was a man who killed two snakes to protect the girl and the land. Al-Khaḍr was a prophet who taught Moses the right way. He is a very different figure in Islam. And besides, Muslims don't pray to saints. We pray directly to God, because only God can answer our prayers.

This Muslim official objected both to the elision of the saints' identities and to the practice of shrine visitation, perhaps because it involves the imitation of Christian practices.[18] Abuna Theophilos similarly ridiculed the popular elision of the saints' identities. He described a Muslim who wanted to write a book about the church in al-Khaḍr:

> I asked him if he knew when Khaḍr lived. He said he lived at the time of Moses. So I asked him when Mar Jiryis lived. He said at the time of Jesus. I said, "but Jesus and Moses didn't live at the same time, did they?" He said, yes, that Jesus and Moses and Mar Jiryis all lived at the same time, or just about.
>
> I told him, "You are wrong about three things. First, Moses lived over a thousand and several hundred years before Jesus, and Mar Jiryis

> lived a couple hundred years after Jesus. So Khaḍr at the time of Moses can't possibly be the same as Mar Jiryis." But he said that they were the same...
>
> Khaḍr, the one written about in the Qur'an, they consider him a prophet (*nabī*) and not a saint (*qaddīs*). Just the opposite, we consider Mar Jiryis a saint and not a prophet. Christians don't recognize any prophets after Jesus, except one, and his name was John the Baptist, so Mar Jiryis cannot be a prophet, but only a saint.

When the priest finished his story, his Muslim assistant Ahmad responded, "No. He is one person. Muslims believe that he lived at the time of Moses, and Christians think he lived after Jesus. But he is really the same person. We are not so concerned with the time. He has the same story and the same power." So how do the two saints become one, with "the same story and the same power"?

Boundary Crossings

Muslim baptisms in the church provide an interesting example of convergence in practice. Several Christians told stories of Muslims they know who had baptized their babies in the church. For example:

> I know a [Muslim] woman who had a vision of the Virgin Mary. She had three children who all died when they were babies, like around three months. And she was really worried, and she prayed. The Virgin Mary appeared to her and told her that if she baptized her baby and named him George—which is a Christian name, not a Muslim name—that the baby would live. And so she had a baby, and she baptized him, and named him George, and he is still living.

Curious about these stories, I eagerly awaited the feast day. On two balmy days in May 1996, hundreds of pilgrims, both Muslims and Christians, arrived in family cars and taxis or walked from Beit Sahour, Bethlehem, Beit Jala, or villages to the south. Vendors lined the street to sell shiny painted aluminum icons and crosses, cotton candy and slushes, toy drums and wooden key chains custom carved with your name. Girls in pink dresses and boys in collared shirts clambered for a seat on a small Ferris wheel as parents snapped pictures. Beit Jala's Orthodox scouts stood uniformed at the monastery door, distributing souvenir pins and collecting donations. The pilgrims entered a small alley and ducked left into the church door.

Inside the church in al-Khaḍr village, a young Muslim woman explained to her son that al-Khaḍr protected him. The woman wore a plain blue dress and no head covering. She held her son up before a small icon of Mar Jiryis. Beside her stood an older woman in a bright pink peasant dress, a white scarf over her hair. Realizing I had overheard, the first explained:

> I came because this is the feast of Khaḍr—peace be upon him—and my son is named Khaḍr. I named him Khaḍr and had him baptized in the church as a vow. You see, my mother-in-law had four children and three of them died. The only one to survive was my husband. So I decided to baptize my babies so they would go on living. I baptized not only Khaḍr but also my other son.

With a somewhat quizzical look, I ask how a Muslim could baptize children in the church, and she responded defensively:

> I baptized them like anyone baptizes their children. Like the Christians. I believe in *ʿĪsā, ʿalayhī as-salām* [Jesus, peace be upon him].... Look, this is his godmother [introducing a second middle-aged woman next to her and pointing to a large pendant of the Virgin that hung from her neck. The second woman nodded in affirmation]. She is a Christian, and she was here when the priest baptized him!

Outside the church on the same day, a young woman cuddling a redheaded baby told me, "I came to the church because... my little boy is named George. Mar Jiryis appeared to me in a dream when I was pregnant and told me I had to name my son George. So I did, and that's why I'm here." Explaining her reluctance to baptize her child in this church, she pointed to her friend:

> I'm Latin, and she's Orthodox... I know this man, and he is Latin [Catholic]. He made a vow and called his son George, and he came here to have his son baptized. So the son will remain Greek Orthodox, but his father is Latin. But he made this vow. This is how it goes.

So this is how it goes. But *it* seems to go in a number of different directions. In the church in the midst of a Muslim village, Muslims and Christians gather to venerate a saint they call by different names. Muslims baptize their babies, and Catholics have reservations about baptizing theirs. A shared popular religious tradition provides the symbolic "proof" of interreligious harmony, and yet, such sharing and harmony are not uniformly accepted even in the Bethlehem district.

The interreligious community around this shared saint is most visible, however, in the ritual action on the feast days. In the vestibule, pilgrims touched and kissed a gold-clad icon of Mar Jiryis to the left of the sanctuary's archway. Caretaker Ahmad and a Christian woman from nearby Beit Safafa sold candles, ranging from beeswax candles about two feet long to long white ones almost six feet tall. Inside the small church, its walls brightly painted in sky blue, most of the icons on the four square pillars seem stylistically modern. The iconostasis, rather imposing for the size of the church, holds traditional icons of Jesus, the Virgin Mary, John the Baptist, two angels, Elijah (the traditional Jewish form of George and Khaḍr) and Mar Jiryis.

Much of the activity of pilgrims took place around a glass-encased icon on the center right wall of the nave. Dated 1713, the central panel of the triptych depicts a young mounted soldier with spear in hand, its point in the mouth of a supine red dragon. One side panel depicts the torture of Jiryis in boiling water and the resurrection of a dead man before the emperor Diocletian. The opposite side panel depicts the beheading of Mar Jiryis, with a small image of St. Alexandra hovering reclined in the prison window. Below, the saint arranges miraculous transport to Palestine for a church pillar donated by a young woman from Istanbul/Constantinople. The glass doors encasing the triptych hold photos, jewelry, bills, and coins, offerings to the saint on behalf of loved ones in need. Many pilgrims touched and kissed this icon and placed their candles in the adjacent stands.

During the Sunday liturgy on the morning of *yawm al-shaṭḥa* (lit., "day of escape, adventure"; the first of two pilgrimage days), a few dozen worshipers lit candles and venerated icons while priest and chorus intoned the prayers and readings. Most attention focused on the liturgical action, though people entered and left intermittently. On the feast day, however, standing room was scarce during the liturgy, at which an Arab archimandrite presided and the chorus was large. Candles blazed in the stands as people pushed toward the icons. Incense and candle smoke filled the church as attendants rushed busily to extinguish bent candles and prevent injury to the pilgrims.

A Muslim woman from Bethlehem explained her presence in the church:

> Today is the feast day of Khaḍr, and we wanted to come and celebrate, because we believe in al-Khaḍr. We are Muslims, but there is no

> difference between Christians and Muslims. This is a holy place, and we respect it. Also, my father has been ill, and we wanted to come because of that. We light candles and everything. We believe in Khaḍr like the Christians do. Maybe it's because we live with Christians all the time, I don't know. And also, we came because we wanted to take a trip, to "smell the air." We came here in the morning, and we brought food, and we'll stay all day.

Religious celebration within a holy place and time, the need to intercede with the saint, and the affirmation of an imagined interreligious community are blended in this act of pilgrimage.

Intercession and Baraka

Amira, a young Muslim professional, explained why she lit a candle in the church in al-Khaḍr:

> I am a Muslim, but I had a Christian friend when I was young, and she used to light candles for us. I would go to the Church of the Nativity with her, and we would light candles. Whenever one of my family was sick, she used to light candles for us. It just became like a tradition for me. Now, whenever I go into a church, I like to light candles. Whenever one of us is sick, I still like to go to the Church of the Nativity and light candles. This time I lit one for [my sister] and one for [my brother-in-law, under administrative detention in an Israeli prison].

Lighting candles in a church is a Christian practice that she and other Muslims have adopted through observing and accompanying Christian friends.

A group of youth from the Lutheran church in Bethlehem entered the church. When asked why they came, a young woman replied, "That's a tough question. My mother told me I had to come and light a candle for my brother. So I came. I don't always come to the feast of al-Khaḍr, but it is just something you do, because it's here, I guess." Such responses were fairly common among both Muslims and Christians. A long history of social custom for lighting candles in this church on the feast day is the only reason many pilgrims need.

Imm Hasan, a middle-aged Muslim woman from Dar Rahhal village, brought a friend from the Jewish settlement of Efrat that surrounds her village "to see our traditions." She had brought a gift to the church for her mother, adding, "For a long time, we have lit candles or brought something whenever we had a sick child, and we have prayed that he would get well."

The pervasiveness of such petitionary prayer to the saint is perhaps illustrated best by George, a young man from Beit Sahour, lighting candles beside the large icon in al-Khaḍr. A self-described Marxist-Leninist, he explained: "Perhaps I have a different idea about the saint than most. I can't say I believe in him like other people. But I came here to light a candle for my mother, because she has cancer." Asked why Mar Jiryis was important, he replied, "Because he is a Palestinian saint. He was from here. Perhaps it is also because he is close to the people, and the churches are nearby, easily accessible to the people." Even for those whose secular political ideologies shape their primary identity, the saint provides a last resort in times of family health crises. Mar Jiryis is a "Palestinian saint," accessible because he is locally present. One might locate George at the opposite end of the spectrum from the elderly Abu Hani, who explained that the faithful who pray most diligently in this church in al-Khaḍr can hear the hooves of Mar Jiryis' horse and see him riding into the church.

These petitioners address Mar Jiryis/Khaḍr for both general and specific problems. Pilgrims insist, "Whatever you ask of him, he will answer." A young Orthodox Christian woman articulated her understanding of the intercession (*wasṭa*) of the saints:

> Saints are instrumental in aiding Christians to interpret the scriptures. There is a verse about God giving to the apostles the authority to forgive sins and loose things on the earth, and this authority was given then to the saints and then to the priests. One needs the *wasṭa* of saints, because God cannot be approached directly. Saints are not ordinary persons, but the Holy Spirit is working in them.

She then offered an example of how Mar Jiryis is particularly efficacious:

> A while ago, I was a student at Talitha Kumi [Lutheran School]. I had a test that I didn't study for. I came here to the church and lit a candle and asked George to help me. I went to the test, and I didn't even answer all the questions or anything, but I got a good grade. I believe that this is from Mar Jiryis, that when the teacher was grading the paper, she didn't see the wrong things. Some people think things just happen. Others say, "*Yā Khaḍr!*" because they think Mar Jiryis has a role in these things.

Many of the pilgrims with whom I spoke on the day of the feast came seeking such quotidian interventions.

The practice of seeking intercession from the saint has various explanations, though this young woman's explanation is not far from that of Abuna Theophilos:

> God cures the people who come here. Mar Jiryis intercedes, mediates for the people before God... I pray in the church in front of the icon of Mar Jiryis so that somebody will be cured. It is not I who cures them, but God through me and through Mar Jiryis. But even more than it depends on me and on Mar Jiryis, it depends on what is inside the person who is asking for the help. If inside him is purity and strong faith, then the prayer will be answered.

The sense of proximity to the saint in the churches dedicated to him, and particularly in the icons, suggests a concentration of the *baraka* of the saint in certain objects and places. Pilgrims who brushed their hands across the face of the icons explained that they wanted to partake of the *baraka* of the saint, a power that would protect them from harm and disease.

An elderly Muslim woman brought her son's family to the church. She guided them over to the icon of Mar Jiryis, quickly dipped her whole hand in the oil candle beside it, and, with quiet laughter, smeared it liberally on the forehead and hair of her grandchildren and their parents. She smiled brightly as they left the church.

Christian pilgrims dipped two or three fingers of their right hand into the candle oil and then made the sign of the cross on their head and chest. Muslim pilgrims usually placed some of the oil on their foreheads, then ran their hand through their hair. The Muslim gesture is reminiscent of *wuḍū* (ablution) before prayer, suggesting that Muslims and Christians appropriate the *baraka* of the same oil in gestures specific to their ritual traditions.

The story of a child with no hair powerfully illustrates the healing property of the oil from the candle in al-Khaḍr's church. Ahmad the Muslim caretaker agreed with Abuna Theophilos that the people must have faith that God will heal them, and that somehow the saint mediates the power. This time, Ahmad relates, the *baraka* came through the oil in his hands:

> I remember one time when I was here by myself. This couple from Taʿamre [Bedouin villages east of Bethlehem] came. They had a little boy with a strange disease on his head. His hair was falling out, right

> on top of his head. It was like this [demonstrates the smoothness of his own face and wipes his hand across the middle crown of his head].
>
> They wanted me to do something for them. I told them I couldn't do anything for them, and that the priest wasn't here. They really wanted help. They said they had been to I don't know how many doctors and hospitals and had spent all their money on drugs, and nothing worked. I said, "The only thing I know is maybe I can paint the child's head with the oil from the candles in the church." We came into the church, and I painted all over the child's head with the oil, and then they left.
>
> Two days later, they came back, and the child's hair was like this on top of his head [holding his fingers about half an inch apart, eyes wide.] They came back again two weeks later, and all his hair had grown back. They were so happy. Believe me, it was a miracle!

The Muslim couple had faith that the saint's power would heal. In a tangible way, the oil became the vehicle for this miraculous healing, and Ahmad was convinced of the saint's *baraka* and its accessibility without the mediation of a Christian priest.

Baraka *and the Chain*

After the liturgy on both feast days in al-Khaḍr, a large chain was hung in the front right corner of the church, beside the triptych and behind the right front pillar. The gray-silver links formed a long loop, with two-piece neck-shackles the only interruption. Pilgrims placed the shackles over their own necks, clicked them together in front, then brought them back over their heads and kissed the shackles. They repeated this action three times. The third time, many of the pilgrims stepped through the chain loop or passed their children through it. ʿAdnan, an Orthodox Christian from Beit Jala, demonstrated the proper procedure for placing the chain over my neck, kissing it and stepping through. I then asked him why people do this, and he replied, "Because our grandfathers did this. I don't know why." Others suggested it was like making a wish, so they joined in. The chain is an integral part of the local tradition of shrine visitation at al-Khaḍr.

Pilgrims explained the origins of the chain in different ways. Interestingly, none of the Muslims I asked had any explanation of the history of the chain, but Christian informants had a number of theories. Perhaps the most popular of these was that the chain had bound Mar Jiryis during the great persecution, while others suggested it was used to torture him. The scout leader explained that it was not the actual chain, but rather it was symbolic of the chain that bound Mar Jiryis. All agreed, however, that as a result of its association with the torture and persecution of the saint, the chain was endowed with *baraka*. A middle-aged woman from Beit Jala suggested that the chain symbolized the saint's triumph over his persecutors, and a young father from Bethlehem explained that the chain therefore "gives strength and courage and *baraka* and protection." Such explanations represent symbolic reversal, as torture becomes triumph, an instrument of oppression becomes a source of protection and strength. This symbolic reversal mirrors, if only dimly, both Christian theology of crucifixion-resurrection and the mythicized historical construction of contemporary Palestinian political triumph in defeat.[19]

A second explanation of the *baraka* of the chain is its association with the white steed Mar Jiryis rides. Ibrahim's toddler son started crying when he put the chain on the child's neck. The father explained that the saint's horse chain "has the power of the saint in it, to keep you safe, because the saint was strong, and he was a warrior. He was courageous, too, so we believe that the chain gives you courage as well. It is good for you."

Regardless of the explanation of its origin, the importance of the chain lies in its reputation for healing. Nahida, a middle-aged Orthodox Christian, claimed, "If you're sick or there is anything wrong with you, and you put this chain on you, it makes you well." I must have looked doubtful, as she added, "Really!" and explained that "they used to chain the mentally ill with this chain and it would cure them. People would go there and sleep and in the morning they would be well." The healing properties of the chain are the most famous aspect of the church at al-Khaḍr village.

Healing stories of persons with psychological disorders or nervous conditions being chained to the walls of the church or the sanatorium (which was once attached to the church by a metal wire, according to some reports) form the basis of local legend.[20] A young Muslim man from al-Khaḍr village gives a representative example:

> My mother's sister was going crazy, because she had some kind of nerve problem. She couldn't control her actions. This was when she was 12 or 14 years old. My mother took her to al-Khaḍr and asked the priest if she could stay in the church for one or two nights for healing. The priest came and got the keys and locked her in. He gave her a mattress and a blanket, and she was in the church for one night. It was scary in there. There is nothing but one little window up in the top of the

> church. The priest came in the morning to bring breakfast to her or something, and he found her outside. He asked, "What are you doing outside?" She replied, "*He* helped me get out." It was Khaḍr. She was cured. My mother wanted to test her. She said to her, "Let's get you some grapes from the vineyards here at the monastery." She said, "No. This is a holy estate, and we shouldn't take any grapes from here. We can wait until we get home." My mother was convinced that it was a true story. My aunt is an old woman with married children now.

The reputation of the church and its healing chain is the reason many villagers bring families on the feast day. A Muslim woman from an outlying village explained, "I came because my son... can't talk. I put the shackles over there in his mouth, so that maybe he can talk. I hope it will work. I have heard of other people who had children who couldn't talk, and they did this." Asked why she thinks Khaḍr has this power, she admitted, "People say he does. I don't know.... I really have no idea. I just came because I hoped this would help my son. We lit candles and put the chain over the children." The chain ritual is replete with Christian associations. Muslims, who recognize the *baraka* available in the chain but not the etiological story of its source, then emulate the practice.

While the pilgrimage is a religious activity for both Muslims and Christians, it also has a profound social dimension, uniting families, friends, and neighbors across sectarian lines in the celebration of a common saint, Mar Jiryis/Khaḍr. Bowman's statement about a pilgrimage to nearby Mar Elyas (also a site of Christian and Muslim devotion) could likewise apply to al-Khaḍr:

> The festivities... seemed to serve as a "floating signifier" for the people of the region. Each individual was able to attribute to the place and the gathering meanings personal to them, and yet, because the time and the place served as a place of inscription for so many diverse meanings and motives, the feast constituted a community. People recognized that community at the same time as they recognized the multiplexity of its character; it was, in a very real sense, a concentration of the community which they moved through day to day but in a more dilute [*sic*] form.[21]

In the act of pilgrimage, the stories of saints, the traditions of ancestors, and the material objects of devotion connect with the desires of individuals and families for restoration of whole bodies and minds, and the desires of neighbors to share a relationship with each other. The pilgrimage constitutes a "people" across boundaries in the presence of the holy, *baraka*, in this particular place and time.

Vows and Sacrifices

The pilgrims' hopes for the pilgrimage to the church in al-Khaḍr represent only one side of an exchange or negotiation between the saint and the pilgrim. The most common motive expressed for attending the shrine, during the feast or on ordinary days, is the fulfillment of a *nidhr* (*nadhr* in modern standard Arabic) or vow to the saint. People described the vow alternately as a sacrificial gift to the saint or as the fulfillment of a contractual oath. The *nidhr* frames the entire pilgrimage event and forms the basis of all of the ritual action, including the manipulation of the chain. In a sense, the lighting of ordinary candles and the touching of the icons, beyond the simple motivation of receiving *baraka*, is the initiation of a vow to the saint, accompanying the petitions.

Upon arrival at al-Khaḍr on the eve of the feast day, I encounter a mother and daughter, Orthodox Christians from Beit Jala, perspiring from the early morning heat. They explain that they had made a vow to walk from their home to al-Khaḍr. The daughter explained, "We go every year, every single year. And we walk because we made a promise. Lots of people make promises to al-Khaḍr that if something happens they will walk to al-Khaḍr on the feast day. And even if it doesn't happen, you do it, because it is a promise. This is a *nidhr*." The pilgrimage itself and the act of a long, hard walk, sometimes barefoot, constitute a sacrifice of devotion to the saint, the fulfillment of a vow, and a testament to the honor of the individual and the family.

When vows are made, the most common sacrifices are candles, oil, and sheep. Pilgrims speak of gifts, including candles, as a sacrifice. Larger candles—up to six feet tall—carry extra significance as a more expensive sacrifice, though even small candles carry this meaning. While some expressed resentment toward the priests for "changing money in the church" by selling candles, others saw the expense as essential to the sacrifice. A Christian woman from Bethlehem stated simply, "If you ask for something from Mar Jiryis, then you buy a candle or sacrifice an animal as your *nidhr* to show your gratitude."

Pilgrims bring small bottles or large plastic canisters of oil, depositing them under icons or quietly at the back of the church. The Muslim woman who brought oil at her mother's behest quietly asked me what exactly the oil was used for in the church. She merely needed to fulfill the *nidhr* and to light candles as she had done with her mother and grandmother in previous years, both an individual and a familial commitment to maintain the tradition.

Abuna Theophilos explains that vow-making represents a cultural tradition, not a practice regulated by the church:

> The people, when they are having trouble, they will say "*Yā Mar Jiryis! Yā Khaḍr!*" And they will promise Mar Jiryis to give him something if he helps them and answers their prayer. The *nidhr* is according to the possibilities and abilities of the person. Whatever they promise they have to fulfill. It is a promise they make to the saint, and I have nothing to do with it. There are no fixed amounts or anything.... If they promised a candle, they can't bring a sheep to slaughter. They have to bring what they promised.

The sacrifice of a sheep or goat to the saint, however, is more precious than oil and candles. Animal sacrifice resonates with major themes in both the Islamic and Christian traditions. On the occasion of ʿĪd al-Aḍḥā, Muslims sacrifice a sheep or goat in commemoration of Abraham's near-sacrifice of his son, for whom the animal was substituted. I was unable to find a Muslim pilgrim who offered such a sacrifice to verify whether Muslims consciously connect this narrative and the popular *nidhr* practice, though a Christian pilgrim connected it to the near-sacrifice of Isaac and to Jesus as sacrificial lamb. A wide network of symbolic connections associates primary symbols of the tradition with the popular practice of fulfilling a *nidhr* to the saint.

Abuna Theophilos generally tries to dissociate himself from the actual slaughter and is happy that few pilgrims perform the sheep sacrifice. In fact, the priest has so little involvement in the sheep sacrifice that one young Christian couple had difficulty arranging one. With their small child, they led a sheep around on a leash, tethering the animal when they entered the church. The young woman explained simply, "One day when something was wrong. Our son was sick. I said, '*Yā Khaḍr!*' And I made a vow to bring a sheep." The couple found the priest to pray and cut the ear of the sheep, smearing the blood in the sign of the cross on a short column to the right of the church door. They waited for hours for someone to slit the sheep's throat, but they finally decided to leave the sheep tied up in the inner courtyard of the monastery. The young father said to me as they left, "We have fulfilled our vow. The meat is supposed to go to the poor; we can't take any of it. [The priest] can do what he wants with it." While tradition seemed to mandate that they also slaughter the sheep they brought, they were satisfied that their vow was fulfilled without the actual slaughter; they shifted responsibility to the priest for the distribution of the meat or the funds from selling the sheep.

The priest told another sheep story, though, in which the sheep played a decisive role:

> One time this Muslim man came with his daughter. She was very small, only about eight or nine years old. They had a large sheep with them. The man got the sheep out of the car and asked me if I would pray over the sheep so he could take it home and sacrifice it. He said he had made a *nidhr* to al-Khaḍr, but he wanted to take the sheep home and sacrifice it there.
>
> He asked me what I thought about this. I told him that it was his choice. He was free to do whatever he wished. But in my opinion, I think that if you promised the sheep to al-Khaḍr, you should sacrifice it here in the monastery. The little girl spoke up, and she said, "The priest is right. You should do it here if it is for al-Khaḍr." He agreed, and so I told Ahmad here to go find a butcher and bring him to the monastery. He said, "Where am I going to find a butcher?" I told him to go through all the streets around here until he found a butcher. So he went and he asked up and down the streets, but he couldn't find anybody.
>
> The man with the sheep said, "OK. I will take the sheep back and get a friend to come and we will sacrifice the sheep. So he opened up the car, and the sheep was standing behind the car. But all of a sudden, the sheep dropped on the ground like it was dead. I said, "What is this? You brought a sick sheep here to sacrifice?" He said, "No. I swear it was fine when I brought it." It was almost as if the sheep was insisting on staying at the monastery. It really looked like he was dead.
>
> The man looked very scared and he got in his car with the little girl. He came back a few minutes later with his friend, and they had brought a butcher as well. They parked and got out. The sheep rose up, and it was fine. Then they took it over behind the church and slaughtered it. Is this a miracle or what? There are many stories like this of things that happened here—miracles!

While the man's motives for taking the sheep home for slaughter are unclear, the priestly narrator indicates that bringing the sacrifice to the holy place is of primary importance in fulfilling a *nidhr* to the saint, whatever happens to it upon arrival. The story lends his opinion miraculous authority. The pilgrims who journey to the village demonstrate that for them, too, the place of their sacrifice is of utmost importance, for the saint is most present in the shrine dedicated to him. Here the *baraka* is focused in the icons and the chain, and here the saint receives the gifts of candles, oil and sheep, gold and coins. The means of sacrifice is unimportant, and though the sacrificial objects are defined by custom, the place itself is central to the ritual.

Dedicating Children

Parents frequently make a *nidhr* for the healthy birth of children. At some churches, couples carry girls in white dresses with a blue sash, the colors of the Virgin Mary, and present them to the priest for prayers of blessing. Throughout the feast days at al-Khaḍr, several little boys ran about in green shirts and pants, red capes embroidered with a gold cross, and riding caps of red, gold, and green satin with coordinated feathers, often with a yellow plastic sword and scabbard hanging at their side. The little boys were dressed as the soldier-saint himself.

The feast days serve as "name-days" for all sons whose parents have dedicated them to the saint and given them his name. The young mother who led the sheep to al-Khaḍr said, "Today is the feast of al-Khaḍr. So anyone whose name is George, Jiryis or Khaḍr comes to celebrate. We celebrate them on this day. Like [my husband] . . . his father is named George, and our son is, too."

The dedication of a child to the saint is a ritual act in fulfillment of a *nidhr*. The boys costumed as Mar Jiryis become, in a sense, living sacrifices, and by their names they are drawn to this particular place and into relationship with this particular saint throughout their lives. A couple with a small child stood with their extended family behind the church as the crowds flowed out from the feast-day liturgy. The child's aunt explained that they were planning to dress the boy as Khaḍr for the next six months as a vow. The boy's father commented, "I have two brothers who were dressed like Mar Anton (St. Anthony) when they were young. But even though we are Latin, we are going to dress him like Mar Jiryis and change the tradition." The aunt added, "We are all Latin, but why not? We come here to Mar Jiryis." Among the pilgrims, dedication to the saint partially transcends such sectarian boundaries.

Shirin, a middle-aged Orthodox woman from Bethlehem, explained that, if the parents had petitioned Mar Jiryis for a healthy boy, the parents bring the child on his fortieth day to the saint's shrine to be blessed by the priest. They then promise to dress the boy like the saint. A young Christian mother holding her green-clad child in al-Khaḍr explains, "Well, I made a vow before he was born that if he was born healthy, I would dress him like Khaḍr for six months. Some people vow to do it for a year or three months, but I plan to take it off after six months. Every time we take him out, we dress him like this, as a *nidhr*."

The naming and dedication of children returns us to the discussion of baptism, noting that even the name may highlight significant sectarian boundaries among the local Christian communities. While the saint relates to believers ecumenically, and they share the feast, the vows, and dedication of children, the rite of baptism and consequent church membership creates a barrier not easily overcome between Catholic and Orthodox Christians.

Transcending Sectarian Boundaries: "Palestinian" Religion?

The baptism of Muslim infants in Christian churches, in the name of Khaḍr, represents an amalgamation not only of the saint, but also of rituals, that calls attention to the significance of Mar Jiryis/Khaḍr as a shared symbol and link at the level of popular religious practice between Christians and Muslims in Bethlehem. Muslims and Christians in Bethlehem consider Muslim baptism evidence of harmonious interreligious coexistence. Shirin, an Orthodox Christian, commented that Muslims believe in Mar Jiryis more than the Christians, citing as proof the example of Muslims baptizing their infants in the church. When I told her that Abuna Theophilos denies that such Muslim baptisms ever happen, she retorted, "He is from Greece, and they are a little fanatical there. I know they do that. [The Muslim I know] is related to Rashida next door. You can ask her." When Rashida came over later that day, she exclaimed, "That's right! He's my cousin. I went to the baptism, and I ate the cake!"

The overlap of Christian and Muslim interpretations of the ritual action suggests that, on a fundamental level, Palestinian Christians and Muslims in the Bethlehem area share common religious conceptions. The first is that the divine power of blessing, *baraka*, is tangibly accessible in certain sacred objects in particular sacred places associated with a saint or holy person. Contact with such power may heal physical, mental, or spiritual illness and may protect from evil and harm. The second is that one may gain benefits from the *baraka* through oaths and bargains struck in the name of the saint as mediator of this divine power.

On this level, one could say, firstly, there is a "Palestinian religion" associated with a Palestinian saint, in contrast to the more universal traditions. In the conversation with Shirin and Rashida, for instance, the Christian woman offers "proof" that belief in the saint, symbolized by the sacrament of baptism, unites Christians and Muslims. Both Muslims and Christians attest to the participation of local Arab priests in such rituals. Shirin interprets the Greek priest's denial as a product of his Greek-ness and labels him "fanatic," in contrast with the tolerance and intermingling of religious rituals characteristic (for her) of "native" Palestinian society. This delineation of identity is not exactly "national," though it asserts a "Palestinian" cultural identity opposed to a foreign church hierarchy.

Secondly, sectarian boundaries are transcended but simultaneously reinforced here; the saint as unifying symbol is refracted through layers of identity.[22] Herzfeld demonstrates how icons or divine images may become fragmented according to the "segmentary logic" of local social relations.[23] The Muslim woman who baptized her sons for protection insists that she did so "like anyone baptizes their children, like the Christians." While she sees baptism as a normal practice for "anyone," it is a *normative* Christian practice; it is shared, but it is also "theirs."

Muslims who have their children baptized in the church and name them George or Khaḍr do not consider the ritual of baptism an initiation into the Christian tradition. While maintaining their Muslim identity, they use baptism to ensure the protection of their child from evil and harm. Motivated by dreams in which either the saint or the Virgin appears to them and demands that their child be named after Mar Jiryis, they come to the church for a "naming ceremony" that is baptism. The baptismal water is linked to the other objects in the church, the chain and the oil and the icons, from whose healing and protective *baraka* they seek to benefit.

While Muslims know the connection of baptism with Jesus, this connection is secondary, and they do not explicitly seek identification with Jesus through baptism. The Muslim woman justifies baptizing her sons by asserting her faith in *ʿĪsā, ʿalayhī as-salām*, something she claims to share with the Christians. The vocabulary of this assertion is distinctly Muslim, however, as my Muslim associate noted after this conversation. Christians refer to Jesus using the name *Yesūʿ* and do not repeat *ʿalayhī as-saḷām* (peace be upon him) after the names of prophets, as Muslims commonly do. Again, Jesus is shared, but he is also a Muslim Jesus.

In both instances, those asserting the unity of their practice of baptism called a member of the other tradition as witness. Thus, transgression of sectarian divisions provides, simultaneously, both evidence of unity on the level of personal and local relationships, and an acknowledgment of these divisions on the communal level of identity. Transgression requires boundaries.

As Kertzer reminds us, symbols have power often precisely because they are ambiguous and multivalent, allowing them to foster political solidarity in divided societies.[24] The baptism ritual for those who participate in it at the shrine of al-Khaḍr has multiple meanings. For Latin Christians who dedicate their babies to the saint and visit the shrine but hesitate to baptize them, identifying with the saint does not supersede sectarian identity. Some Muslims, however, have apparently crossed this boundary. Sectarian boundaries between churches thus seem more significant for some Christians than the boundary between Christian and Muslim ritual seems for some Muslims. Mar Jiryis becomes a symbol of Christian-Muslim unity on the level of "local" traditional culture (Mar Jiryis *is* Khaḍr in al-Khaḍr village), even while the particular church in which he is venerated retains its significance as a sectarian symbol. In the pilgrimage acts, the symbolic person Mar Jiryis/Khaḍr is refracted through the national-cultural discourse of Muslim-Christian unity and the discourse of personal relations.

During one conversation with the *waqf* official who condemned Muslim participation as "ignorance," even "contradictory to religion," I told him about the many people who speak of this pilgrimage as an important common tradition that brought Christians and Muslims together as Palestinians. He responded:

> I am not against going to al-Khaḍr. If Muslims go to any holy place, they can pray there. Muslims should go and visit all the holy places in this land, because they belong to them. They should visit all the places of the prophets. And in any place that is holy, they can pray to God. But if they go to solicit a favor from Khaḍr, then I say, "No." But the holy places and Khaḍr belong to all.

For this "official" Muslim authority, then, the shrines to Khaḍr assimilate with all "holy places" that "belong to" Muslims as a part of their historical religious inheritance; and yet, stripped of supernatural power as merely a place to pray to God, they "belong to all." The argument against this particular pilgrimage is part of a broader censure of the visitation of saints' tombs and shrines, characteristic of Salafi reform movements (see Damrel's essay, in this volume). The place remains important, but the practices and beliefs that draw most pilgrims are contrary to "true Islam." Swedenburg suggests that Salafi movements in the late Ottoman period in Palestine threatened "unifying folk practices," such as shared shrine visitation, at a time when state-sponsored mosques "replaced local *maqams* [shrines] as village centers of worship." He claims,

> The chief reason for the suppression of saint worship was the localism it expressed. Though such folk practices were not immediately wiped out, they were forced into regression as more and more peasants were "educated" and came to regard such activities as "un-Islamic."[25]

In al-Khaḍr village today, this struggle between local "unifying social traditions" and the official tradition of the *ʿulamā* continues.

These official reformist tendencies are not merely "middle-class" objections to peasant religiosity.[26] The portrayal of practices as old, superstitious, and backward is a common trope in the religious discourse of modernity. Orsi's portrayal of the post–Vatican II moralizing and rationalizing reforms of Marian devotion[27] have interesting parallels to Salafi discourse in Palestine. Attempts to deny particular groups the experience of *praesentia* in holy objects represent struggles for cultural and political power. The recent rise of Hamas as a governing authority in the Palestinian territories may stimulate greater conflict over these local "unifying social traditions."[28]

A few pilgrims in al-Khaḍr expressed concerns about these issues. A woman in the group from Dar Rahhal village reprimanded her older companion for telling me she used to light candles at the church with her parents and ask the saint to heal sick relatives: "This is *tashrīk*, *shirk* ('ascribing partners to God'; idolatry or polytheism), a practice of the *mushrikīn* (polytheists)! We don't associate anyone with God! There is only God, and we pray to him! We don't pray to Khaḍr. He is just a *nabī* (prophet)." She began a heated debate with the man accompanying the group about whether Khaḍr was a *rasūl* (messenger, the highest degree of prophet), a *nabī*, or a *walī*. They continued for a few minutes, before the older woman interrupted, "*Khalāṣ* (Enough)! He is a good man. We were ignorant then, and we would light candles for them." The woman who rebuked her said, "We are just visiting, just to watch what is going on. We will just visit the church after the prayer and then leave." The older woman delivered her *nidhr* of oil and lit a candle, and the man listened for a while to the liturgy, standing in the back of the sanctuary, before the group left.

Such arguments between Muslim pilgrims were not common during the feast, though occasionally my questions sparked them. A group of Muslim secondary school girls emerged from the church. One of the older ones told me, "We just came to visit, because of the feast. We are Muslims, but we visit the church and light candles. Just for a visit. We don't pray (*ma minṣallīsh*) here, but we pray in the mosque." Her younger companion added, "We light candles and we ask for things from al-Khaḍr, because he performs miracles." They left the monastery arguing over whose answer was right.

The ambiguity and ambivalence represented in these public and private debates about "orthodoxy" is part and parcel of how religious symbols and holy presences operate. Pilgrims to the shrine in al-Khaḍr and devotees of Mar Jiryis/Khaḍr address the everyday troubles of their lives and walk around within the "floating signifier" of community that the saint's *baraka* creates.

Palestinian Politics and the Palestinian Saint

The continuing presence of the protector Mar Jiryis/Khaḍr has implications for the imagined community of Palestine at the civic and political level as well. Many Christians, most of them men, reflect on the religious and political meaning of the saint in the context of Palestinian society. Elder Abu Hani of Beit Jala recalls a version of the story:

> The people believe that he was a soldier who became a Christian, and they tortured him in a lot of ways. Finally, they cut his head off and cut his body to pieces and sent it to all parts of Palestine. But God brought all the parts together and he came back to life. This shows God's power over death.... Here in al-Khaḍr, they just have a piece of his bone, like from his hand. But he is present here. The people have faith that he answers prayers.

The resurrection story of a scattered, dismembered Palestinian saint resonates loudly with the discourse of the post–Oslo II (1995) dismemberment of Palestinian land through "Bantustanization" and the perpetual scattering of Palestinian refugees awaiting their "right of return."

The sermon preached by Arab archimandrite Atallah Hanna in the church of al-Khaḍr on the feast day explicitly linked the theme of resurrection to "the Palestinian saint." The archimandrite urged the congregation to "remember our resurrection" and to be "free from the fear of death, even under harsh circumstances." The archimandrite explained privately the pervasive presence of the saint's image:

> Mar Jiryis is so important first and foremost because he is Palestinian. He was from Lid (Lydda), and he is buried there. He was a beautiful youth, very gifted, and he suffered much because of his faith. He is also a symbol of heroism. His martyrdom was heroic. He is a real saint of the people, the most important saint in Palestine. He is a *qudwa* (exemplar), and people want to be like him. There are reports of many miracles that occurred in Palestine because of him.

The themes of "being Palestinian," miraculous powers, suffering for the faith, and heroic martyrdom form a web of significant connections for local believers.

Clergy outside the Orthodox Church more explicitly identify Mar Jiryis with themes of contemporary Palestinian identity. A Roman Catholic priest in Bethlehem suggests that the primary reason for the saint's popularity among Palestinians is that "he was a *muḥārib* (fighter). He was a Roman soldier." In a society bearing scars of military occupation and in streets patrolled by foreign soldiers, the most popular saint is a "soldier-martyr." A Greek Catholic priest in Bethlehem draws the connection:

> In Christian history, all the saints, like Jiryis, didn't they resist and fight for freedom from oppression?... There is martyrdom for the nation, for the family, for God, for your father; in protection of the nation, your house, your family, your religion. This is in the wider sense of martyrdom, of course, not in the narrow sense.

In the vision of this Catholic priest, Mar Jiryis shares with contemporary Palestinians the experience of martyrdom in the cause of resisting oppression and fighting for freedom.[29] A Palestinian Lutheran pastor—though quick to point out that Lutherans do not venerate the saints like their coreligionists (i.e., the "presence" of the saint is symbolic, not *real*)—suggests an even closer link: "Saint George is very important to the people, because he has overcome the dragon in a miraculous way. The people hope they can overcome the dragon of the occupation, too."

Popular Muslim legends of Khaḍr parallel such Christian political reflection on Mar Jiryis. A young Muslim man from al-Khaḍr village recounted one of many stories that link al-Khaḍr to the struggle of the Palestinians:

> In 1967, the Israeli general who invaded the village established a governor's camp there. The first night al-Khaḍr came and wanted to kill him,

> grabbing his throat. The general was scared. He had his soldiers trying to find the man who had strangled him. The next night he came back again, and the general made so much noise, the soldiers started shooting thousands of rounds at anything that moved. All they found was a cat. This happened three nights in a row. The general then went to see the *mukhtār* (leader) of the village and demanded that he find the man that had attempted to kill him and turn him over to the soldiers. The *mukhtār* explained, "This is not a man. You are dealing with something heavenly, something prophetic. I have no control over it, and neither do you. I can only advise you to leave." The general said he would not leave; he wanted one more night to find out what was going on. That very night the soldiers packed up and left al-Khaḍr village.

The legend may certainly serve a political function, to deflect blame from any villagers and thus to avert military reprisals for such resistance, but it also reflects a direct connection between the saint and the contemporary Palestinian nationalist struggle in popular religious discourse. Beit Jala Christians reported that Mar Jiryis rode along the border to protect the town from Israeli incursions during the al-Aqsa Intifadah, which began in 2000.[30] The saint with his *baraka* becomes literally a boundary protector.

The common practice of Muslims and Christians, and the unity signified by it, resonate with the narrative of a "secular" Palestinian nation undivided by religious strife. For pilgrims, the reasons for visiting the shrine are multiple and taken for granted; no particular justification is needed until an outsider raises the issue. The fact of the feast day and the accessibility of the powerful figure at the center of it draws pilgrims whose belief in such spiritual forces is strong, though they may be "ignorant" from the perspective of the priest or the imam. The "field of faith and local community which [makes] the people feel at home" may be assailed by those claiming the saint, the pilgrimage, or the shrine as belonging to their particular sect.[31] Nevertheless, the combined saint seems to accommodate these claims.

Appeals for national unity on secular grounds are not exclusive of such local religious acts of solidarity. In fact, Christians and Muslims who participate in the pilgrimage regard the saint as not only locally accessible but also as "Palestinian." They, and others in the secular nationalist movements who do not participate in the pilgrimage as a religious act, imagine the shared community created by the pilgrimage as an effective symbol of the interreligious unity characteristic of Palestinian society and, by extension, the Palestinian nation.

This interreligious harmony is, however, subject to strain and ambivalence. In al-Khaḍr, the crowd of pilgrims is perhaps more Muslim than Christian, and awareness of the shared customs is high. But an elderly Christian couple from Beit Sahour gives voice to an undercurrent of suspicion. They initially spoke fondly of the feast as a gathering place for local Christians and Muslims in the old days, repeating the familiar refrain, "The Muslims, they believe in al-Khaḍr as much as we do." Later, in the same conversation, one confessed to my associate (unbeknownst to them, a Muslim from the refugee camp in Beit Jala) their concern that "in Beit Jala, the Christians are selling the land to the Muslims. The Muslims are ruining the place." Some of this ambivalence may be explained in terms of class differences and provincial prejudices, as the "Muslims" recently settling in Beit Jala, as in Bethlehem, are either rural migrants from the southern West Bank, around Hebron, or refugees moving out of the camps in the area. "Muslims" may be included in the unifying symbol of Mar Jiryis and yet simultaneously excluded on another level. Local, communal, and national identities coexist in their contradictions.

Fernandez warns of the dangers of articulating shared symbols too explicitly, as the "moral community created by... ritual may be actually threatened by an attempt to achieve moral community on the cultural level where the symbolic dimensions of interaction must be made explicit."[32] Many Islamist and secular nationalist activists in the Bethlehem area recognize the need to preserve "moral community" on the cultural level, which is, however heretically, one of the values of the pilgrimage practice itself. Such traditional forms of moral community have quite frequently succumbed to modernist ideologies based on scientific rationalism and "progress" in other societies. With the building of the Israeli "security fence" or "separation wall" that separates Palestinians from each other and from their lands, it may be Israeli policy rather than narrow religious orthodoxy or modernization that cuts people off from this symbol of Palestinian cultural, national, and spiritual unity.

The stories shared and interpretations given by pilgrims at the al-Khaḍr shrine selectively appropriate the narratives of the saint from the Islamic and Christian traditions, though most of the Islamic *narrative* is obscured. Such practice and interpretation challenge notions of official orthodoxy and yet constitute a significant aspect of the religious lives of people who call themselves Christians and Muslims in the district around Bethlehem. The religious and political, the Christian and Muslim dimensions of the symbolic person Mar Jiryis/Khaḍr, cannot neatly be separated, nor are they neatly blended into one voice. This is not syncretism, though some meanings are surely elided and harmonized with one another; rather, it is an often-ambiguous, highly fluid process of adding supplementary meaning to one's religious tradition, whether from another religious tradition or from the Palestinian nationalist discourse. The complex and multifaceted moral, political, and religious imagination of pilgrims in the presence of *baraka* simultaneously preserves, transcends, and blurs boundaries between heaven and earth, and between the people who inhabit the religious worlds that intersect in the shrines of saints.

Postscript

Glenn Bowman made the observation that the Israeli military checkpoint installed between the Mar Elyas church and Bethlehem after the first Intifada in the early 1990s significantly disrupted the shared nature of Christian-Muslim pilgrimage to the site. Christians had to apply to the Israeli military for permits to attend the feast day at Mar Elyas, and Muslims rarely attended. The pilgrimage to the church in al-Khaḍr has not suffered the same fate, despite the shifting of checkpoints since 1996 and the ongoing construction for the past decade of an eight-meter-high wall (variously called the separation barrier or apartheid wall) along the village border. Al-Khaḍr village, however, remains on the "Palestinian side" of the wall. Pilgrims from the southern West Bank are still able to navigate to the village. My contacts in al-Khaḍr, neighboring Beit Jala, and Bethlehem report that, in 2010, Muslims and Christians continued to join in the pilgrimage, though the picnic grounds and olive orchard are now walled off from the church complex. As one put it, "because of the political situation, people are not celebrating as much as before." The shared saint and pilgrimage as a signifier of Muslim and Christian local tradition and of the Palestinian nation may ebb and flow with the national mood, perhaps giving new meaning to the term "floating signifier."

Bibliography

Anderson, Benedict R. O'G. *Imagined Communities: Reflections on the Origin and Spread of Nationalism*. Rev. ed. London: Verso, 2006.

Attwater, Donald. *The Penguin Dictionary of Saints*. Vol. 30, Penguin Reference Books. Baltimore: Penguin Books, 1965.

Boff, Leonardo. "Martyrdom: An Attempt at Systematic Reflection." In *Martyrdom Today*, edited by Johannes Baptist Metz, Edward Schillebeeckx, and Marcus Lefébure, 18–23. Edinburgh: T. & T. Clark, Seabury Press, 1983.

Bowman, Glenn. "Nationalizing the Sacred: Shrines and Shifting Identities in the Israeli-Occupied Territories." *Man* (n.s.) 28 (1993): 431–60.

Brown, Peter Robert Lamont. *The Cult of the Saints: Its Rise and Function in Latin Christianity*. Haskell Lectures on History of Religions. Chicago: University of Chicago Press, 1981.

Canaan, Tawfiq. *Mohammedan Saints and Sanctuaries in Palestine*. Jerusalem: Ariel Publishing House, 1927; repr. ed., London: Luzac, 1980.

Evans-Pritchard, E. E. *Nuer Religion*. Oxford: Clarendon Press, 1956.

Hanauer, J. E. *Folklore of the Holy Land*. New and enlarged ed. London: Sheldon Press, 1935.

Hasluck, Frederick William, and Margaret Masson Hardie Hasluck. *Christianity and Islam under the Sultans*. Oxford: Clarendon Press, 1929.

Hertz, R. "Saint Besse: A Study of an Alpine Cult." In *Saints and Their Cults: Studies in Religious Sociology, Folklore, and History*, edited by Stephen Wilson, 55–89. Cambridge: Cambridge University Press, 1983.

Herzfeld, Michael. "Significance of the Insignificant: Blasphemy as Ideology." *Man* 19, no. 4 (1984): 653–64.

Kertzer, David I. *Ritual, Politics, and Power*. New Haven, Conn.: Yale University Press, 1988.

Khalidi, Rashid. *Palestinian Identity: The Construction of Modern National Consciousness*. New York: Columbia University Press, 1997.

Lusi, Janette Andoni. "The Life of the Exalted Saint among the Martyrs, George Clothed in Victory" [Arabic pamphlet]. Bethlehem, West Bank: n.p., 1988.

Omar, Irfan. "Khidr in the Islamic Tradition." *Muslim World* 83, no. 3–4 (1993): 279–91.

Orsi, Robert A. *Between Heaven and Earth: The Religious Worlds People Make and the Scholars Who Study Them*. Princeton, N.J.: Princeton University Press, 2005.

Riches, Samantha. *St. George: Hero, Martyr, and Myth*. Stroud: Sutton, 2000.

Sobrino, Jon. "Political Holiness: A Profile." In *Martyrdom Today*, edited by Johannes Baptist Metz, Edward Schillebeeckx, and Marcus Lefébure, 12–17. Edinburgh: T. & T. Clark, Seabury Press, 1983.

St. Augustine's Abbey (Ramsgate, England). The Book of Saints: A Dictionary of Servants of God Canonized by the Catholic Church. 4th ed. London: Adam & Charles Black, 1947.

Swedenburg, Ted. "The Role of the Palestinian Peasantry in the Great Revolt (1936–1939)." In *Islam, Politics, and Social Movements*, edited by Edmund Burke and Ira M. Lapidus, 169–203. Berkeley: University of California Press, 1988.

Taylor, Christopher S. "Saints, Ziyara, Qissa, and the Social Construction of Moral Imagination in Late Medieval Egypt." *Studia Islamica* 88 (1998): 103–20.

van der Veer, Peter. *Religious Nationalism: Hindus and Muslims in India*. Berkeley: University of California Press, 1994.

Notes

1. Tawfiq Canaan, *Mohammedan Saints and Sanctuaries in Palestine* (Jerusalem: Ariel Publishing House, 1927; repr. ed., London: Luzac, 1980). In this chapter, the Muslim saint will be referred to as *Khaḍr* to reflect Palestinian colloquial Arabic pronunciation, rather than the standard Arabic (and scholarly convention in Islamic studies) spelling, *Khiḍr.*
2. Hasluck, in discussing the *tekke* of Mamas in Turkey as a site of Christian and Muslim pilgrimage, or, in his words, "for so amicable a juxtaposition of religions," draws an "analogy between the *tekke* of Mamas and a Christian monastery of S. George situated in a Mohammedan village near Bethlehem and venerated by both religions." He adds that "S. George is in Syria particularly susceptible to identification with the Moslem saint Khiḍr, whereas Mamas has no Muslim affinities." See Frederick William Hasluck and Margaret Masson Hardie Hasluck, *Christianity and Islam under the Sultans* (Oxford: Clarendon Press, 1929), 46.
3. Riches notes that the standard motif of St. George rescuing a princess from a dragon was not recorded before the tenth century CE, but it became popular after being included in the mid-thirteenth-century *Golden Legend* version of the Life of St. George. For variations on the life of the saint, see Samantha Riches, *St. George: Hero, Martyr, and Myth* (Stroud: Sutton, 2000), 3; for examples of the localization of the saint's cult, see pp. 17–20.
4. Robert A. Orsi, *Between Heaven and Earth: the Religious Worlds People Make and the Scholars Who Study Them* (Princeton, N.J: Princeton University Press, 2005), 61.
5. Christopher S. Taylor, "Saints, Ziyara, Qissa, and the Social Construction of Moral Imagination in Late Medieval Egypt," *Studia Islamica*, no. 88 (1998): 105.
6. Benedict R. O'G Anderson, *Imagined Communities: Reflections on the Origin and Spread of Nationalism*, rev. ed. (London: Verso, 2006).
7. Taylor, "Saints," 105.
8. Glenn Bowman, "Nationalizing the Sacred: Shrines and Shifting Identities in the Israeli-Occupied Territories," Man (n.s.) 28 (1993): 432. Bowman (1993, p. 432) employed Hertz's (1983) concept of contested holy place to Palestinian pilgrimage sites. R Hertz, "Saint Besse: A Study of an Alpine Cult," in *Saints and their Cults: Studies in Religious Sociology, Folklore, and History*, ed. Stephen Wilson (Cambridge: Cambridge University Press, 1983).
9. Peter Robert Lamont Brown, *The Cult of the Saints: its Rise and Function in Latin Christianity*, Haskell Lectures on History of Religions (Chicago: University of Chicago Press, 1981), 22.
10. Orsi, *Between Heaven and Earth*, 12.
11. Taylor, "Saints," 106. Cf. Brown, *The Cult of the Saints.*
12. Orsi, *Between Heaven and Earth,* 49.
13. Janette Andoni Lusi, "The Life of the Exalted Saint among the Martyrs, George Clothed in Victory" [Arabic pamphlet] (Bethlehem, West Bank: n.p., 1988).

14. St. Augustine's Abbey (Ramsgate, England), *The Book of Saints: A Dictionary of Servants of God Canonized by the Catholic Church*, 4th ed. (London: Adam & Charles Black, 1947), 259.
15. Donald Attwater, *The Penguin Dictionary of Saints*, vol. 30, Penguin reference books (Baltimore: Penguin Books, 1965), 148. Hasluck notes in *Christianity and Islam Under the Sultans*, 321 n. 1 that "It is curious that, while in the West legend relates the rescue by S. George of a princess from a dragon, this is by no means the case generally in the East... Early western travellers to the East mention his martyrdom and his burial at Lydda (Diospolis), but say nothing of his dragon fight... the saint is represented in Coptic eikonography as a horseman with a lance but no dragon, the slaying of the dragon being foreign to the Coptic legend... In fact, according to Baring Gould... the first mention of the princess and the dragon is in de Voragine's *Golden Legend*, that is, not earlier than the end of the thirteenth century." In fact, Riches (*St. George*, p. 3) notes an example from the tenth century.
16. The figure of Khaḍr (alt. Khiḍr) is often associated with sites of Christian-Muslim interaction in the Eastern Mediterranean (as discussed in Wolper's essay in this volume).
17. Irfan Omar, "Khiḍr in the Islamic Tradition," *Muslim World* 83, no. 3–4 (1993): 286.
18. See discussions of similarly complex objections in Cuffel's essay in this volume.
19. According to Khalidi, the narrative of "triumph in defeat," of the proud and dignified *fidā'iyyīn* revolutionary fighters defined the Palestinian nationalist movement, particularly during the 1970s and 1980s. Cf. Rashid Khalidi, *Palestinian Identity: The Construction of Modern National Consciousness* (New York: Columbia University Press, 1997), 146–49. Palestinian National Authority leader Yasser Arafat embodied this *fidā'ī* tradition for many Palestinians, especially upon his triumphal return to the Occupied Territories in 1995.
20. Cf. Canaan, *Mohammedan Saints and Sanctuaries in Palestine*; J. E. Hanauer, *Folklore of the Holy Land*, new enl. ed. (London: Sheldon Press, 1935).
21. Bowman, "Nationalizing," 438.
22. The metaphor of refraction is from E. E. Evans-Pritchard, *Nuer Religion* (Oxford: Clarendon Press, 1956). Herzfeld notes that "Campbell's (1964:344) adoption of the metaphor of refraction seems peculiarly apt here. Icons are doctrinally non-autonomous; their ownership, especially their association of particular saints with specific families or villages, shows that they are interpreted in terms of existing social relations" (Michael Herzfeld, "Significance of the Insignificant: Blasphemy as Ideology," *Man* 19, no. 4 [1984]: 654).
23. Herzfeld, "Significance," 654.
24. David I. Kertzer, *Ritual, Politics, and Power* (New Haven, Conn.: Yale University Press, 1988), 11.

25. Ted Swedenburg, "The Role of the Palestinian Peasantry in the Great Revolt (1936–1939)," in *Islam, Politics, and Social Movements*, ed. Edmund Burke and Ira M. Lapidus, *Comparative Studies on Muslim Societies* (Berkeley: University of California Press, 1988), 176.
26. Cf. Peter van der Veer, *Religious Nationalism: Hindus and Muslims in India* (Berkeley: University of California Press, 1994), 57–58.
27. Orsi, *Between Heaven and Earth*, 51–58.
28. Though I have not done so here, Alexandra Cuffel's analysis (see her essay in this volume) of the gendered nature of objections to shared shrine visitation might well be applied to the pilgrimage to al-Khaḍr village. The large majority of those who performed the "unofficial" ritual acts of the pilgrimage (outside the formal liturgical period on each of the feast days) were female. The predominant themes of healing, toleration, relationships with family and neighbors, and boundary crossing in the discourse of female pilgrims stand in stark contrast to the more nationalistic, militant interpretations of the significance of the Palestinian saint expressed in primarily male discourse. Though one cannot make a rigid division between these two tendencies, this interpretation needs to be explored more systematically.
29. It is worth noting here that the traditional Christian notion of martyrdom is more passive, and that in the traditional story of St. George, he stands up to the emperor and refuses to recant his faith. The saint does not "fight" other than at the emperor's behest, and he does not militantly "resist" the emperor's attempted suppression of his Christian faith. The elision of freedom fighter and martyr may owe more to the reflections of liberation and political theologians within the contemporary Catholic Church, who have struggled with ways to articulate the "political holiness" of Christian activists who sacrifice their lives for the poor and with the "martyrdom" of non-Christians, not for the Church, but "for the kingdom of God." See Jon Sobrino, "Political Holiness: A Profile,"; and Leonardo Boff, "Martyrdom: An Attempt at Systematic Reflection," both in *Martyrdom Today*, ed. Johannes Baptist Metz, Edward Schillebeeckx, and Marcus Lefébure, 12–17, 18–23 (Edinburgh: T. & T. Clark, Seabury Press, 1983).
30. Hala Nasser, Yale University, personal communication, November 2003.
31. Bowman, "Nationalizing the Sacred," 438.
32. Quoted in Kertzer, *Ritual, Politics, and Power*, 68.

3

Christmas in Cambérène, or How Muhammad Begets Jesus in Senegal

Eric Ross

CONTEMPORARY SENEGAL HOSTS a Muslim religious order, called the Layenne, which has integrated the figure of Jesus into its beliefs and observations to an unprecedented extent. Muslims have always recognized Jesus (or 'Īsā in Arabic) as a prophet and one of God's messengers. The Koran and Hadīth attribute to Jesus many of the same qualities as Christians do. Jesus is the "Messiah" (*al-masīh*, the "anointed one") who brought the Gospels (*Injīl*). He is the "Spirit from God" (*rūhun min Allāh*) as well as the "Word of God" (*kalimat Allāh*). He was of virgin birth and his death was only apparent; God removed him from this world (Glassé: 208–9). While this latter belief is not exactly the same as the Christian doctrine of the Resurrection, Jesus *lives* in Islam too. Moreover, as in various Christian traditions, there exist Islamic traditions, expressed in *hadīths*, according to which Jesus will return at the end of time to defeat the anti-Christ (*al-dajjāl*). The status of Jesus in Islam is thus elevated beyond that of most other prophets and messengers. As a prophet he is surpassed only by Muhammad and Abraham.

For the Layennes of Senegal, however, Jesus is far more than an important prophet from the past. He has been reincarnated in a contemporary historical figure: Seydina Issa Rohou Laye (1876–1949). The Layenne doctrine of Jesus's reincarnation is part of a larger theological construct involving Issa's father, Seydina Mouhammadou Limamou Laye (considered the reincarnation of the prophet Muhammad) and it builds on Sunni eschatological and millenarian conceptions of the *mahdī* ("the guided one") and the anti-Christ.

This study discusses the various Christian, or apparently Christian, elements to be found in Layenne culture. These elements range from theology and historiography, through architecture and religious practice, to imagery and vocabulary. Of particular significance to this study is the annual Christmas

Day celebration held in the Layenne shrine of Cambérène. Each time a Christian, or an apparently Christian, element is identified, an attempt is made to determine its probable origin and the significance of its expression within Layenne culture. The wider significance of this phenomenon for the Christian-Muslim encounter in Senegal is discussed.

The Layennes: One of Senegal's Sufi Orders

Over 90 percent of Senegal's population is Muslim and worships according to the Sunnī-Malikī rite. Islamic practice in that country is further conditioned by a number of Sufi *orders*, called *ṭarīqah* (pl., *ṭuruq*) in Arabic.[1] These orders are mass organizations, with hundreds of thousands and even millions of affiliates. All of them were established in the last decades of the nineteenth century, a crucial period in Senegal's history corresponding to the defeat of precolonial states and to the consolidation of French colonial rule.[2]

Despite significant differences with regard to demographic base, social milieu, and place of origin, these religious orders share common historical and organizational traits. Each was initially set up by a charismatic founding figure, a sheikh, often from an already-well-established lineage of scholar-clerics.[3] Following the deaths of these founders, the orders became institutionalized under the leadership of their sons and grandsons, the caliphs, who have succeeded each other in order of primogeniture. The orders have varying degrees of internal hierarchy, but these hierarchies all tend to be based on genealogy and lineage (with both patrilineal and matrilineal filiation being important). The orders are primarily spiritual and religious institutions. They manage mosques and Koranic schools. They also constitute powerful social networks, regulating relations between individuals, between families and even between individuals and the state. Consequently, they have become powerful economic forces, wielding considerable weight in the sectors of agriculture, transportation, retail commerce, real-estate, and the construction industry. Each of Senegal's Sufi orders is centered on one or more shrines, containing the mausoleum of the founder, and organizes regular commemorative pilgrimages which are held according to either the lunar-Islamic or the solar-Gregorian calendar.[4]

The Layenne order, object of this present study, is by far the smallest of Senegal's Sufi orders in demographic terms. Its membership is estimated at between twenty and thirty thousand men, women, and children (Laborde: 9). The Layenne order is also more regionally and ethnically based than Senegal's other Sufi orders. Layennes belong, for the most part, to the Lebou ethnicity of the Cape Vert peninsula, and they are concentrated in the Lebou villages and neighborhoods of the greater Dakar agglomeration (Yoff, Cambérène, Thiaroye, and Rufisque). The Lebous number about fifty thousand people in all. They constitute a subgroup of the Wolof, distinguished historically by their principal economic activity, fishing, and by their political independence.[5] Outside the Cape Vert, there are small communities of Layenne affiliates (called *dahiras*), in the cities of Kayar, Mboro, Thiès, and Mbour, and as far away as Saint Louis, Kaolack, and Ziguinchor. These communities are the result of recent Layenne migration from the original heartland. So too are the Layenne communities abroad, in France and Italy especially.

The Layenne order is the legacy of Seydina Mouhammadou Limamou Laye (1845–1909), born Libasse Thiaw. He is believed by members of the order to be both the *mahdī* (the messianic leader who some Muslims believe will come at the end of time) and the reincarnation of the prophet Muhammad. The name Seydina Mouhammadou Limamou Laye is Wolofized Arabic. Limamou derives from *al-imām*,[6] while Laye comes from "Allāhi" (declined in the genitive case, as in the expression *al-hamdu li-llāhi*). Seydina Mouhammadou Limamou Laye thus translates as "Our Lord Muhammad Imam of God." Moreover, all members of the Layenne order attach "Laye" or "Lahi" to their family names and use the term to greet each other. One explanation for this is that the common adopted name washes away distinctions of lineage and caste expressed by traditional family names.[7] All members of the order thus become social equals.

The story of the Layenne order's foundation, recounted in the hagiographies, is full of marvels and mystic Koranic references.[8] Libasse Thiaw was born in the Lebou fishing village of Yoff, on the night of the 15th of Sha'bān,[9] during an earthquake (Laborde: 15, Lô: 500). Limamou Laye had been resting "for over a thousand years" in a cave. This cave, "Xóotum Ngor" in Wolof, is located near Ngor at the western tip of the Cape Vert peninsula (and thus at the western extremity of *dār al-islām*). From a mystic perspective, it lies at "the confluence of the two seas," the place where Moses meets Khiḍr (a personification of esoteric knowledge) in the *surah* "the Cave" (Koran 18:60). This westernmost cape is otherwise called "Pointe des Almadies" on maps. For many Layennes, this toponym, which has existed for centuries, refers to the *mahdī* and it thus prophesized the coming of Limamou Laye.[10]

Unlike the founders of Senegal's other Sufi orders, Libasse Thiaw was not born into a clerical family and does not seem to have had much religious instruction. As in the case of the prophet Muhammad, Libasse was illiterate. He gave all his sermons in Wolof, not in Arabic (Laborde: 20). Like the

Prophet again, as a young man Libasse showed no overt signs of a spiritual calling. Like most other men of Yoff, he worked as a fisherman. However, on the first day of the month of Sha'bān 1301 (May 24, 1884),[11] shortly after the death of his mother, Libasse Thiaw announced to the world that he was the *mahdī*. This announcement occurred when he was in his fortieth year. This is important because, according to *hadīth*, forty was the age of the prophet Muhammad when he received the first revelation from God.

At the time, many in Yoff thought Libasse was mad. Other people farther away, however, including members of important clerical lineages, heard of him and began flocking to Yoff. In response, Libasse Thiaw, now known as Seydina Mouhammadou Limamou Laye, established himself and his followers in a new neighborhood called Yoff-Layenne, outside of the old village. The foundation of Yoff-Layenne was miraculous in that it occurred on a stretch of beach newly exposed after an exceptionally high tide had "cleansed" Limamou Laye's house (Lô: 504). Moreover, the saintly founder's settlement was blessed by a miraculous spring of fresh water that sprang up only meters from the ocean's salty waves; "with his foot he removed the sand and water sprang forth." (Sylla & Gaye 1985: 20)

As more and more disciples began arriving in Yoff-Layenne, local Lebou leaders and the French authorities in Dakar decided to take action against the "troublesome marabout." In 1887, three years after Limamou had announced his mission, they decided to have him arrested. A detachment of police arrived in Yoff but Seydina Limamou had already left. In order to disperse his followers, the police set fire to the houses at Yoff-Layenne. Meanwhile, Limamou Laye was in spiritual retreat in an isolated spot near the village of Malika, a place now known as Nguédjaga. After three days of retreat, he voluntarily gave himself up to the authorities, who imprisoned him on the island of Gorée.[12] While in prison, Seydina Limamou was attended to by a Christian woman, Michelle Sène, designated for that purpose by the authorities (Sylla & Gaye 1985: 92). It eventually became apparent to those preparing to prosecute Limamou that the charges of possessing arms and inciting public disorder were spurious. He was released from prison after three months of confinement. The formula "three years, three days, three months," which Limamou Laye is said to have repeated prior to these events, is considered a prophesy of his three years of predication, three days of seclusion and three months of imprisonment (Lô: 510).

Following his release from prison, and having come to an accommodation with both the Lebou and the colonial authorities, Seydina Limamou Laye rebuilt Yoff-Layenne. However, members of his entourage who were not native to the village of Yoff were not permitted to reside there. Consequently, Seydina Limamou set up a second village three kilometers east of Yoff that he called Cambérène,[13] a reference to the holy city of Medina (Sylla 1971: 628) The reference alludes to the fact that Limamou Laye was following the model of the prophet Muhammad who, when opposed by the authorities in Mecca, moved his community to a new place, Medina.

Layennes consider Seydina Mouhammadou Limamou Laye to be a *mujaddid*, a "renewer" of the faith. The crux of his teachings related to the need for a strict practice of Islam (i.e., prayer, fasting, alms-giving, etc.) and the abandonment of the non-Muslim, traditional practices (such as excessive expenses and feasting at weddings and funerals), which characterized Lebou culture at that time. He was also adamantly opposed to the caste structure which underlay Lebou society.

Seydina Mouhammadou Limamou Laye lived out the remaining twenty years of his life entirely peacefully, administering to the needs of his growing community. Layennes interpret this as confirmation of his prophetic status, as God would never permit a false *mahdī* to prosper thus. When he died, in 1909, it was in Yoff-Layenne that Mouhammadou Limamou was buried.

Seydina Issa Rohou Laye: Jesus Reincarnate and First Caliph of the Layennes

Seydina Mouhammadou was succeeded by his eldest son, Seydina Issa Rohou Laye (1876–1949), who is believed by the Layennes to be the reincarnation of Jesus. His Wolofized Arabic name translates as "Our Lord Jesus, Spirit of God," in direct reference to one of the names of Jesus in the Koran.

Seydina Issa Rohou Laye came to the stewardship of the Layenne order at thirty-three years of age, the age of Jesus Christ when he fulfilled his earthly mission. During Seydina Issa's forty-year caliphate, the Layenne order, despite its heterodox doctrines, became a respected and influential institution on the Cape Vert peninsula. First of all, in contrast to his father, Issa received a complete and advanced education in Islamic sciences and in Arabic. He studied under a number of master scholar-clerics and was attending the school of Sëriñ Mamour Diakhaté in Ngakham at the time of his father's death (Sylla & Gaye 1985: 104). Second, Seydina Issa Rohou is believed to have received official recognition of his status as a descendent of Muhammad from a *sharīf* in Mecca named Sādiq b. Abū Bakr (Sylla & Gaye 1985: 84–85).[14] A metal seal to this effect is said to have been procured in Mecca by a Layenne pilgrim named Balla Silwi Sène. The seal, which states: *'Īsā Rūh Allāh ibn imām kul imām*, is

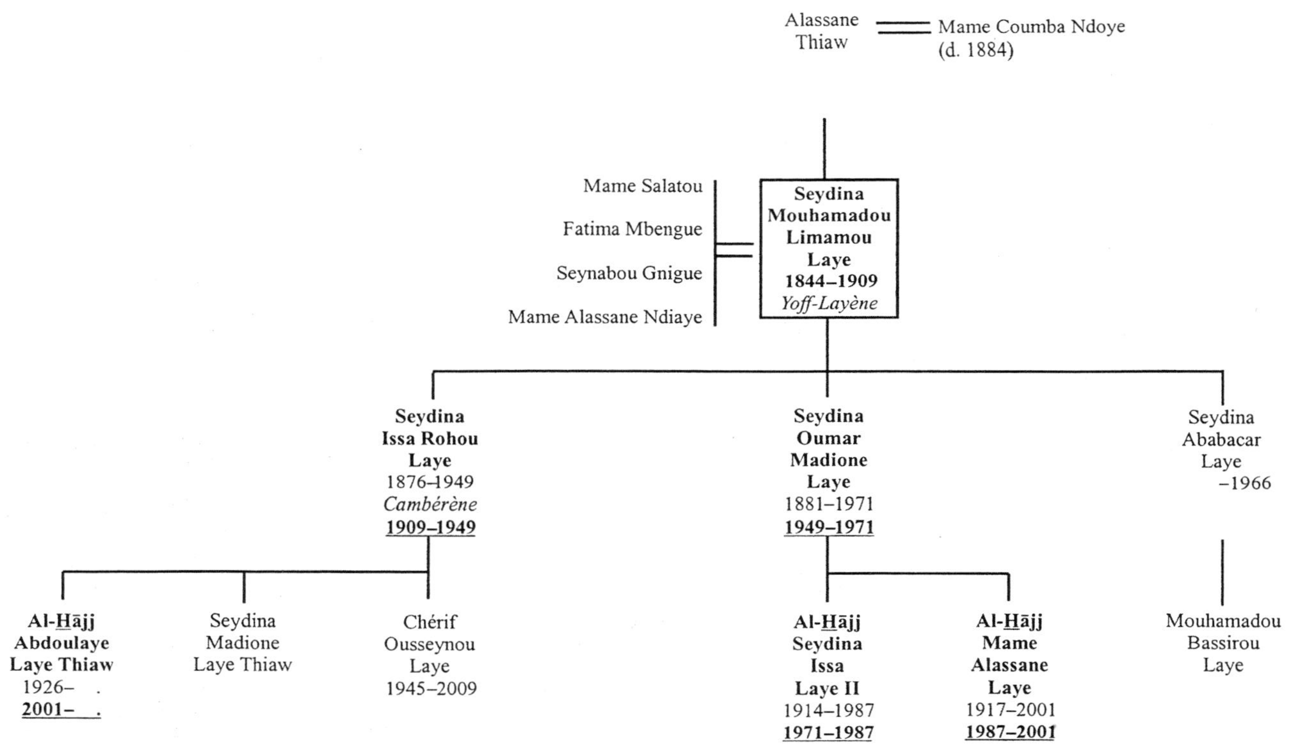

FIGURE 3.1 Genealogy of the Laye-Thiaw Lineage (© Eric Ross).

signed "Imām al-Haramayn" and is dated 1339.[15] The seal is preserved to this day in Seydina Issa's mausoleum in Cambérène.[16]

Seydina Issa Rohou was also decorated with the highest civic honors by the French Republic,[17] and he was a guest of honor at the Colonial Exhibition in Vincennes, on the outskirts of Paris, in 1931 (Sylla & Gaye 1985: 108).[18] The civic medals, which figure prominently on portrait photographs of the period, were awarded for the caliph's contributions to fighting epidemics and recruiting soldiers during both world wars.[19] In addition to his Islamic and civic credentials, Seydina Issa Rohou Laye is considered a social modernizer and a "builder" (he is called *le bâtisseur* in French) and is remembered locally for being the first African to be driven around in his own chauffeured automobile.[20]

Seydina Issa's reputation as a modernizer and builder date to 1914 when Dakar and the Cape Vert peninsula were afflicted by a plague epidemic. Among the affected localities was his father's settlement of Cambérène, which was devastated. As a result, Seydina Issa Rohou Laye resettled the surviving inhabitants in a new location, which he also called Cambérène, only a few kilometers away but on a healthier site, by the beach. The old site, known today as Ndingala or Guentaba,[21] is still revered as a holy place. It features a baobab tree and a well, both of which are held to be blessed. While building the new settlement, Seydina Issa is reputed to have personally overseen the erection of houses, making sure that they were properly aligned.[22] He also endowed both Cambérène and Yoff-Layenne with new "solid" mosques.[23]

When Issa Laye died, in 1949, he was buried in Cambérène. The caliphate of the Layenne order passed first to his brother, Seydina Oumar Madione (1949–71), and then to two of Madione's sons: Al-Hājj Seydina Issa II (1971–87) and Al-Hājj Mame Allasane (1987–2001). Only after the death of Allasane did the eldest of Seydina Issa Rohou's own sons, Al-Hājj Abdoulaye (b. 1926), accede to the caliphate. At the time this study was undertaken Seydina Issa Rohou Laye's three sons: Abdoulaye, Madione, and Ousseynou, were the most senior religious figures in the order and constituted its highest moral authority (see fig. 3.1).

Layenne Doctrines and Practices

Clearly, many Layenne beliefs and doctrines related to the *mahdī*, Muhammad's reincarnation, and the Second Coming of Jesus, are at odds with normative Sunnī Islam. While the messianic figure of the *mahdī* is a central doctrine in Shīʿī Islam,[24] there is far less doctrinal consensus about the *mahdī* in Sunnī tradition. Where it exists, the coming of the *mahdī* is often linked to a Second Coming of Jesus and to the defeat of the anti-Christ. There are a number of cases in history when individuals have claimed to be the *mahdī*.[25] Apart from Seydina Mouhammadou Limamou Laye, occurrences of mahdism in Senegal include: Hamme Ba (1790–1862), father of the Tijānī jihadist Cheikhou Ahmadou; and Abdoulaye Iyakhine Niakhité Diop (1886–1943), a Baye Fall Murid whose community is based in Thiès.[26]

While the concept of the *mahdī* might be tolerable to Sunnī theologians in principal, instances when men have actually claimed to be the *mahdī* have usually met with rejection on their part and with repression by political authorities. Groups which claim to follow a *mahdī* are considered "beyond the pale" of Islam by religious scholars and secular authorities. Such groups include the Druzes and the Ahmadis, who have suffered persecution at the hands of mainstream Sunnī and Shī'ī regimes.[27] This has not been the case of the Layennes. Apart from the three months during which the French colonial authorities imprisoned its founder, the movement has been able to thrive peacefully on the outskirts of Senegal's capital city.

More contentious even than the issue of the *mahdī* is the Layenne doctrine of prophetic reincarnation. While Layenne intellectuals and apologists (Sylla & Gaye 1985; Thiam 2006) maintain the legitimacy of this belief by citing a number of *hadīths*, there seems to be no precedent for these arguments in Sunnī sources.[28] Nor is reincarnation a traditional religious belief in Senegal. The Layenne doctrine of reincarnated prophets is thus unprecedented in the region.

Beyond its implications within Islam, the Layenne doctrine of reincarnation becomes significant when placed within the pan-African context of the era. Reincarnation features in several more-or-less Islamic African-American millenarian and prophetic movements of the early twentieth century. The founder of the Moorish Science Temple, Noble Drew Ali (1886–1929), claimed he was a prophet sent to redeem African-Americans. Following his death, several of his disciples, including Wallace Fard Mohammad (d. 1934?), claimed to be Drew Ali's reincarnation (Nance 2002: 150; Wilson 1993: 46). Wallace Fard Mohammad established the Nation of Islam which, upon his death, passed to the leadership of Elijah Mohammed (1897–1975). Elijah Mohammed claimed he was a prophet and that Wallace Fard Mohammad was Allah incarnate. This trend in African-American Islam continues with Isa Muhammad (a.k.a. Malachi Z. York, b. 1935, founder, among other things, of the Ansarullah Community of "Muslims for Jesus"), who claims to be the embodiment of the Second Coming of Christ (Malone O'Connor 1998: 511). In Africa itself, prophetic movements have characterized Christianity rather than Islam. Among the "Ethiopian" churches of southern Africa is the Nazareth Baptist Church founded by Isaiah Shembe (1867–1935). Shembe is considered by his followers to be both a prophet and a messiah sent to the Zulus. Likewise, William Wade Harris (1865–1929) in Liberia and the Ivory Coast and Simon Kimbangu (1889–1951) in the Belgian Congo both claimed to be prophets sent by God to their respective peoples, and both founded independent Christian churches.

All these contemporaneous African and African-American prophetic movements involve a measure of Black nationalism, or at least race consciousness. In each case, a Black prophet established an independent religious institution to meet the needs of his people. The "blackness" or African-ness of the prophet is important to the identity of the newly established community and contrasts with the perceived "whiteness" of mainstream Christian culture and institutions. These types of anti-colonial, Afrocentric and Black-empowerment readings lie just below the surface of contemporary Layenne discourse. Both Mouhammadou Limamou and Issa Rohou Laye are presented as "Black prophets" sent by God to Africans in the darkest days of colonial subjugation. They serve to counter the perceived white supremacy of colonial Christian and ethnocentric Arab discourses. To different degrees and in different ways, both of these universalizing religions have been accused of culturally alienating Africans. The Christianity propagated in Black Africa by missionaries, exemplified by the images of a blond, blue-eyed Jesus which they circulated, has been interpreted as integral to a hegemonic colonial project to alienate Africans from their own spirituality. And while "race" has never figured in Islamic representations of the faith, the Arabic language of the Koran and the Arab ethnicity of the prophet Muhammad have. There is a notion among the Layennes that God chose to reincarnate the Arab Muhammad and the white Jesus in the bodies of two Black prophets in order that proud imperial peoples be humbled and that downtrodden Africans be uplifted. The career of Sheikh Ahmadu Bamba Mbacké (who never claimed to be anything other than a Sufi master) is seen by many Murids in similar anti-colonial terms, as the triumph of Black Muslim spirituality over the alienating European/Christian colonial project. Ironically, at the very moment delegates at the Fourth International Convention of Negroes of the World, meeting in New York City in 1924, declared Jesus to be black (Pinder 1997: 223), unbeknownst to them a Black Jesus was leading a Sufi order on the home continent.

Despite the contentious doctrines at its heart, the Layenne order has secured a peaceful niche for itself within Senegalese society. This may partly have to do with the profoundly tolerant and democratic nature of this society generally, where all religions are practiced within the framework of a secular state (Gellar 2005). The social and political acceptance of the Layenne order can also be attributed to the mainstream manner in which it projects itself publicly. While the millenarian, messianic, and reincarnationist doctrines at the heart of its identity are held and defended by the order's spiritual, moral, and intellectual leaders, the order as a whole sees itself as one of a number of Sufi orders active within a national society. Though it is the smallest of these orders, it maintains fraternal relations with the others. For instance, the Layennes seek to highlight the deep spiritual commonalities between the saintly founders of all of Senegal's orders rather than to trumpet any inherent superiority of Seydina Mouhammadou Limamou Laye. Moreover, when non-Layenne Muslim leaders criticize the order, they are far more likely to take exception to the high visibility of Layenne women at mosques and during religious observances than to reprimand it for its non-normative doctrines about the *mahdī* and reincarnation.

The proper role of women within an Islamic community is one of the central preoccupations of Layenne teachings. Seydina Mouhammadou Limamou Laye was a steadfast opponent of what he considered un-Islamic practices. Many of these practices related directly to the social and spiritual lives of women. For example, Lebou women had privileged knowledge of, and access to, *tuur* and *rab* spirits, who could be either malevolent or beneficial depending on circumstances. Women were the ones able to communicate with these spirits and to exorcise them if need be through *ndëpp* ceremonies involving music, dancing, and animal sacrifice. Such ceremonies are forbidden by the Layenne, as they are by all of Senegal's Muslim and Catholic authorities. Layenne women are also forbidden from participating in any type of dancing, a very popular form of female sociability in Senegal, and the scope they have to indulge in wedding and baptism ceremonies is curtailed. Traditional Lebou funerals, especially, were known for the excessive, and ruinous, feasting and gift-giving which they occasioned. This practice too was banned by the founder of the Layenne order. Moreover, women are expected to turn over household finances and the revenues they earn to their husbands, which is at variance with gender roles in wider Senegalese society. The order advocates unrestricted polygamy, meaning that men are permitted to take more than the four wives allowed for by normative Islamic family law, and Layenne girls are betrothed almost from the day of their birth.

Yet the role of women within the Layenne order is paradoxical. While, on the one hand, the order promotes a form of hyper-patriarchy that restricts the social space of women, on the other, it advocates the full participation of women in the religious and devotional sphere (Laborde 1995). Layenne women are expected to be as assiduous and devout as men. They should attend mosque for all the canonical prayers; a separate space is allocated to women in Layenne mosques. As children they attend Koranic school with the boys. They have their own local devotional associations, called *dahiras*, placed under the moral authority of respected mothers, where they recite *dhikr* as loudly as men do.[29] This contrasts with practices in Senegal's other Sufi orders, and in the Tijāniyya in particular, where women cannot recite out loud and may not be permitted in mosques.

However, despite its rhetoric about the equality of women and men before God, when compared to Senegal's other Sufi orders, the Layenne order is actually quite restrictive when it comes to women in positions of religious leadership. In all of the other orders, a small number of women have attained the high spiritual rank of "*sheikhah*." For example, there are two *sheikhahs* in the Qādiriyya order: Adja Khar Mané and Oumy Souko, while Soxna Mariama Niass (b. 1932) of the Kaolack branch of the Tijāniyya is a reputed Islamic scholar specializing in women's issues. In her day, Soxna Maïmouna Mbacké (1926–2000), Ahmadu Bamba's youngest daughter, had a large following of male and female disciples. She organized a major religious commemoration each year during Ramadan and her mausoleum in Touba is now a popular stop on the Murid pilgrimage circuit. Senegal's most well-known female Sufi was Soxna Magat Diop (1917–2004), also a Murid. She was the daughter of the Murid Baye Fall *mahdī* Abdoulaye Iyakhine Niakhité Diop, mentioned above. She inherited leadership of her father's disciples when he died (Lake 1997). Like Soxna Maïmouna Mbacké, Soxna Magat Diop taught the Koran to both male and female students. Moreover, when she died, leadership of this branch of the Baye Fall Murids passed to two other women: her younger sister, Soxna Seybata Aïdara in the city of Thiès, and her eldest daughter, Soxna Bintou Massamba Mbacké (b. 1934) in the Dakar neighborhood of Parcelles Assainies. There are no similar cases of female spiritual leadership in the Layenne order, though a few Layenne women have become practicing mediums.

Known as *marabouts* in popular idiom, mediums combine Islamic and traditional esoteric practices for paying clients. These practices include: geomancy, astrology, numerology, confecting amulets and talismans, using holy waters and potions, holding divination sessions, and dream interpretation.

Marabouts operate both within and outside of Sufi structures and the vast majority are men. Yet some Layenne women have succeeded as *marabouts.* Such is the case of Coumba Keita, who became a *marabout* after having had visions of both Seydina Issa Rohou Laye and of the Virgin Mary (Gemmeke 2007: 37). The appearance of the Virgin Mary in a Senegalese Sufi context seems even more unlikely than that of Jesus. And yet, Mary (Maryam in Arabic), like Jesus, is exalted in Islam. Her virginity is proclaimed in the Koran (3:47), where there is an entire chapter named for her (*sūrah* 19). Maryam was consecrated to God while still in her mother's womb (Koran 3:35) and Muslims address her as *sayyidatunā*, or "Our Lady" (Glassé: 260–61).

Senegalese Sufism has singled out specific women, namely the mothers, wives, and daughters of sheikhs, for special devotion. The most well-known case of this is Mame Diarra Bousso (1833–1866), Sheikh Ahmadu Bamba's mother. Since the 1950s, her tomb in Porokhane has become a pilgrimage center in its own right (Evers Rosander 2003). Two Layenne women—Mouhammadou Limaou's mother, Mame Coumba Ndoye, and one of his wives, Mame Salatou Laye—are likewise revered by Layennes (Laborde: 97). These women are considered paragons of feminine virtues: piety, fidelity, decency, discretion, sobriety, and obedience—virtues extolled in both Muslim and Christian traditions.

Christmas Day in Cambérène

The Layennes hold a variety of annual festivals. Most, such as the Tabaski,[30] Korité,[31] and Mawlud[32] celebrations, are common to all of Islam and are held according to the lunar-Islamic calendar. The Layenne also have their own specific celebrations, such the Wooteba festival held annually on the first of Sha'bān to mark Seydina Mouhammadou Limamou Laye's public appeal as *mahdī*. Likewise, there are annual pilgrimages to Xóotum Ngor (the cave by the sea where Seydina Limamou Laye resided prior to his birth), Ndingala-Guentaba (the original site of Cambérène), and Nguédjaga (the site near Malika where Seydina Limamou Laye spent three days in seclusion; Laborde: 28).[33] These all constitute sacralized places where Layennes assemble to commune together. They are also *lieux de mémoire*, memory places where the Layenne community constructs is past and affirms its present identity.[34] They mark Layenne space just as the pilgrimages they harbor punctuate the yearly cycle (see fig. 3.2). Commemorations and exhibits are integral to this identity-building and affirmation process.

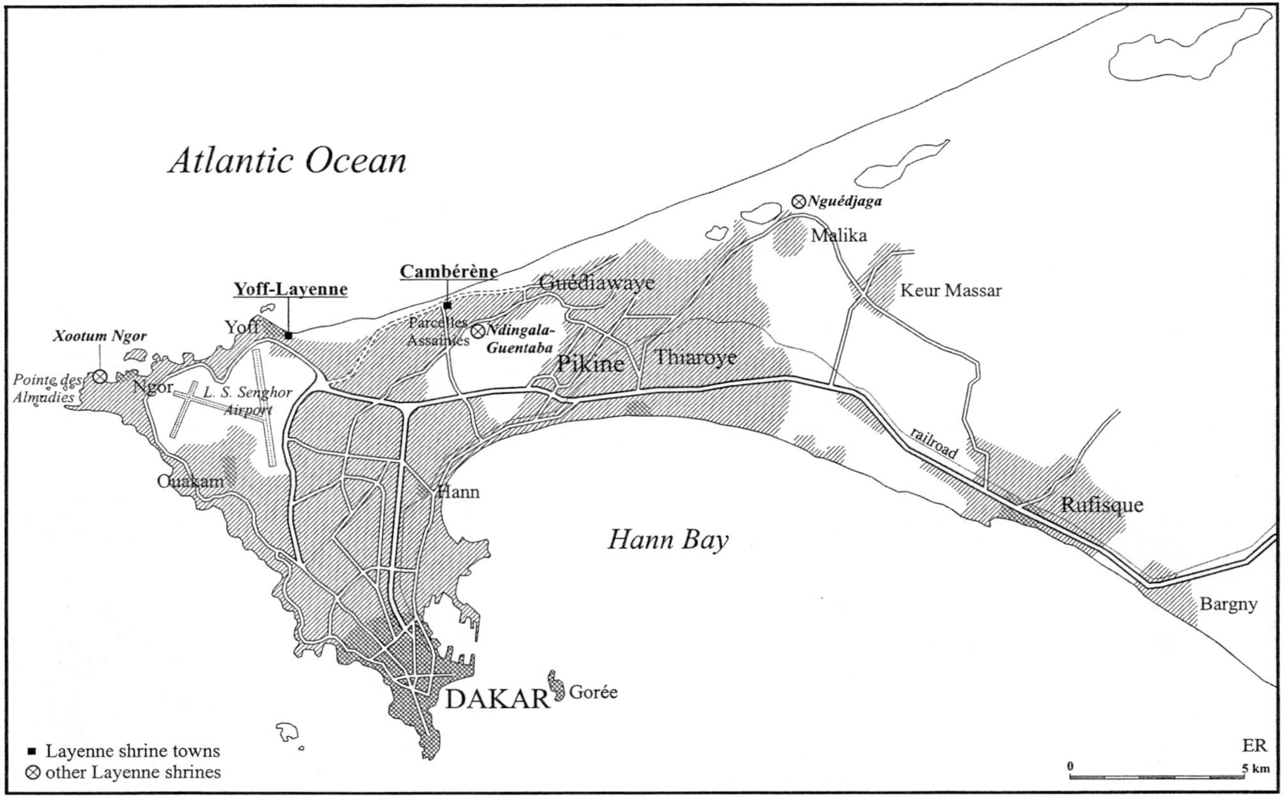

FIGURE 3.2 Map of Layenne shrines on Cape Vert Peninsula (© Eric Ross).

While all the major Layenne celebrations are held according to the Muslim calendar, one secondary Layenne event, the celebration at Cambérène on December 25, is held on a Christian date. Cambérène was established by Seydina Issa Rohou Laye in 1914 after his father's settlement of that name had been devastated by an outbreak of the plague (Sow: 51–60). The site and layout of the new settlement resembled the older settlement of Yoff-Layenne, established by Seydina Mouhammadou Limamou Laye in the mid-1880s. Like Yoff-Layenne, Cambérène consists of two distinct spaces: the "village" and the Diamalaye (see fig. 3.3). The "village"[35] is a densely-built-up neighborhood centered on a Friday mosque[36] and public square. Most of the square is covered over by an *mbaar*, a hangar-like structure that gives shelter from the sun. Together, the mosque and the square lie at the geographical and religious heart of the community. The mosque is used for all canonical prayers, by both men and women. Furthermore, in Layenne tradition each prayer is preceded by collective *dhikr* recitation. These recitations take place in the covered square in front of the mosque. Like the mosque, the square is sacred ground; it consists of fine clean sand and shoes are removed upon reaching it.

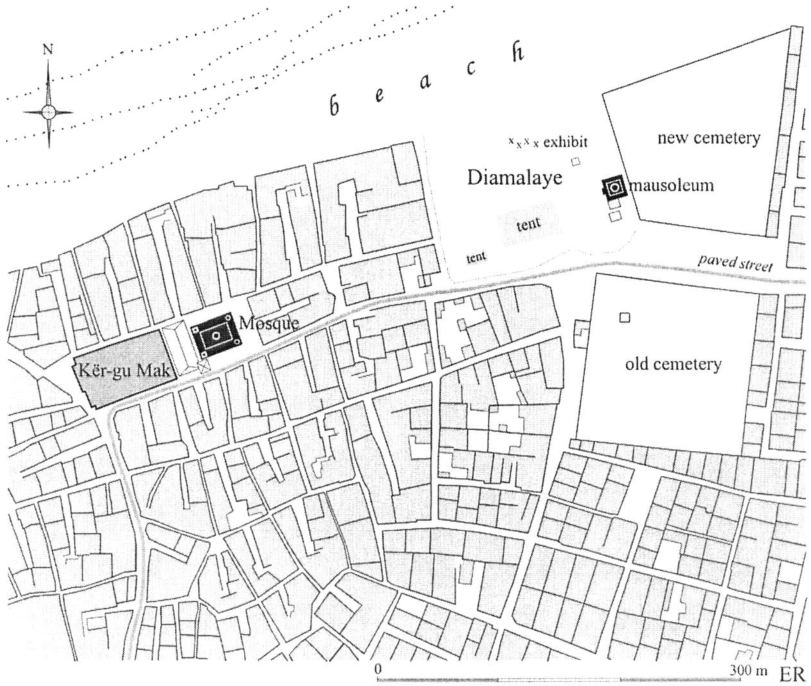

FIGURE 3.3 Plan of Cambérène on Christmas Day 2006 (© Eric Ross).

The mosque, erected in 1937, is the main monument of the village (see fig. 3.4). Architecturally, it resembles a church. It has a pair of minarets on the front façade, flanking an entrance narthex beneath a triangular pediment, just as most classically designed churches of Western tradition do. It also has Gothic-style arch windows. These Gothic elements should not however be seen as a direct Christian influence on the Layenne movement. Rather, they reflect the state of the building professions in the early twentieth century. Masonry architecture in brick and cement was introduced along Senegal's coast by Europeans and masons were initially trained to erect buildings for use by Europeans. It seems that the impetus for using monumental masonry architecture for mosques came from the colonial authorities, rather than from practicing Muslims or the clerical elite. When the first masonry mosques were erected in colonial cities, in Saint Louis's North Ward in 1844–47 and in Dakar in the early 1880s (the Carnot Street Mosque), the neo-Gothic architectural style then in vogue for church architecture was adopted (Sinou 1993). By the 1930s, when the Cambérène mosque was built, this Church-inspired plan had become standard in mosque design. Seydina Issa Rohou Laye had already used it when he had the Yoff-Layenne mosque rebuilt in 1925. Moreover, this church-like plan (minus the overtly Gothic elements) is still the vernacular for mosque construction in Senegal and other West African countries today.[37]

The houses that surround the mosque and square are inhabited by the extended families of senior members of the Layenne order, many of whom are related to the Thiaws and to each other. These compounds are built in a U-shape. In each compound, subunits within the extended family occupy separate houses facing a common alley-courtyard which opens onto the street. The senior family unit occupies the oldest house, which closes the alley at the back end of the compound. This U-shaped configuration is characteristic of Layenne family compounds generally. It is claimed to be conducive to congenial family life within the compound and to cohesive community life outside the front gate. It constitutes a settlement model found also in Yoff, but which seems to have been most completely implemented by Seydina Issa Rohou Laye in Cambérène. The compound on the western end of the square is called "Kër-gu Mak."[38] Seydina Issa lived in this house and it is still used by Layenne caliphs today.

The second spatial component of Cambérène, after the village with its square, is called the Diamalaye. It consists of a large open sandy space on the beach. It is kept scrupulously clean and is delimitated from the surrounding streets by a row of half-buried used tires. People must take their shoes off upon

FIGURE 3.4 Cambérène's mosque as seen from the Diamalaye (© Eric Ross).

entering the Diamalaye as it is considered sacred space just like a mosque. The Diamalaye is used for special congregational prayers on holy days, and it is where Cambérène's Christmas Day celebration is held. On the east side of the Diamalaye, that is to say on the *qiblah* axis, the direction of prayer to Mecca, is Seydina Issa Rohou Laye's mausoleum. It is important to note that when setting up Cambérène, Seydina Issa Rohou was replicating the two-part layout of his father's settlement in Yoff-Layenne, which also consists of a village with mosque and square, and a Diamalaye prayer ground with attendant mausolea and cemetery on the beach.

Both Yoff-Layenne and Cambérène are holy places and are administered directly by the Layenne caliph. Despite the facts that they are integrated into the fabric of Senegal's secular civil territorial administration and that they are completely embedded within greater Dakar's urban sprawl, public life and activities are subject to Islamic prescriptions and proscriptions. For instance, neither alcohol nor tobacco can be consumed there.

The Christmas Day celebration in Cambérène is a recent tradition and is a by-product of the youth outreach activities of Chérif Ousseynou Thiaw-Laye, a son of Seydina Issa. Chérif Ousseynou is a charismatic and enterprising figure within the Layenne order (Laborde: 81–82).[39] He is fluent in French and has traveled extensively in Africa, the Middle East, Europe, and America. He has also personally overseen the conversion to Islam of a number of Westerners, including a French vice-countess, Anne de Lignière (Farlu ci Diiné-ji: 5–6). Chérif Ousseynou has been an important figure in the Layenne order for several decades. However, since the accession of his brother Abdoulaye to the caliphate in 2001, the authority he commands has increased, as he is now the caliph's official spokesperson. Indeed, should he survive his two older brothers he will, in all likelihood, be designated caliph of the entire Layenne order.[40]

In 1986, Chérif Ousseynou set up an association called Farlu ci Diiné-ji ("Mobilization in Religion") whose express purpose was the organization of the various Layenne celebrations and events (Laborde: 82). Such celebrations (called *gàmmus*, *màggals*, *mawluds*, cultural days, etc.) are common to all of Senegal's Sufi orders and require a good deal of logistical organization and coordination: press releases, liaising with the authorities, transportation, provisioning of food and drinking water for pilgrims and guests, rental and setting up of tents, chairs, loudspeakers, maintenance of security, and so on. There are thus organizations similar to the Farlu ci Diiné-ji in the other Sufi orders.[41] In practical terms, the organization of such religious events requires the mobilization of youth—young men mostly—because they are the ones with time and energy for the intensive work involved. The focus of the Farlu ci Diiné-ji thus expanded from its initial narrow mandate of event organization to a broader one of structuring Layenne youth. Again, there are similar youth associations in Senegal's other Sufi orders.[42]

The need to "guide" youth was explained thus by Chérif Ousseynou:[43] Urban youth especially are afflicted by unemployment and underemployment and are vulnerable to a number of social "threats," principally drugs, alcohol, prostitution, and criminality.[44] During visits to the West, Chérif Ousseynou was struck by the prevalence of crack, cocaine, and heroin use among its youth.[45] Left to themselves, Senegalese youth will be destroyed by these "Western" practices.[46] Thus, the mobilization of youth during religious celebrations is complemented the rest of the time by education sessions, traveling exhibitions, and the distribution of video cassettes and pamphlets. Farlu ci Diiné-ji operates like a non-governmental organization, setting up fishing cooperatives, organizing professional training sessions, and networking with foreign donor agencies.

In 1994, Chérif Ousseynou's desire to educate youth was taken a step further when he organized a new religious celebration, called "Appel de la Jeunesse" (Call to Youth). This celebration was held on the second and third of January, the first day in Yoff-Layenne and the second in Cambérène. The next year, the date was moved to December 25, and it has since become a fixed annual event.

There may be several reasons for holding the celebration at Christmas time. First, the celebration of the symbolic "birthday" of a saint is common practice in Sufi orders.[47] The dates chosen are often symbolic because "true" dates of birth are rarely known or recorded.[48] For example, the celebration of the Prophet Muhammad's birthday, called the *mawlid*, occurs on the 12th of Rabīʿal-Awwal, which is in actuality the recorded date of his death. In the case of the "Appel de la Jeunesse" celebration, the association of Issa (the reincarnation of Jesus) with Christmas is evident. Though the practice was discontinued many centuries ago, Muslims in the Middle East used to celebrate the prophet ʿĪsā's birthday along with Christians, on the Christian birth date. Closer at hand, Christian observances on Senegal's Atlantic coast date back to the era of Portuguese trade, and Christmas has been celebrated by Catholic communities there continuously since then.

More importantly, however, given the youth audience targeted by the event, Christmas time was chosen because it is very much a time for partying in Senegal's cities, and in Dakar in particular. Though the Senegalese are overwhelmingly Muslim in faith, the Senegalese state is secular, more or less on the French model. Both Muslim and Christian holy days are official holidays in Senegal, and alcohol is legally available for purchase. Moreover, the worldwide secular aspects of Christmas and New Year's celebrations, namely late-night partying, drinking, clubbing, and so on, and the youth culture associated with these forms of entertainment, thrive in Dakar. From an Islamic perspective, the Christmas holiday season is thus a time when youth are particularly at risk of succumbing to dangerous temptations. According to its initiator, the intention of the "Appel de la Jeunesse" celebration is to allow Layenne youth to focus attention and energy on a "virtuous" enterprise and thus resist the temptation to go out and party.

During the "Appel de la Jeunesse" celebration, youth and those responsible for them, that is, parents, educators, religious guides and people in positions of authority, assemble under the spiritual mantle of Issa/Jesus. For that purpose, a large assembly tent, banners, and an exhibit are set up on Cambérène's Diamalaye, next to his mausoleum. By Senegalese standards, this religious celebration is a very small affair. On December 25, 2006, less than a thousand people were present at the event at any given time.[49]

The program of the "Appel de la Jeunesse" celebration varies from year to year. In 2006, it lasted one day and involved two principal sessions. The day began with a morning visit (*ziyārah*) to Seydina Issa Rohou's mausoleum, though it was undergoing reconstruction at the time. This was followed by a *dhikr* session held in the tent. Layenne *dhikr* consists of loud rhythmic repetition of "Allāhi Allāhi" (Wolof pronounciation: "Laye Laye"), the clicking of fingers, and the movement of arms and the upper body. Participants and spectators sat on the sand. The *dhikr* was attended mostly by men but many women were also present. People wandered in and out, joining the *dhikr* and greeting acquaintances (see fig. 3.5). As in all Layenne religious gatherings, men and women shared the same religious space, though women sat in their own circles. They were, however, every bit as vocal as men in their recitations. Everyone wore white clothing, in conformity with Layenne practice, for white is considered a sign of purity. The young men and boys who were helping organize the event, presumably members of Farlu ci Diiné-ji, all wore white tee-shirts or tunics with a black photo-image of Issa's face printed on both front and back (see fig. 3.6). The morning *dhikr* session ended around 12:30, lunch-time.

The afternoon session started around 15:30, after noon prayer.[50] Once again sheltered in the shade of the tent, the afternoon session, called the "official ceremony," had a more formal aspect than the morning one. Rows of chairs

FIGURE 3.5 Dhikr recitation beneath the tent on the Diamalaye (© Eric Ross).

FIGURE 3.6 Young members of Farlu ci Diiné-ji wearing tunics with the image of Issa Rohou Laye printed on both front and back (© Eric Ross).

were set up and important guests, officials, and notables, were in attendance. After loud *dhikr* recitations, Al-Hājj Abdoulaye, caliph of the Layennes, arrived to preside over the congregation. He was greeted by the assembly but did not speak. It was Chérif Ousseynou who addressed the gathering, in Wolof. At sunset prayer, Al-Hājj Abdoulaye blessed the congregation and it dispersed. Later that evening, small groups of Layenne disciples, groups of men and groups of women separately, held nocturnal *dhikr* recitations in private homes.

The Exhibit

During the entire Christmas Day event, an exhibit of Layenne history was displayed on A-frame panels that had been set up on the Diamalaye. This exhibit can be assembled, dismantled, and moved as needed and it is displayed at all Layenne religious and cultural events. It uses photographs, montages, and short texts (in French) to narrate the history of the order. The photographs and pictorial montages are particularly interesting as significant Christian elements are present.

The photographic history of the order begins with an iconic portrait of Seydina Issa Rohou Laye. It depicts an adult Issa, posed standing, clothed in an ankle-length black robe and white cape. Issa's head is also covered in a black and white turban.[51] He holds a pair of white gloves in his left hand. His right hand rests on a pedestal. Five medals are arrayed across his chest. This photo was clearly taken in a studio. There exist other photos of Seydina Issa Rohou Laye, all of them formal in nature: group photos with dignitaries and officials, at holy-day prayers, inaugurating mosques, and the like, but it is the early twentieth-century black-and-white studio photo that is most widely reproduced and integrated into a variety of pictorial compositions.[52] One finds a portrait version of it (head and shoulders only) on the cover of publications, on storefront signs, on tee-shirts, painted on canvas or on walls, sometimes in color (though the original photo is black and white). Various versions of this photograph, and of its derivatives, can be viewed on the web (see, for instance, http://www.layene.sn/new/l_francais/rohoulaye.php).

The ubiquitous use of this image of Issa Laye has parallels in Senegal's other Sufi orders. The Murids have developed an especially rich iconography around the single known picture of Sheikh Ahmadu Bamba, taken in 1912 (Roberts & Nooter Roberts 2003). While less widespread among Tijānīs, the practice is not unknown. Two photographs, taken in Tivaouane and first published in 1916, depict Al-Hājj Malick Sy in the shade of an open parasol (Marty 1916: 369–71). These two pictures are at the origin of the incongruous iconography of this saint.

While there are absolutely no photographs of Mouhammadou Limamou, Issa Rohou was photographed on numerous occasions. The photographic polarity between the father, Muhammad, and son Issa is significant. Islamic tradition generally discourages the pictorial representation of Muhammad. Thus, the facts that no picture of Seydina Mouhammadou Limamou Laye exists and that he is never represented pictorially are in keeping with the traditions pertaining to the prophet Muhammad. In Christian tradition and practice, on the contrary, images of Jesus Christ play a central role: the Christ-Child with Mother Mary, Jesus of the Sacred Heart, Jesus on the Cross, and so on. The ubiquity of Seydina Issa Rohou Laye's image is thus compatible with Christian practice, though not necessarily derived from it.

Alongside two reproductions of the studio photo of Issa (one of the entire figure, the other of the head only), displayed in the exhibit was a Christian devotional picture of Jesus of the Sacred Heart (see fig. 3.7). This image of Christ is Catholic in origin, produced by Catholics for Catholic devotional purposes. In fact, it is exactly the kind of Christ image some commentators

FIGURE 3.7 Devotional image of Jesus of the Sacred Heart displayed at the exhibit (© Eric Ross).

have argued was alienating to African Christians. A bearded Christ with locks of blond hair resting on his shoulders parts his red cape to expose his heart shining through the white tunic. The heart is crowned by flames and wears a belt of thorns. There is nothing extraordinary in such an image of Christ being available to the Layennes. The image of Jesus of the Sacred Heart is quite common to contemporary Catholic piety.[53] Dakar has a large Catholic community, several hundred thousand strong, and numerous Catholic educational and charitable institutions operate in the city. What is extraordinary is that the Layennes have integrated such a Christian image into their own Islamic visual culture.

Also prominently displayed at the exhibit was a composite image of Jesus/ Issa. This composite image combines Jesus and Issa in a single face (see fig. 3.8). The right side of the face is that of the iconic long-haired, bearded, blond Jesus of the Sacred Heart image, while the left side of the face is the turbaned photo portrait of Issa Rohou Laye (with civic medals just within sight at the bottom). The two halves of the face are separated by the wake of a gold-colored star or comet (perhaps the Nativity Star), which shoots upward through its center. Clearly in this case the Christian tradition of Jesus portraiture has been adopted and integrated into the Issa imagery. The image on display was a photograph of an original work which looks like it was done in colored pencil and watercolor.[54] Other photographs of this image were on sale at the site during the Christmas Day event.

FIGURE 3.8 Composite image of Jesus/Issa displayed at the exhibit (© Eric Ross).

The other images displayed at the exhibit included photos of the other Layenne caliphs as well as photos of the current Layenne leadership. Chérif Ousseynou, principal organizer of the event, was shown in a variety of contexts (see fig. 3.9). There were photos of him with his brothers in a position of authority and submission, and there were photos where he was shown with members of his personal following—including the French vice-countess who converted to Islam through his good graces. He was also photographed in the company of some Catholic nuns.[55]

This Layenne use of imagery, not to mention patently Christian imagery, is in apparent contradiction with the oft-cited proscription of images in Islam. Yet imagery of all sorts, including figurative imagery, abounds in Muslim devotional practice and within Sufi groups in particular. Such pious imagery includes representations of major holy places (the Ka'ba, Mecca, the Mosque of the Prophet in Medina, the Dome of the Rock in Jerusalem), pictorial representations of Koranic prophets, scenes from Islamic history, portraits of Sufi masters who established orders, and photographs of living Sufi sheikhs and of popular shrines. While there is no disputing that there is a strong iconoclastic current within Islam, based on *hadīths* and expounded in numerous theological and legal treatises, outside of the libraries, on the street and in people's homes popular religious imagery thrives throughout the Muslim world.

FIGURE 3.9 Photo of Chérif Ousseynou kneeling before his brother Al-Hājj Abdoulaye, Caliph of the Layennes, displayed at the exhibit (© Eric Ross).

In Senegal, most religious images relate quite specifically to one of the Sufi orders. The most common representations are portraits of Sheikh Ahmadu Bamba Mbacké, Seydina Issa Rohou Laye, Al-Hājj Malick Sy, Sheikh Ibra Fall, or others from Senegal's pantheon of modern Muslim "saints." These depictions are iconic—each has a standardized form derived from an original historic photograph—and they serve a number of purposes. Primarily, the image of a holy man on a building or a vehicle brings *baraka*, or God's blessings, to the premises. The image of a saint will also identify the owner as a member of a specific Sufi order, or of a specific sub-branch of the order affiliated to one particular sheikh or another. There are few small or medium-sized businesses in Senegal that do not display such images. Senegal's Islamic visual culture also includes painted glass *sous-verre* pictures, calendar art, murals depicting scenes from local Islamic history, and portrait pendants worn over clothing.

All of these art forms can be found among the Layenne and on the streets of Cambérène. The pictures at the exhibit, however, have special significance. They are officially sanctioned by one of the highest moral and spiritual authorities within the order and they are displayed at a holy place, the Diamalaye, during a commemoration involving the whole community. They are thus integral to the *lieux de mémoire*. They contribute to creating the master narrative of Issa/Jesus. Along with the *dhikr* and the speeches and the prayers and the architecture of the place, they help define Issa/Jesus for Layenne believers and disciples.

Jesus/Issa and the Muslim-Christian Encounter in Senegal

The most significant aspect of the Christmas Day celebration in Cambérène, from the standpoint of trans-faith interactions at shrines, is the extent to which Christian concepts have been integrated into an otherwise Senegalese Sufi event. Several Christian or Christian-like elements can be observed. The church-like architecture of the mosque has already been dealt with. The origin of this plan lies in Western European church architecture, but it had already become the standard design for masonry mosques in Senegal prior to the establishment of Cambérène.

A second Christian element observed among the Layennes is the use of French Catholic vocabulary. The Layenne do not hesitate, for example, to use the French term "le Messie" to designate Seydina Issa Rohou Laye. While Jesus is called *al-masīh* in the Koran, he is not usually referred to as such in

Islamic literature. "Le Messie" as used by the Layennes is a loan from French Catholic usage. Similarly, God is called "le Bon Dieu" in Layenne texts. God is referred to by 99 Divine Names in the Koran, but "The Good" is not one of them. "Le Bon Dieu" is a French Christian formulation equivalent to the English phrase "the Good Lord." While such linguistic francisims occur in other Senegalese Sufi discourse—Sheikh Ahmadu Bamba Mbacké for instance is commonly referred to as "le Cheikh" by Murids—it seems that it is especially pronounced among the Layennes. This might be due to the proximity of Dakar, where French permeates the Wolof language to a greater extent than elsewhere in Senegal and where Catholic literature in French circulates quite freely.

There is an even stronger borrowing from French Catholic tradition in the visual display. A typical Catholic devotional image of Jesus of the Sacred Heart is displayed alongside historic photographs of Seydina Issa Rohou Laye. Moreover, some Layenne disciple-artist has combined the two images as a composite, and this composite image is displayed along with the rest. Ironically, in this case, it is the supposedly alienating image of the blond Jesus which has been appropriate and integrated into the representation; Blond Jesus and Black Issa share a single face.

Catholic piety is also evident in at least one instance of a Marian vision. Catholic images of the Virgin Mary are as easily available in Dakar as those of Jesus Christ. The Layenne medium who had a vision of the Virgin, along with visions of Seydina Issa Rohou Laye, would have visual references to situate her visions. She knew exactly who the vision was of. Visions of Sufi masters, in dreams or in wakeful state, are common to the Sufi experience, as are visions of the Prophet Muhammad. The medium in question did not therefore have a Catholic Marian experience. The Virgin Mary she saw was equivalent to one of the Sufis or prophets more usually seen in Sufi visions.

There is evidence in the display, namely in the photo of Chérif Ousseynou Laye and the nuns, that the Layennes engage with Catholics directly, though the precise nature of these relations was not ascertained.

Finally, the date chosen for the event, Christmas Day, is clearly inspired by Christian practice. Yet here too, a deeper reading reveals that the date was chosen at least partly because of the secular, irreligious practices associated with Christmas. The choice of date was an attempt by Chérif Ousseynou to prevent partying and alcohol consumption among Layenne youth at the moment each year when they face the greatest temptation to indulge in these activities.

Bibliography

Aqeron, Charles-Robert & Pierre Nora (1997). *Les lieux de mémoire: vol. 1*. Paris: Gallimard.

Ba, Amadou Hampate (1976). *Jésus vu par un Musulman*. Dakar: Nouvelles Editions Africaines.

Basse, Ababacar Laye (2003). *Les Enseignements de Seydina Limamou Lahi (psl)*. Dakar: self-published.

Charles, Eunice A. (1975). Shaykh Amadu Ba and Jihad in Jolof, in *International Journal of African Historical Studies*. 8 (3): 367–82.

Duchemin, G. J. (1948). Urbanisme rural, le village de Cambérène, in *Notes africaines*. (39): 17–18.

Evers Rosander, Eva. (2003). Mam Diarra Bousso—The Mourid Mother of Porokhane, Senegal. *Jenda: A Journal of Culture and African Women Studies*. (4).

Farlu ci Diiné-ji (1995). *Kureel bu Yiw bi: 114e anniversaire de l'appel de Seydina Limamou Laye*. Yoff/Cambérène: Farlu ci Diiné-ji.

Friedman, Yaron (2001). Al-Huasayn ibn Hamdān al-Khasībī: A Historical Bibliography of the Founder of the Nusayrī-'Alawite Sect. *Studia Islamica*. 93: 91–112.

Gellar, Sheldon (2005). *Democracy in Senegal: Tocquevillian Analytics in Africa*. New York: Palgrave/Macmillan.

Gemmeke, Amber (2007). Women Reconfiguring Esoteric Economies, in *ISIM Review*. (19): 36–37.

Glassé, Cyril (1991). *The Concise Encyclopedia of Islam*. San Francisco: Harper Collins.

Laborde, Cécile (1995). *La confrérie Layenne et les Lébou du Sénégal: islam et culture traditionelle en Afrique*. Bordeaux: Institut d'études politiques de Bordeaux, Centre d'études d'Afrique noire.

Lake, Rose (1997). The Making of a Mouride Mahdi: Serigne Abdoulaye Yakhine Diop of Thies, in *African Islam and Islam in Africa: Encounters between Sufis and Islamists*. David Westerlund & Eva Evers Rosander, editors. London: Hurst & Co., pp. 216–53.

Lô, Cheikh Mahtar (1972), trans. Assane Sylla. La vie de Seydina Mouhamadou Limāmou Laye, in *Bulletin de l'IFAN*. Vol. 34 série B, (3): 497–523.

Malone O'Connor, Kathleen (1998). The Islamic Jesus: Messiahhood and Human Divinity in African American Muslim Exegesis, in *Journal of the American Academy of Religion*. 66 (3): 493–532.

Marty, Paul (1915–1916). Le groupement tidiani d'Al-Hadj Malick, in *Revue du monde musulman*. 31: 367–412.

Mbacké, Khadim (2005), trans. Eric Ross, ed. John Hunwick. *Sufism and Religious Brotherhoods in Senegal*. Princeton: Markus Wiener Publishers.

Nance, Susan (2002). Mystery of the Moorish Science Temple: Southern Blacks and American Alternative Spirituality in 1920s Chicago, in *Religion and American Culture*. 12 (2): 123–66.

Nemoy, Leon (1940). Biblical Quasi-Evidence for the Transmigration of Souls. *Journal of Biblical Literature*. 59 (2): 159–68.

Pinder, Kymberly N. (1997). "Our Father, God; Our Brother, Christ; or Are We Bastard Kin?": Images of Christ in African American Painting, in *African American Review*. 31 (2): 223–33.

Roberts, Allen A. & Mary Nooter Roberts (2003). *A Saint in the City: Sufi Arts of Urban Senegal*. Los Angeles: UCLA Fowler Museum of Cultural History, University of California Press.

Ross, Eric (2006). *Sufi City: Urban Design and Archetypes in Touba*. Rochester: University of Rochester Press.

Samson, Fabienne (2005). *Les marabouts de l'islam politique: Le Dahiratoul Moustarchidina wal Moustarchidaty, un mouvement néo-confrérique sénégalais*. Paris: Karthala.

Sanneh, Lamine (1989). *The Jakhanke Muslim Clerics: A Religious and Historical Study of Islam in Senegambia*. Lanham: University Press of America.

Schimmel, Annemarie (1975). *Mystical Dimensions of Islam*. Chapel Hill: University of North Carolina Press.

Sinou, Alain (1993). *Comptoirs et villes coloniales du Sénégal: Saint-Louis, Gorée, Dakar*. Paris: Karthala.

Sinou, Alain & Bachir Oloudé (1988). *Porto-Novo: ville d'Afrique noire*. Marseille: Parenthèses/Orstom.

Sow, Abdourahmane (1962). Monographie du village de Cambérène, in *Notes africaines*. 94: 51–60.

Sylla, Assane (1971). Les persécutions de Seydina Mouhamadou Limāmou Laye par les autorités coloniales, in *Bulletin de l'IFAN*. Vol. 33 série B, (3): 590–641.

Sylla, Assane & El-Hadji Mouhamadou Sakhir Gaye (1985). *Le Mahdi: Mouhamadou Seydina Limamou Laye du Sénégal*. Rufisque: Imprimerie nationale.

Sylla, Assane & El-Hadji Mouhamadou Sakhir Gaye (1976). Les sermons de Seydina Mouhamadou Limāmou Lahi et de son fils Seydina Issa Rohou Lahi, in *Bulletin de l'IFAN*. Vol. 38 série B, (2): 390–410.

Thiam, Mame Libasse Laye (2006). *Hayāh ʿĪsā ibn Maryam dhimn al-Āyāt al-Qurāniyyah wa al-Ahādīth al-Nabawiyyah* (The Life of Jesus son of Mary in Quranic Verses and Prophetic Traditions). Dakar: self-published.

Wilson, Peter Lamborn (1993). *Sacred Drift: Essays on the Margins of Islam*. San Francisco: City Lights Books.

Notes

1. The Arabic term *ṭarīqah* translates literally as *path* or *way* to God. While the term "way" conveys well the spiritual essence of Sufism, it does not adequately convey the institutional character of the Sufi *ṭarīqah*. *Ṭuruq* are organized associations of Sufis, more or less hierarchical in structure. The term is often translated as *brotherhood* in

English (*confrérie* in French). Yet the Arabic term *ṭarīqah* does not carry with it the gender bias of these European-language terms. The Sufi path to God has always been open to women, and in Senegal and sub-Saharan Africa generally, women can have elevated rank within the institutions. The gender-neutral term "order" is thus preferable. For an introduction to Sufism, read Annemarie Schimmel, *Mystical Dimensions of Islam* (Chapel Hill: University of North Carolina Press, 1975).

2. Briefly, other than the Layennes, Senegal's Sufi orders include the following groups: (1) The oldest order is the Qādiriyyah, a world-wide order whose spiritual center is the tomb-shrine of Sheikh 'Abd al-Qādir al-Jīlānī (1077–1166) in Baghdad. There is one major Senegalese branch of the Qādiriyyah (called the "Khadrs" locally), that established by Sheikh Buh Kounta (1844–1914) in Ndiassane. Other important Qādirī branches operate out of the Mauritanian towns of Nimjat and Boutilimit. (2) The Tijāniyyah order, first established by Sīdī Ahmad al-Tijānī (1738–1815) in Fez, Morocco, is the largest order in Senegal in terms of number of adherents, but it is fractured into several competing branches: the Tivaouane branch founded by Al-Hājj Malick Sy (1855–1922), the Kaolack branch established by Al-Hājj Abdoulaye Niass (1844–1922), the "Mahdiyyah" branch in Thiénaba founded by Amary Ndack Seck (1830–1899), and the Madina Gounass branch of Al-Hājj Ahmadou Seydou Ba (1898–1980). There is also the "Omarian" branch of the Tijāniyyah that remains faithful to the descendents of Al-Hājj Omar Tall (1794–1864). (3) Senegal's most well-known (and well-studied) order is that of the Murids, established by Sheikh Ahmadu Bamba Mbacké (1853–1927) and centered on the holy city of Touba. A sub-branch of the Murids called the Baye Fall was established by Sheikh Ibra Fall (1858–1930). For an analysis of Senegal's Sufi orders, see Khadim Mbacké, *Sufism and Religious Brotherhoods in Senegal*, trans. Eric Ross, ed. John Hunwick (Princeton: Markus Wiener Publishers, 2005).
3. It is often stated that there is no clergy in Sunni Islam. Nonetheless, religious authority exists and it usually rests with religious scholars, the *'ulamā'*, who, collectively and preferably by consensus, guide and sanction religious practice. In precolonial Senegambia, Islamic scholarship developed as a family profession that was passed down from father to son. Together, these lineages constituted a distinct nearly endogamous "order" within society. Such religious authorities are called *sëriñ* in Wolof, *cerno* in Pulaar and *karamoxo* in Mandinka. The French term *marabout* often designates them in the literature, but it has pejorative connotations akin to "charlatan." The neutral term "cleric" is thus preferred here. The clerics themselves use a host of specialized Arabic terms, such as *shaykh*, *muqaddam*, *'ālim*, *qādī*, *imām*, etc., depending on their rank and function. For an analysis of the origin and early development of Muslim clericalism in Senegambia, see Lamin Sanneh, *The Jakhanke Muslim Clerics* (Lanham: University Press of America, 1989).
4. For a full description of Senegal's Sufi shrines, see Eric Ross, *Sufi City: Urban Design and Archetypes in Touba* (Rochester: Rochester University Press, 2006).

5. The Lebou first secured independence from the kingdom of Kayor in the 1790s. They then created a federal state on the Cape Vert peninsula under the sovereignty of a lineage of Muslim clerics, the *sëriñs* of Ndakarou. Whereas all the other precolonial polities and titles were abolished following independence, the Sëriñ Ndakarou is still recognized as the leader of the Lebou by the Senegalese government. The Lebou are the original landowners of the greater Dakar region (an agglomeration of nearly three million people), a fact of considerable political and economic importance for Senegal's capital.
6. *Imām* means "leader" and refers specifically to the one who leads prayer.
7. This explanation was given by Chérif Ousseynou Thiaw-Laye during an interview, Cambérène, January 10, 2007. Like other Senegambian societies, the Lebou were differentiated by "castes." Artisan castes (blacksmiths, leatherworkers, woodworkers, weavers and *griots*) were socially inferior to "free" people like farmers and fishermen, and mixed marriages were forbidden. While these distinctions and proscriptions have weakened considerably over the last century and a half, they have by no means disappeared from contemporary Senegalese society.
8. The main hagiography of Seydina Mouhammadou Limamou Laye was written in 1931–32 by his *muqaddam* Cheikh Mahtar Lô. Originally entitled *Busarā' al-Muhibbīn wa Tayqīz al-Jāhilīn* (Discernment of the Friends and the Awakening of the Wayward), it was translated by Assane Sylla and published as "La vie de Seydina Mouhamadou Limāmou Laye," *Bulletin de l'IFAN série B* 34 (3): 497–523, 1972. The colonial archives were explored by Assane Sylla, "Les persécutions de Seydina Mouhamadou Limāmou Laye par les autorités colonials," *Bulletin de l'IFAN série B* 33 (3): 590–641, 1971.
9. The date has mystic significance. The Night of Mid-Sha'bān is called by some Sufis "the Night of Destiny" because it is believed that the destinies of mortals are determined each year on that night. For others, it is "the Night of Abrogation" because God, in His Mercy, has the power to erase one's past sins from His Ledger. On that night believers can appeal to God to do so.
10. It is more likely however that "Almadies" derives from the Portuguese term "almadya," or pirogue.
11. *Nurul Mahdi*, official website of the Layenne order, http://www.layene.sn, retrieved September 2, 2005. The emergence of Limamou as *mahdī* in 1301 of the Hijrī calendar is understood by the Layennes in millenarian terms; popular traditions in the Muslim world often situate such events at the opening of a new century.
12. The island of Gorée has deep historic resonance as one of the main ports of the infamous Atlantic slave trade. Though this trade was long over by 1887, the symbolism of the "Black prophet" being sequestered there by European colonizers is not lost on present-day Layenne consciousness.
13. The etymology of the toponym Cambérène, and how this toponym may relate to Medina in Arabia, are not known to the author.

14. By definition, a *sharīf* (literally "noble") is a patrilineal descendant of the prophet Muhammad. In Sunni practice, the title is bestowed on the descendants of 'Alī (the Prophet's nephew) and Fatīma (the Prophet's daughter). Historically, the Sharifs of Mecca have been the custodians of the official register of descendants of the Prophet.
15. Translates as: "Jesus Spirit of God, son of the imam of all the imams," signed by "Imam of the Two Sanctuaries" (i.e., Mecca and Medina). The year 1339 of the hijrī calendar corresponds to 1920–21 CE.
16. Seydina Issa Rohou's mausoleum was under reconstruction at the time of the 2006–7 field work session and the author was not able to gain entry.
17. By this time, Dakar had been incorporated as a French "commune" (municipality). It was considered part of French territory and those of its inhabitants born there or literate in French had the legal status of French citizens.
18. Information confirmed during an interview with Chérif Ousseynou Thiaw-Laye, Cambérène, January 10, 2007.
19. Interview with Chérif Ousseynou Thiaw-Laye, Cambérène, January 10, 2007.
20. Interview with Babacar D., a Layenne disciple, Cambérène, January 10, 2007.
21. The Wolof term *gent* refers to an abandoned settlement.
22. *Nurul Mahdi*, http://www.layene.sn, retrieved September 2, 2005.
23. The concept of "solid" architecture refers to the construction materials used. Cement, concrete, stone and brick masonry, and tiles are considered "hard" (*en dure* in French), as opposed to more perishable traditional materials such as earth, wattle and thatch.
24. Ithnā 'Asharī Shī'ites believe that the *mahdī* is the Twelfth Imām. Currently "hidden," he will reappear prior to the Day of Resurrection in order to reestablish pure faith on earth.
25. Among the most famous historical figures to have claimed to have been the *mahdī* we find: 'Ubayd 'Allāh (874–934), founder of the Shī'ī Fatimid dynasty; Ibn Tūmart (1077–1130), founder of the Almohad Empire; Muhammad Ahmad ibn 'Abd Allāh (1843–1885), who led the revolt against Egypto-Ottoman rule in the Sudan; and Mirza Ghulam Ahmad (1835–1908), founder of the Ahmadiyyah movement in the Punjab.
26. For Hamme Ba see Eunice Charles, "Shaykh Amadu Ba and Jihad in Jolof" (*International Journal of African Historical Studies*, 8 (3): 367–82, 1975). About Abdoulaye Iyakhine Niakhité Diop see Rose Lake, "The Making of a Mouride Mahdi: Serigne Abdoulaye Yakhine Diop of Thies" (*African Islam and Islam in Africa: Encounters between Sufis and Islamists*, David Westerlund & Eva Evers Rosander editors, London: Hurst & Co.: 216–53, 1997).
27. The Druzes hold the Fatimid caliph al-Hakim (d. 1021) to be an incarnation of the Divine who will return as *mahdī*. The Ahmadiyya community was founded by Mirza Ghulam Ahmad of Qadian (1835–1908) in 1889 and is thus contemporaneous with Senegal's Layenne order. Mirza Ghulam claimed to be a *mahdī* and a

messiah (note here the use of the indefinite article "a," rather than "the") as well as an avatar (or embodiment) of previous prophets: Krishna, Buddha, Jesus and Muhammad. The Ahmadiyya community has been subject to persecution, most notably in Pakistan, in part because of these doctrines.

28. The concept of transmigration of souls was debated in the literature of the 'Abbāsid era, notably by Ya'qūb al-Qirqisānī in his *Kitāb al-Anwār* (written in 937 CE). Actual claims of reincarnation have only be been made by fringe Shī'ī groups like the Nusayrī-'Alawīs, who consider Jesus, Muhammad, the twelve imams and the *mahdī*-to-come as incarnations of a single soul. See Yaron Friedman, "Al-Huasayn ibn Hamdān al-Khasībī: A Historical Bibliography of the Founder of the Nusayrī-'Alawite Sect," *Studia Islamica*. 93: 91–112, 2001) and Leon Nemoy, "Biblical Quasi-Evidence for the Transmigration of Souls," *Journal of Biblical Literature*. 59 (2): 159–68, 1940).
29. *Dhikr* (literally "remembrance" of God) is the most common and widespread of Sufi devotional practices. *Dhikr* often consists in the recitation of Divine Names, or of special litanies containing Koranic phrases. *Dhikr* practice varies greatly from one Sufi group to another. For some it is an individual practice; for others it is collective. For some it is silent, recited in the mind; for others it is done out loud. Layenne *dhikr* is collective and very vocal.
30. Tabaski designates the 'Īd al-Kabīr or 'Īd al-Adhā festival (10th Dhū-l-Hijjah) which commemorates the story of Abraham and corresponds to the culmination of *hajj* pilgrimage to Mecca.
31. Korité corresponds to 'Īd al-Fiṭr (1st Shawwal) which closes the holy month of Ramadan.
32. The Mawlud al-Nabī is the Prophet's Birthday (12th Rabī'al-Awwal).
33. See also http://www.layene.sn, the official website of the Layenne order.
34. The concept of *lieu de mémoire* was developed by Charles-Robert Aqeron and Pierre Nora in a three-volume work entitled *Les lieux de mémoire* (Paris: Gallimard, 1997), which dealt with the construction of collective historical memory in France, and particularly with the fixation of this memory in the landscape. Buildings, monuments, battlefields, ceremonies, commemorations, festivals, etc., all contribute to the production of collective memory.
35. Cambérène is still called a "village" despite the fact that, since the early 1980s, it has become heavily urbanized and entirely embedded in the urban fabric of Parcelles Assainies, a dense working-class suburb of Dakar (pop. 340,000 in 2004). The population of the *arrondissement* (ward) of Cambérène is 40,000, but the Layenne "village" (neighborhood) itself has only about 6,000 inhabitants (Laborde: 10).
36. Like all Muslims, the Layenne distinguish "ordinary" or "neighborhood" mosques (Ar. *masjid*, *jàkka* in Wolof), used for regular prayers throughout the week, from "Friday" or "congregational" mosques (Ar. *masjid jāmi'*, *jumaa* in Wolof), which can also be used for the *khutbah* mid-day prayer on Fridays.

37. Most famously, the Friday Mosques of such major nineteenth-century ports as Lagos and Porto Novo are redolent with Baroque Catholic designs attributable to the importance of Afro-Brazilians to civic life in those cities at that time. See Sinou & Oloudé 1988.
38. Kër-gu Mak can be translated as "the Master's House" or "the House of the Senior One."
39. Chérif Ousseynou appears to be the only member of the family to use the title *sharīf*, which denotes descent from the prophet Muhammad. It is not clear whether he is using the term as a title, or whether Sharīf is actually part of his first name, in which case he is named for Sharīf Husayn (624–80), Muhammad's revered grandson.
40. Chérif Ousseynou Thiaw-Laye died of an undisclosed illness on July 1, 2009, at the age of 64.
41. In the Murid Order, it is the Hizbut Tarqiyya association which gave itself the mandate of organizing Touba's "Grand Màggal" each year. Similarly, the annual *gàmmu* in Tivaouane is organized by a Tijānī association called Dahira du Comité d'Organisation au Service du Khalife Ababacar Sy, or COSKAS.
42. The Tivaouane branch of the Tijāniyyah has a mass youth organization called Dahiratoul Moustarchidina wal Moustarchidaty, which operates nationally under the "moral authority" of Sëriñ Moustapha Sy (see Fabienne Samson, *Les marabouts de l'islam politique*, Paris: Karthala, 2005). Murid urban youth in search of structure in their lives tend to gravitate towards the Hizbut Tarqiyya association headquartered in Touba, which began as a students' association at the University of Dakar, or else they join "Général" Sëriñ Modou Kara Mbacké's organization, the Mouvement Mondial pour l'Unicité de Dieu.
43. Interview with Chérif Ousseynou Thiaw-Laye, Cambérène, January 10, 2007. The French term used by Chérif Ousseynou during the interview was *encadrer*, literally "to frame" youth.
44. This religious reading of social threats is identical to the Christian notion that the Devil finds work for idle hands. Not just youth, women too are thought to be particularly susceptible to Satan's tricks.
45. During the interview, Chérif Ousseynou used body language and gesture to indicate smoking up, snorting, and shooting up.
46. Satellite television, AIDS, cancer, and diabetes are also seen as dangerous "modern illnesses." (Farlu ci Diiné-ji: 4)
47. In Morocco, the birthday celebrations of many saints (called *mawsim*, lit. "season") are scheduled according to the solar calendar, not the Islamic lunar one, so that they correspond to the agricultural seasons. Most *mawsims* are held in late summer, following the grain harvest, when rural people have time and some money to spare. In Egypt, a saint's birthday celebration is called a *mulid* and is also an occasion for pilgrimage and the holding of a fair.

48. In Christian tradition as well, the dates chosen for Christmas celebrations (25th of December for some, 6th of January for others) are symbolic. The "true" date of Jesus' birth is not known.
49. By contrast, the annual Grand Màggal in Touba and Gàmmu of Tivaouane attract well over one million pilgrims each.
50. In Senegal, noon prayer is held relatively late, at 14:15. By tradition, the Layenne pray later still, around 15:00.
51. All subsequent Layenne caliphs have worn a double turban of white and black cloth.
52. The author has been unable to determine the source, date, or circumstances surrounding this studio photograph.
53. The cult of the Sacred Heart of Jesus, twinned with that of the Sacred Heart of Mary, first appeared in France during the Counter-Reformation. They were especially promoted by the Catholic Church during the second half of the nineteenth century, when most Catholic institutions in Dakar were established. Images like the one displayed at the Layenne exhibit are an important part of this Catholic cult. David Morgan (Valparaiso University, Indiana), personal email communication, June 1, 2007.
54. The artist of the original composite image is not known to the author. Photographs of the image were on sale at the Christmas Day event, but the vendors could not say where the original was.
55. Chérif Ousseynou appears to have excellent relations with Catholics, but during the brief interview with him the author was unable to ask about the significance of the photo with the nuns.

4

Environmental Disasters and Political Dominance in Shared Festivals and Intercessions among Medieval Muslims, Christians, and Jews

Alexandra Cuffel

FOCUSING ON REACTIONS to shared festivals and rituals of intercession by Jews, Christians, and Muslims living in Egypt, the Levant, and to a lesser extent al-Andalus and the Maghrib, I argue that shared processions and festivals "stretched" and redefined both communal and gender boundaries. They also served as a vehicle for Muslims, Christians, and Jews to *reassert* such boundaries through their interpretations of these joint festivals and holy spaces. I further suggest that while some of these customs were clearly very old (some are still being practiced!), participation in, anxiety about, and the impulse to manipulate or interpret them advantageously increased beginning in the eleventh and twelfth centuries and continued through the early sixteenth century. The tensions and contradictions in reactions to shared festivals and saint veneration mirror similar tensions and contradictions between Jews, Christians, and Muslims during this period, and between men and women. Yet, interreligious or gender anxieties were not the only contributing factors. Rather, these festivals or joint intercessions were used as venues for working out broader issues of identity, political power, and fears regarding ecological threats beyond anyone's control. The abandonment of customary identities was an unofficial, yet inherent and necessary component for the efficacy and the simultaneously sacred and playful nature of these festivals. Whether political officials were willing to tolerate the temporary dissolution or weakening of religious and gendered boundaries depended on the degree to which identity boundaries as a whole appeared to be threatened. In times of universal crisis, such as plague, the participation of the other was co-opted as a *necessary* part of the ceremony.

Theoretical Frameworks

Already in early Islam, Muslim authors recognized and fretted about the attraction that Jewish and Christian religious rituals held for their coreligionists, particularly the practice of visiting holy gravesites and shrines. In al-Bukharī's ḥadīth collection dating from around the mid-ninth century of the common era, we find the following saying attributed to the Prophet Muḥammad and an explanation: "'Allah cursed the Jews because they built the places of worship at the graves of their Prophets."[1] Elsewhere in the same collection:

> Um Salama told Allah's Apostle about a church which she had seen in Ethiopia and which was called Mariya. She told him about the pictures which she had seen in it. Allah's Apostle said, "If any righteous pious man dies amongst them, they would build a place of worship at his grave and make these pictures in it; they are the worst creatures in the sight of Allah."[2]

In another version, *two* women, Um Salama and Um Ḥabība, both describe the images they had seen in the Ethiopian church.[3] Neither account indicates what the woman or women themselves thought of the images. That they asked the Prophet about what they saw, however, shows that the church had clearly made an impression and aroused their curiosity. The inclusion of their query in one of the standard compendia of ḥadīth also suggests that al-Bukharī and others thought it and the Prophet's answer would prove important to later generations of believers. In this account, the women's interest prompts a sharp condemnation, indicating Allah's utter disapproval of Christian image making, and in particular, such images' connection with the graves of the holy dead. By implication, any Muslim who imitated such practices would also be disgraced in the eyes of God, or following the first ḥadīth, share in the cursed status of the Jews who also venerated gravesites.[4]

These ḥadīth and later medieval sources about Muslim interest in and sharing of non-Muslim religious practices reveal a continual tension—attraction and participation in these rituals on the one hand, and condemnation of them as "un-Islamic" on the other. The second ḥadīth further underscores another characteristic of much of the medieval Muslim literature about shared saints and festivals, namely the attribution of interest in and practice of "foreign" and inappropriate religious customs to *women*. Suggestions that certain "undesirable" religious customs were foreign and/or primarily the purview of women were a polemical effort to create categories of "right" versus "heretical" religious customs.[5]

In the context of similar phenomena in early medieval western Europe, Peter Brown has suggested that expressions of disapproval regarding festivals and visitation of the dead also reflect a less explicit tension between family and community, namely the needs and abilities of individuals and specific families in contrast to those of the broader community. Within these very practices lay both the tension and its potential resolution, namely festivals and saint veneration as a way of creating community across social and even religious divisions.[6] He was drawing from the work of Victor and Edith Turner, who stressed the liminal status of pilgrims. According to these anthropologists, the process of travel removes the pilgrim from his or her daily routine and secular concerns as he or she focuses on the sacred meanings of the journey, and yet the traveler still must function in the physical world, albeit a very different one than the one to which he or she is accustomed. Pilgrims visiting the holy dead or other holy sites occupy a kind of halfway space between the divine world and the human one, the living and the dead.[7] Furthermore, the Turners associated two forces at work in pilgrimage: "social structure" and "anti-structure" or "*communitas*." The former deals with the normative rules and sanctions of a given society, whereas the latter refers to a spontaneous and shared sense of belonging, even among people of different identities, by those brought together through the pilgrimage process.[8] A variety of scholars have applied the theories of Peter Brown and Victor and Edith Turner to the phenomenon of *ziyāra*, that is, visiting graves and shrines, among Muslims and Jews in the Middle East.[9] Those scholars who have worked on shared practices have mostly concentrated on identifying the common rituals and the meaning that they had for each community. In applying the theories of Victor and Edith Turner, historians of premodern pilgrimage in Europe and the Middle East have often overlooked the Turners' qualifications about pilgrimage and *communitas*, as well as subsequent anthropological critiques of their theory.[10] Victor Turner in particular developed a three-tiered concept of *communitas*, the first involving the spontaneous abandonment of quotidian restraints and hierarchies, the second, "normative *communitas*" in which the spontaneity of the first is at least partially "captured" and bound by social rules, and finally, "ideological *communitas*" wherein the participants seek to establish a utopian society.[11] Later anthropologists and ethnographers have questioned the validity of or attempted to refine the universal applicability of Turner's theory and have argued both for the need to consider differences between cultures in the comparative study of pilgrimage and the presence of multiple goals, ideologies, and interpretations on the part of the participants within a single pilgrimage or festival.[12] Indeed, John Eade and Michael Sallnow deplored the tendency, based on applications of Turner's theory, to reduce pilgrimage to a dichotomous struggle between the dissolution and reinforcement of social norms, maintaining that pilgrimage should be viewed "not merely as a field of social relations but also as a *realm of competing discourses*."[13] Other anthropologists have emphasized the need to address the somatic aspects of certain types of pilgrimage, such as illness, pain, and sexuality.[14]

Rather than dealing solely with travel to gravesites and the rituals surrounding pilgrimage, I focus on shared festivals, holy sites, and processions. These are closely related to pilgrimage, for they involve travel and the creation of sacred space and time. The interpretations of sharing, in and of itself, by the different religious communities, and the ways in which anxiety about gender boundaries were interwoven with those regarding religion demonstrate that these activities were very much part of a "realm of competing discourses" relating not only to social and religious hierarchies, but to gendered and sexual ones as well. Individuals, especially rulers, played with these competing discourses as needed. The festivals, processions, and their interpretations were shaped by particular social, political, religious, and even environmental contexts of the Fāṭimid, Ayyūbid, and Mamlūk eras.

Bidaʿ, Polemic, and Festivals: Reflections of Religious, Political and Ecological Tensions

Despite clear evidence of shared religious practices in earlier periods of Islamic and even pre-Islamic history, beginning in the eleventh century, the development and proliferation of two genres: *bidaʿ* treatises (treatises dedicated to defining and, usually, condemning *bidaʿ*, that is, "innovations" to standard, accepted Muslim practice), and anti-Coptic polemical tracts testify to a shift in attitude toward the participation in religious rituals by multiple communities. Sunni Muslim authors following the Mālikī legal school in al-Andalus and the Maghrib began composing books dedicated entirely to the identification and refutation of *bidaʿ*. The first of these was written in 900 CE; however, the majority were written between the twelfth and sixteenth centuries CE.[15] Authors from the other legal schools also composed *bidaʿ* treatises, the most famous of these being Ibn Taymīyya (d. 1328 CE), a Syrian Ḥanbalī; however, the majority of these were Mālikī, some of whom, such as al-Ṭurṭūshī (c. 1060–1126 CE) and Ibn al-Ḥājj (d. 1336 CE), brought their ideas from al-Andalus and the Maghrib to Egypt and the surrounding regions as they themselves emigrated east.[16] Not only did Sunni objectors to shared practices travel from the western Mediterranean eastward, so too did the Shi'i followers of the Fāṭimids, along with Sufis and their adherents, such as Aḥmad al-Badawī (1200–1276 CE) and his family. Both the Fāṭimids and many Sufis, both those originating from the Maghrib and those native to the Levant and Egypt, encouraged some of the practices against which the Mālikī legalists, and others who followed their example, fought in their anti-*bida'* treatises.[17]

As Maribel Fierro points out, discussions of innovations involving Muslim imitation of non-Muslims do appear in other genres of literature, such as ḥadīth (like those discussed above), the legal compendia by the founders of the four major law schools, *fatāwā* and *ḥisba* collections, and historical chronicles.[18] However, I suggest that the rise of a genre specifically dedicated to refuting practices that were often identified as Jewish or Christian in origin and favored by women indicates a heightened anxiety on the part of many Muslim legalists about what they perceived as the increased blurring of the boundaries between Muslims and non-Muslims, and men and women. That the majority of these treatises were written in regions and periods during which conflict between Muslims and non-Muslims as well as between Shi'a and Sunni was quite high further suggests that they sprang from social, religious, and political conflicts between these groups.[19] I argue that three major factors affected Jewish, Christian, and Muslim relations generally and Muslims' receptivity to shared religious practices specifically: (1) fears of betrayal by the indigenous Christian population to other Christian powers such as Byzantium or the Latin West; (2) environmental threats which increased with the arrival of the "Black Death"; (3) the spread of the Fāṭimid custom of broadening spheres of influence through gifts of clothing and food to religious rivals.

Speaking of the 'Abbāsid caliph, al-Manṣūr (754–775 CE), Jean Maurice Fiey noted that the caliph's treatment of Jacobite and Melkite Christians who lived in the borderlands near Byzantium differed considerably from his treatment of the Nestorians who lived in the heart of Baghdad.[20] Fiey suggests that fear of the Byzantines and a potential alliance between them and Christians living near the border prompted al-Manṣūr to enforce dress regulations on the *dhimmi*, that is, the "protected minorities," which included Jews, Christians, and Zoroastrians, and to displace them from the frontier.[21] Similar fears and tensions arose regarding the power of *dhimmi* in al-Andalus, Egypt, and the Levant.[22] Mohammed-Tahar Mansouri argues that North African Christians who were attracted by the new Fāṭimid regime because of its receptivity to employing non-Muslims faced pressures to convert to Islam to avoid suspicion that they might ally with outside Christian forces. Fāṭimids drew sharp criticism in the Maghrib for what the Sunni majority perceived as their tolerant or even preferential treatment of *dhimmis*, to the point that the Fāṭimids were strongly associated with Jews, both because they appointed Jews to governmental positions and because like the Jews they traced their identity through the female line; their ancestry from the Prophet Muḥammad, and thus their claim to power, derived from Muḥammad's daughter, Fāṭima. Such accusations followed them to Egypt.[23] Similarly, in al-Andalus, *dhimmi* regularly attained positions of power and mingled freely on a daily basis with Muslims, much to the consternation of some Muslim poets and legalists.[24] Thus in both al-Andalus and the Maghrib the Muslim leadership regularly provided Jews and Christians with opportunities of advancement, which in turn heightened resentment and anxiety about the *dhimmi* in other sectors of the Muslim population, especially those who saw themselves as guardians of Islamic law.

Fears of *dhimmi* power and alliance with Christians outside Muslim rule became more acute during the Crusades. From the late the Fāṭimid into the Ayyūbid and Mamlūk periods in Egypt and the Levant, many Muslims both feared that Coptic Christians would ally with European or Ethiopian Christians and betray the Muslims to them, and they resented the prevalence of non-Muslims in governmental positions that granted them power over Muslims—a violation of Muslim law, but a law that had been frequently disregarded. The production of a substantial number of polemical treatises against religious minorities during this period, many of which focused primarily or exclusively on the Copts and the specter of their potential political betrayal of the Muslims along with their economic oppression of the Muslim populace, indicates that fears of oppression and betrayal through enemy alliance were major issues during the height of the crusading period and its aftermath, when Europeans still aspired to free Jerusalem from Mamlūk control.[25] Further indication of rising tensions between Muslims and Copts is that after 1354 CE, Mamlūk authorities enforced the requirement for the sons and families of Coptic men who converted to Islam to become Muslim as well, were less lenient about allowing or ignoring the return to their original religion on the part of Coptic converts to Islam, and placed greater pressure on Copts to become Muslim.[26]

Civil unrest, increasingly conservative religious reforms, the *reconquista* in the Maghrib and al-Andalus, the Crusades, international trade, and exploration and expansion on the part of the Western Europeans, all served simultaneously to increase hostility and fear about the religious other, and also to encourage, even force, Jews, Christians, and Muslims to interact and cooperate in new ways. Environmental threats as well as political and religious tensions also inspired conflict between different religious communities while at the same time pushing those communities to cooperate in the face of a danger common to all. Paula Sanders has noted that Fāṭimid Egypt, from the reign of al-Mustanṣir (1035–1094 CE) suffered from a number of low inundations from the Nile which caused drought and famine.[27] Starting in the mid-fourteenth century, the so-called "Black Death," which most scholars still agree was the bubonic plague and its variants, placed additional pressure on all communities, not merely because of the numerous deaths it caused and the constant specter of its return, but because of the need to create theological explanations, sources of blame, and relief.[28] Stuart Borsch has also recently demonstrated that the plague caused further agricultural distress because of the decrease in labor to manage the dikes and canals of the Nile as well as to till farmland. Farmers fled to the cities in search of assistance, and Bedouins began to take over farmland.[29] Religious minorities, women, and "bad" religious and social behaviors all served as a focus of blame, but, I will argue, as source of relief as well.

In medieval Islamic law, the status of *dhimmi* entailed a variety of rights and restrictions.[30] These legal systems established hierarchies which, while allowing marginal groups to exist, also constructed boundaries between religious groups by regulating food, dress, marriage, inheritance, and so on. These barriers served to preserve the religious identity of each of the groups in question.[31] Yet in her examination of ritual in Fāṭimid Cairo, Paula Sanders maintains that the Fāṭimid caliphs and their viziers used festal processions with accompanying gifts of food and clothing to create a familial-like bond across divisions between the Isma'ili caliphs and their followers, and their subjects comprised of other types of Shi'a, a Sunni majority, as well as Jews and Christians.[32] Such inclusiveness encouraged participation in festivals and pilgrimage across denominations and seriously challenged the carefully drawn lines of hierarchy that separated religious groups. They also challenged gender and social hierarchies. Indeed, Boaz Shoshan, in attempting to account for the simultaneous participation of the religious, political, and learned elite in festivals with artisans, merchants, peasants, and the very poor of both genders and for the strenuous objections that members of the elite expressed toward these celebrations, suggests that they found some of the extreme behavior in both state-sponsored and "popular" festivals threatening to the very status quo that some of the state festivals had been designed to establish, and thus condemned the practices.[33] In other words, Fāṭimid and later Mamlūk authorities attempted to create "normative *communitas*" to use Turner's term, but they and religious leaders feared that such occasions fostered "spontaneous *communitas*" with its concomitant disregard for hierarchical distinctions. These concerns prompted legislation to ban a number of Coptic festivals that attracted Muslim participants and, according to *bidaʿ* writers, lewd behavior.[34]

Shared Festivals and Contested Hierarchies

The relationship between fears of *dhimmi* economic and political power and shared religious practice are especially evident in the writings of two Mamlūk chroniclers, al-Maqrīzī (1364–1442 CE) and Ibn Taghrībirdī (1411–1470). Al-Maqrīzī, who frequently contented himself with describing the religious customs of non-Muslims and Muslim participation in them without comment, at the beginning of his discussion of Coptic festivals and beliefs, warned that Muslims who celebrated with the Copts became like them.[35] Huda Lutfi has argued that al-Maqrīzī systematically attempted to portray Coptic religious practices as worthless and in decline both in his *Khiṭaṭ*, which is dedicated to describing the topography and religious practices of Egypt, especially Cairo, and in his historical chronicle, *Kitāb al-Sulūk li-maʿrifat duwal al-mulūk*, as part of a program to claim Muslim hegemony in the region.[36] That he targeted Copts in particular should be seen as a reflection of the growing tension between Muslims and Copts.[37] Copts especially suffered from measures to purge the government of non-Muslims because so many were in fact government officials. For example, according to the *History of the Patriarchs of the Egyptian Church*, during the caliphate of al-Ḥāfiẓ (1131–1149 CE), so many Christians served as administrators in Egypt that the people went to one of the Muslim amirs and begged him to take power away from the Christians lest some of the Muslim population convert to Christianity.[38] However, the level of resentment and its tie to fears of Muslim adoption of non-Muslim identity may be seen best in a poem that both al-Maqrīzī and the fifteenth-century historian Ibn Taghrībirdī cite in protest to the Sultan al-Malik al-Ashraf's appointment of a man of Christian descent as confidential secretary of Egypt:

> He went backwards each day, and exchanged urine for excrement
> He was one time a Jew, then a Christian by practice
> If the Shaykh's life is long, he'll join the Magi (Zoroastrians)[39]

The poem was originally composed in the eleventh century in response to the Emir of Granada's appointment of a Christian as vizier after the death of the Jew who had held the post previously.[40] Both in the poem's original context and in response to al-Malik al-Ashraf's actions, the non-Muslims are compared with dirty bodily fluids as a way of making both the non-Muslims themselves and the choices of the Muslim leaders as despicable as possible to the audience. More important for our purposes is that the Muslim leaders are accused of adopting the practices or religion of non-Muslims by their willingness to allow non-Muslims to take government positions. Thus, accusations of improper religious affiliation or practice within the Muslim world are part of a wider anxiety about the disintegration of appropriate hierarchies of power between Muslim and *dhimmi*. Not only was the Muslim-*dhimmi* hierarchy threatened, but according to this poem, Muslim identity dissolves entirely due to the adoption of non-Muslim practice. This fear is expressed even more clearly by Ibn Taymīyya. For him, one of the worst sins a Muslim could commit was to become like his/her non-Muslim neighbors. Adopting the symbols of another religion, he wrote, implied accord with the beliefs those symbols represented and, eventually, all differences between Muslim and non-Muslim would disintegrate.[41] Despite strong criticism from individuals such as Ibn Taghrībirdī and Ibn Taymīyya, however, the willingness on the part of some Muslim amirs and sultans to appoint Jews and Christians to office also indicates a willingness to disregard such hierarchies.[42]

The tension between complicity and condemnation in regard to shared festivals evident in the writings of Mamlūk chroniclers like Ibn Taghrībirdī and al-Maqrīzī was a long-standing one. For example, the Christian chronicler, Yahya ibn Saʿid of Antioch (11th century CE) describes the celebration of Palm Sunday in Jerusalem:

> In Jerusalem it was the custom of the Christians, done every year on Palm Sunday, to carry a great branch from an olive tree from the church called al-Lʿazaria [St. Lazarus] to that of the Resurrection. It was carried through the streets with readings and prayers. The cross was carried publicly. The governor of the town rode on horseback with all his cortege accompanying the Christians and pushing away the crowd. In Egypt as well as in the rest of the country the practice existed during

> this festival to decorate the churches with olive branches and palm fronds and then distribute them on the same day to the people as a form of benediction. That year (1007–1008 CE) al-Ḥākim [the caliph] prohibited the inhabitants of Jerusalem to observe this practice and thereafter prohibited it in all the provinces of his empire; he forbade the carrying of olive or palm branches in any church. Nothing like these should appear in the hands of a Muslim, or a Christian, or anyone else. The prohibition was extremely strict.[43]

What becomes clear in this passage is that Muslims regularly joined in the Christian celebration; al-Ḥākim's prohibition against carrying palm or olive branches explicitly included Muslims, suggesting that they joined in at least some of the festival and perhaps saw these branches as imparting blessing, much like their Christian neighbors. Furthermore, according to Ibn Sa'id, the governor, presumably a Muslim, joined the procession, though whether as part of the celebration or simply to provide crowd control is not entirely clear. Even if only the latter, his willingness to do so and his presence indicated local governmental support of a very public Christian festival that violated several rules set forth in the Pact of Umar (the document—in various versions—that set down the basic rights, obligations, and prohibitions of *dhimmi* living under Muslim rule). Therein, Christians are forbidden from carrying their crosses or books publicly or from singing loudly. Riding horses (as opposed to mules and donkeys) was also forbidden to *dhimmi*.[44] The Christians themselves do not ride horses in this narrative; however, the presence of the governor and other officials on horseback as part of the procession would have added a level of dignity that some Muslims may have found inappropriate for a Christian festival.

Presumably, all of these violations prompted the caliph to attempt to abolish the practices. However, even al-Ḥākim himself, well known for his severe treatment of *dhimmi*, and indeed of any individual of whose behavior he did not approve, seems to have participated in or at least observed and taken pleasure in Christian festivals.[45] Slightly later in his account, while describing Epiphany, Ibn Sa'id notes that "[f]or many years al-Ḥākim attended them (the festivities) in disguise and watched them."[46] Eventually, the caliph forbids even the mention of the holy day and the rites surrounding it "by all people, whoever they might be," let alone its practice.[47] Even the caliph himself, therefore, was not immune to the attractions of non-Muslim festivals, in this account. Nor was al-Ḥākim unusual in his interest and participation. A number of other caliphs, sultans, and governors also participated in Coptic festivals to varying degrees.[48] For example, another Fāṭimid caliph, al-Ẓāhir (1021–1036 CE), assisted with the cost of lighting during the festival al-Ghiṭās (Epiphany) and watched the Christian procession with his entire family—an event which, like the festival described above, included the public display of crosses and the singing of hymns.[49] Again, a Muslim leader willingly tolerates and even encourages joint Muslim-Christian celebrations despite the violation of hierarchical symbols designed to mark Muslims as superior to *dhimmi.* We know from al-Maqrīzī and other Muslim sources that some Muslim attendees were far more active in their participation. Ibn Taymīyya complains about al-Ghiṭās: "Many ignorant women have begun to bring their children to the bathing pool at this time. They claim that this benefits the child. This is from the religion of the Christians."[50] Individuals such as Ibn Taymīyya , Ibn al-Ḥājj and even al-Maqrīzī may have objected vociferously to shared customs, holy places, and festivals—however, much of the Muslim population did not.

The Christian chronicler, Ibn Sa'id, offers little in the way of explicit interpretation or commentary about al-Ḥākim's interest in or even condemnation of these shared festivities; however, by presenting both rituals and Muslim participation in and sanction of them as long-standing and widespread, this chronicler indirectly argues for the continuation of the Christian celebrations and the extra privileges to set aside the customary restrictions on the display of non-Muslim religious symbols and songs. Al-Ḥākim's prohibitions come across as anomalous, and his own behavior as contradictory. Similar to Western European Christian and Jewish travelers' reactions to Muslim presence at Christian and Jewish holy sites or participation in Christian and Jewish festivals or fasts, Ibn Sa'id never protests Muslim participation; rather, he boasts about it, suggesting that in his eyes it added honor and validity to the ceremony.[51]

Descriptions from Muslim authors such as al-Ṭurṭūshī, Ibn Taymīyya, Ibn al-Ḥājj, and al-Maqrīzī writing in al-Andalus, Syria, and Egypt from the twelfth to the fifteenth centuries and from Western Christian pilgrims such as the late fifteenth-century Swiss friar Felix Fabri or the fourteenth-century Irishman Simeon Symeonis, indicate that al-Ḥākim's efforts to abolish either Christian or Muslim participation in either Palm Sunday or Epiphany failed utterly.[52] Indeed, Muslim participation and the resultant mixing of Muslim and non-Muslim, men and women increased, as did anxiety about it. Consider Ibn al-Ḥājj's (d. 1336 CE) discussion of Palm Sunday:

> And this is what some of the Muslims do on one of the festivals of the Copts which is called *'Id al-zaytūnah* (Palm Sunday). On this day the

> Christians enter a place called *al-Maṭarīyah* to a well there named the well of Balsam; it is very well known there. On that day a great crowd gathers, many from the Copts and non-Copts from many lands they come to bathe in its water. Then some of the Muslims do that and they rush to it like what the Christians do, and they bathe themselves for their ablution and they uncover for this most [of their bodies?]. And this is what was mentioned previously about uncovering arousing parts glorifying the festival of the people of the book as [mentioned] before. And this increases [so] that women, men, and elderly travel to it from distant places and they assemble there and they uncover inside it as outside it. And in their gathering [there are] scandalous deeds as previously stated. But this is an increase of another scandalous matter and it is that the *dhimmi* woman looks at the body of a Muslim woman. And it is forbidden. The *'ulamā'* forbade it, may God have mercy on them. Furthermore even if bathing in this water were permitted, it is done but in a time different than their gathering.[53]

Ibn al-Ḥājj is focusing on a particularly Egyptian way of celebrating Palm Sunday. He objects to Muslims imitating Christians. He suggests that going to the pool might be allowed, but it should be at a different time than the Christian festival. What seems to disturb him most, however, is that men and women, young and old, Muslim and non-Muslim are partially or completely undressed before one another. That non-Muslim women see the bodies of Muslim women naked he emphasizes as especially scandalous. Doing so violated Muslim dignity and the hierarchy of Muslim over Christian, for it allowed non-Muslims to see Muslims in a vulnerable state.[54] He, along with other authors, voiced similar objections to the donning of scanty clothing that then became transparent during the customary water-fights during Nawruz—originally the Persian New Year, but in Egypt the celebration of the rise of the Nile.[55] In other texts from this period and that of al-Ḥākim, bathhouses and bathing were especially singled out as places of inappropriate mixing, in part because when naked, there was no way of differentiating Muslims from Jews and Christians. Rulers attempted to mitigate the situation by requiring Christians and Jews to wear some kind of distinguishing clothing, such as a necklace or colored turban, in the bathhouse, measures that seem to have been observed only sporadically.[56]

In his more general discussion of Muslim participation in *dhimmi* festivals, Ibn al-Ḥājj objects not merely because these events open the possibility that Muslims, Jews, and Christians might engage in activities that would inadvertently violate hierarchies of Muslim over *dhimmi* or make members of the various communities indistinguishable, but because Muslims actively encouraged such behavior. He laments that Muslims treat their Christian neighbors as equals and exchange greetings of peace, gifts, and food, including alcoholic beverages, that they listen to what the Jews say of Muḥammad, and that Muslim women urge their husbands to go shopping among the Christians, a request that the husbands readily obey. He characterizes these activities, like many others, such as dressing up both themselves and then a wooden pole for Shaʿbān, as imitations of the *dhimmi*.[57] Al-Wansharīsī, writing in the late fifteenth century in Fez, recorded similar behavior on the part of Muslims and Christians on *Mīlād*, Christmas, which he compared specifically to the behavior of Muslims and Christians during Nawruz.[58]

What all of these passages seem to portray is a fairly easy, friendly relationship between Muslims and their non-Muslim neighbors, in which little if any effort was expended to recognize and maintain community divisions. This attitude and set of behaviors seem to have increased during festivals, much to the distress of some Muslim legalists. Participants exchanged ideas as well as customs, which potentially violated Muslim restrictions against *dhimmi* speaking negatively of Islam or attempting anything that might constitute proselytizing.[59] The exchanges of food, clothing, and other gifts would have augmented the sense of community belonging across "denominational" lines. These are precisely the practices in which Fāṭimid caliphs engaged in order to create community and loyalty that extended over divisions of Ismaʿili, other Shiʿi and Sunni members of their court, according to Paula Sanders. Independent of governmental agendas to establish political and religious unity and support, shared religious festivals such as those analyzed above served to create or reaffirm existing ties of friendship and social community through shared rituals centered around common, albeit not identical, spiritual understanding of the function of these rituals.

Paula Sanders emphasizes the imitative nature of many Fāṭimid festivals, in terms of both Fāṭimid willingness to borrow practices from extant festivals and the fact that many of these celebrations originated in North Africa from where the Fāṭimids came initially and from where they continued to draw troops and support.[60] Boaz Shoshan also compares "popular" festivals to state festivals, suggesting that in Egypt, the latter served as vehicles to convey state messages and emphasize the legitimate power of particular sultans or amirs. State holidays and processions included many of the festive elements of long-standing celebrations and in this way served to co-opt some of their functions. In turn, he argues, the state festivals were "co-opted" by the populace so that the same behaviors that some of the political and religious elite found so objectionable also became commonplace in the government-sponsored celebrations.[61] "Extremity" of behavior, in particular behavior that involved real or imagined sexual license, was certainly an issue for many chroniclers and composers of *bidaʿ* treatises. I would argue, however, that these authors from the Maghrib and al-Andalus, as well as from Egypt and the Levant, were primarily alarmed by what they saw as inappropriate "mixing." This mixing consisted of Jews, Christians, and Muslims, prompted by common goals of play and worship, laying aside the hierarchical, clearly defined relationships between their different religious communities that many Muslim and Jewish legalists so desired to uphold, and, ironically, that some of the processional, state-sponsored celebrations in Egypt had been designed to underscore. However, this "mixing" was one of gender as well as religious affiliation.

Mixing Faiths and Crossing Genders

Complaints about the intermingling of men and women and Muslim and non-Muslim frequently went hand in hand. Already in the examples cited from Ibn Taymīyya and Ibn al-Ḥājj, women are singled out for special censure. Ibn Taymīyya's comment about al-Ghiṭās gives the impression that only Muslim *women* indulge in the Coptic ritual of bathing on that holiday, yet we know from other Muslim and Christian sources, such as al-Maqrīzī and Ibn Saʿid, that Muslim men were equally involved. Ibn Taymīyya leaves no doubt as to his disapproval of these "women's customs," for he calls those women who participate "ignorant." In Ibn al- Ḥājj's discussion of Palm Sunday, he mentions the presence of men, but he focuses on the shame of Muslim and non-Muslim *women* seeing one another naked, not men. For him, women are behind Muslim willingness to mingle and shop among the Copts, and it is women who dress up the pole on Shaʿbān. Similarly, in a text attributed to the twelfth-century Andalusian, al-Ṭurṭūshī, the author objects to such mixing during a variety of holidays:

> One innovation is that all the people in the land of al-Andalus gather to buy *halwa* on the night of 27 Ramadan (the night on which the revelation of the Qur'an is celebrated), and similarly to buy fruit, like the Christians at the celebration of January (referring to New Year's Eve) and at the celebration of *al-ʿAnṣara* (Pentacost) and Maundy Thursday to purchase fried doughnuts and cheese fritters, both of which are innovative foods. Men go out mingling with the women

> separately and in groups, to enjoy spectacles, and they do the same on Muslim festivals [of 'Id al-aḍḥā (the feast of sacrifice, marking Abraham's willingness to kill a ram instead of his son Ishmael) and 'Id al-fitr (the feast for breaking the fast of Ramadan)] and they go out to the *muṣallā*.... The women set up pavilions there to watch and not to pray.[62]

In an eleventh-century Jewish text from the Cairo Geniza, Jewish officials attempt to ban men from accompanying women and young men who were not related to them, and from bringing any "sinner" (*poshe'a)*, to the festivities at the synagogue of Moses at Dammuh, just outside of Cairo.[63] Texts in the Cairo Geniza regularly use *poshe'a* to designate an "apostate," that is, a Jewish convert to Islam.[64] Jews, like the Muslims described by al-Ṭurṭūshī, not only mix with members of the opposite sex, or attractive members of the same sex, they also play games with one another, dance, watch shadow plays (the Jewish text is more explicit on this point than al-Turṭūshī), make beer, eat special foods, and they do so with Muslims.[65] This Judeo-Arabic text depicts Egyptian Jews behaving very much like their Muslim counterparts at the festivals and certain saints' shrines on the saint's *mawlid* (birth or death day) and provoking very similar reactions from their own religious leadership.[66]

In all of these texts, men are mentioned as participants; however, women's behavior and participation, over and above that of men, and the mixing of men and women, are set aside for special censure. Elsewhere in his discussion, al-Ṭurṭūshī condemned Muslims' imitation of Jewish and Christian women's customs by prohibiting women from going to the mosque regularly, on the one hand, and, on the other, women's habit of raising their hands to pray and using perfume or other forms of adornment when they did go to the mosque.[67] Muḥammad ibn Aḥmad 'Azafi (1162–1236 CE), who was a legalist from Ceuta, exhorted: "Do not be deceived by the one who refers to knowledge and pursues the error of women and children" because they consent to join Christian celebrations.[68] Thus, women became the focus of blame for *all* Muslims' participation in non-Muslim religious rites.[69]

The Jewish document does not single out women as the sole cause of inappropriate religious behavior, including bringing non-Jews to the synagogue; nevertheless, as in many of these Muslim texts, there is a clear worry over women's sexual behavior and mixing with men. Muslim detractors voiced similar objections to women's visiting holy gravesites or the graves of family members by themselves. Ibn al-Ḥājj describes in detail the sexual exploits in which women indulged while on *ziyāra* and participating in various festivals.[70]

Gravesites of the holy dead were so strongly associated with sexual misbehavior, and women's misbehavior in particular, that in his erotic manual, the thirteenth-century Tunisian author Aḥmad al-Tīfāshī chose a graveyard as the scene for a sexual encounter between two women.[71] Cross-dressing and same-sex love were both regularly associated with festivals of all kinds. In a much-discussed passage from al-Maqrīzī describing Nawruz, "effeminates" (*al-mukhannathūn*) or "musicians" (*al-mughanūn*), depending upon the version, and loose women (*al-fāsaqāt*) congregate beneath the caliph's palace, play music, drink beer, and have water fights.[72] The activities described in this passage, from water games to beer drinking, are very similar to those to which the leaders of the synagogue at Dammuh objected. The prohibition in the Jewish text that men should not accompany "a youth and no man that is young unless he is related to him...and no one should risk an action that would cause a rumor..." hints that same-sex liaisons at festivals were a concern within the Jewish community as well.[73] Young men or male youths were considered sexually attractive to other men; within the Islamic world, men's attraction to other men, especially young ones, was considered natural, although acting upon it was prohibited by Islamic law.[74] In this Geniza text, the leaders writing the letter seem to be concerned that the pairing of a young man with an older one might cause scandalous rumors, presumably of a sexual relationship between them.

These practices of play, veneration, procession, and pilgrimage all involved a "mixing" in which boundaries and hierarchies between members of different religious communities and between different genders were disregarded. Indeed, Ibn al-Ḥājj goes so far as to say of men and women celebrating Nawruz privately together: "And they take pleasure in this as that they, on this day, all of them are women."[75] He states that they are all women as opposed to men, both because in Muslim society there was greater concern about women's dress and sexual propriety, and because he sought to feminize men who engaged in these shared practices.[76] The salient point is, however, that he explicitly complains that men and women have become as one gender, much as Ibn Taymīyya argued that when Muslims adopted the practices of *dhimmi*, all differences between the two would disintegrate.[77] Most of the written Muslim sources, and some of the Jewish ones, are hostile toward these shared practices, yet the phenomenon that they describe was widespread among much of the populace at all levels, including sometimes the caliph and government officials, as we have seen. Governmental decrees to abolish or regulate these festivals, or legalists' efforts to polemicize against them, served to reinscribe hierarchy and boundary, and should be understood, as Joel Kramer has quite rightly pointed out, in terms of what Turner called "social structure"—namely, the hierarchical system of legal, economic, and social norms—in conflict with the egalitarian, unstructured behavior and identity characteristic of *communitas* generated during pilgrimages or festivals.[78] What scholars of this phenomenon in the medieval Near East have been less cognizant of is that the temporary disintegration of religious boundaries went hand in hand with the disintegration of gender boundaries and that both, I would argue, are essential to the creation of sanctified time and space.

Disasters, Anxiety, and Borrowing Power

Anxiety about inappropriateness of men's and especially women's behavior at festivals and gravesites and about the inability to distinguish Jews and Christians from Muslims prompted a number of repressive measures during the late fourteenth to fifteenth century, in which women were periodically prohibited from attending funerals, visiting gravesites, or even "displaying themselves" by going outside to the market.[79] These measures were softened to allow slave women to go outside; however, they were required to keep their heads uncovered as a mark of their lower status (to have an uncovered head was shameful for a woman in the Muslim Mediterranean at this time) and to ensure that Muslim ladies did not pretend to be slaves in order to leave their houses. Likewise during this period, dress codes which distinguished the *dhimmi* populations both from one another and from Muslims were more strictly enforced. Mamlūk amirs and sultans, such as al-Malik al-Ashraf, seem to have sought to bring local custom into greater accord with Muslim law and to eliminate "immorality" as a way of appeasing God in hopes that the plague would be lifted.[80] While according to Muslim law plague is not a punishment from God on the Muslims, and any Muslim who dies of it is a martyr and should not flee the plague, by the sixteenth century Muslim leaders were beginning to flee or send their families away from plague-ridden areas, and to consider the possibility that plague was in fact a punishment for immoral behavior.[81] However, while these concerns, along with other worries, such as fears of a new Frankish invasion or alliance with Ethiopia or Egyptian Copts, prompted stricter policing of the boundaries and behaviors of women and religious minorities, they also seem to have opened new avenues of piety that not only allowed for their inclusion, but made it necessary. It is to the latter that I now wish to turn.

Drought, often accompanied by famine, was always a potential threat. In Egypt, such fears centered around whether or not the Nile would flood sufficiently and at the right time, or, conversely, too much and thus destroy crops. Furthermore, illness was strongly associated with Egypt, its winds, and the cycles of the Nile, even prior to the plague.[82] For example, just prior to his discussion of al-Ḥākim, Yahya ibn Saʿid describes the high prices, famine, and then epidemic (*wabāʾ*) that ensued in 983 CE when the Nile failed to rise sufficiently.[83] After the fourteenth century, Muslim and Christian writers alike linked the arrival of plague with the period surrounding Palm Sunday along with the behavior of the Nile and the desert wind, the *khamssin*.[84] Praying for rain and for the alleviation of other natural disasters long predated Islam. Certain talmudic rabbis became known both in life and after death as being good intercessors for rain.[85] The statute regarding appropriate behavior at the synagogue of Dammuh hints that this site also served as a place of intercession during drought: "and he should not pray for rain on the Sabbath unless it is for drin[king(?)]..."[86] Processions with accompanying prayers, which sometimes included the carrying of a saint's relics, became a standard response to invasion, disease, and other natural disasters like drought or famine within the Catholic Church's ritual practice by the sixth century if not earlier.[87] In some regions, Christians co-opted annual Roman processions and rituals for agricultural success.[88] Entire sections of ḥadīth are dedicated to Muḥammad's manner of praying for rain (*al-istisqāʾ*); however, this kind of prayer did not involve processions or large numbers of people praying in its initial form.[89] By the eleventh century, however, Jews, Christians, and Muslims had all adopted processions to a holy place (often associated with a holy person) in order to pray for the alleviation of the threat.[90]

Already in his instructions for prayer for relief against an epidemic, Pope Gregory the Great systematically included clergy, monks, nuns, children, laymen, widows, and married women, each group leaving from a different church but all processing and praying together to the basilica of the Virgin Mary.[91] That all possible members of the community, including children and women of varying status, add their voices to the collective prayer, seems to be an essential aspect of the ritual. A central ingredient to medieval prayers of intercession in the Middle East was that everyone—including members of other religious communities—participate. In a lengthy letter describing the Jewish community's response to an earthquake in 1033, the author says:

> All were in the streets, men, women, and children, imploring God, the Lord of the spirits, to quieten the earth and set it at rest and save both man and animal.... What could the writer [of this letter] do but to address the people, to declare a fast, summon a solemn assembly, that

> the people should go out to the field, the cemetery, in fasting, weeping and lamentation.... Also the governor of the city, with the men in the caliph's [literally: "king's"] employ, pitched tents for themselves outside the town and are still there.[92]

Here, the impetus for the prayer is with the people at large, and then in its more formal manifestation, with the Jewish leader, Gaon Solomon b. Judah. All ages and genders of people participate, as in the procession declared by Pope Gregory; however Solomon b. Judah portrays them as doing so spontaneously as a response to extreme need. Why they proceed to the cemetery is not explained; however, it is likely that they did so in order to petition the holy dead to add their intercession on behalf of the community.[93] The presence of the caliph and his retinue is mentioned in passing, perhaps as a way of underscoring the severity of the disaster. However, the author does not depict his community as joining the Muslims in a common intercessory ritual.[94]

Muslim descriptions of such intercessory processions *do* suggest that Jews and Christians regularly prayed with Muslims in state-sponsored intercessions. As in the Christian and Jewish accounts, every member of the community regardless of gender, age, or wealth participates. A number of the sources also specify that Sufis participated, presumably to add their sanctity to the intercession. Yet Sufis, like women and *dhimmi*, occupied an ambiguous position in Mamlūk society: on the one hand, many believed them to be tremendously powerful and revered them in life and after death, whereas on the other hand, others identified them or veneration of them as being at the root of "unacceptable" and extreme practices by the Muslim populace, especially women.[95] In co-opting the spiritual power of all of these groups—Sufis, *dhimmi*, and women, clothing seems to take on an especially significant role, as we shall see.

In 1450 CE, the Sultan required the market inspector to announce that public prayers for rain would be held in the desert plain because the Nile had not risen sufficiently. The following day the chief qadi went "on foot among masses of students, poor and Sufis.... [T]he caliph and the rest of the qadis were present and they were among a vast throng of people of all classes; the Jews and the Christians also came with their scriptures."[96] The procession and accompanying prayers were held between the grave of the former Mamlūk Sultan, al-Malik az-Ẓāhir Barquq (1389–1412 CE), and the Succor Dome. Ibn Taghrībirdī emphasizes the presence of many types of people—students, the poor, Sufis, people of all classes, *and* Jews and Christians. The presence of multiple types of people seems to have been a necessary component for the success of these prayers, along with great humility, in this case shown by the qadi's choice to travel on foot. The passage is unclear about whether the Jews and Christians came voluntarily or were expected to attend. In either case, Jews and Christians had joined the procession even though the final place of prayer was one holy to the Muslims, not to Jews or Christians. Implicit in the action is that all three parties recognized that the others had some legitimate standing before God, that their prayers would be enhanced by the presence of members of other faiths, and furthermore, that the holy space (i.e., Barquq's tomb and the Succor Dome) and the holy objects (the Torah and Christian Bible) of the religious other held special blessings before God. Similarly, in the late fourteenth century, Ibn Kathir implied that non-Muslims were included in a prayer procession outside the city of Damascus as a matter of course. As the death toll from the plague rose to hundreds per day:

> It was proclaimed in the land that the people should fast for three days. And they went out on the fourth day and it was Friday at the Mosque of the Foot (*al-Qadam*) and they implored God and they asked him to lift the plague from them. Most of the people fasted and the people slept in a group and arose at night like they do during the month of Ramadan. The people awoke Friday, on the twenty-seventh. The people went out on the day of gathering from all sides, and the Jews, and Christians, and Samaritans, old men and old women, and children, and the poor, the amirs, the great, and the judges after the morning prayer. They did not cease to beseech God the Most High there when the river was very elevated and it was a famous day.[97]

While for this Muslim chronicler, the ritual begins with the Muslim people's fast, prayer at the mosque, a special gathering, and prayers at night, once the people leave the mosque, Jews, Samaritans, and Christians join their Muslim neighbors, praying with them. That members of all ages and all genders, as well as all religious communities, participate is integral to the ceremony and carefully emphasized by the Muslim chronicler. In each of these rituals of mass intercession, the inclusion of *all* types of human beings seems to have been an essential part of the ceremony. Yet the desired presence of *dhimmi* in such a ceremony temporarily accorded these non-Muslims a place of religious power, albeit small, as necessary intercessors before God. Women too, despite occasionally being blamed for provoking God's displeasure, are required. Muslims, indeed the entire population, needed *all* spiritual power available: thus these non-Muslims were "borrowed" and incorporated into Muslim ritual. As in the case of Christian and Jewish interpretations of voluntary Muslim veneration of Christian and Jewish holy figures, the barriers of religious distinction were temporarily obscured to create a single faith-community in a moment of crisis.

Another way in which Muslim leaders "borrowed" spiritual power was through clothing. In 1419 CE, Sultan Shaykh al-Malik al-Mu'ayyad led another intercessory procession for relief from the plague:

> After the morning prayer the Sultan rode down from the Citadel without royal regalia; on the contrary he wore a white woolen cloak without any sash at his waist, and over his shoulders a woolen shawl which hung down in back in the Sufi manner.... When the Sultan reached the place of the Friday prayers in the Desert Plain he dismounted from his horse and remained on his feet while the caliph, the qadis, and learned men were at his right and his left, and before and behind him were the various classes of Sufis, shaykhs of the dervish chapels.... The Sultan then spread out his hands and prayed to God... the vast throng looking at him with faith in the efficacy of his prayer. He stood for a long time in prayer while everyone else also prayed to God (Who is exalted) and humbled himself.... From that day the plague began gradually to decrease.[98]

The Sultan, by the simplicity of his dress, and in particular the adoption of Sufi clothing, showed his humility before God, but more particularly, he divested himself of one kind of power—namely, that of political rule—in order to take on another: that of the saints, the friends of God. On either side of him were the caliph, the defender of the faithful, and the qadis, those learned in Islamic law—each representing a type of individual who was particularly devoted to God's service through their roles of protection, judgment, and the interpretation of the Qur'an. Surrounding this entire group, however, were the Sufis. Dressed as he was in the white woolen robe of the Sufis, Sultan al-Malik al-Mu'ayyid became the central figure in a circle of saints.[99] His ability to "borrow" sanctity through clothing ties in with the special place that clothing had in Middle Eastern and Central Asian culture; rulers indicated their approval and granted power to their followers by giving them clothing that they themselves had worn.[100] By the Fāṭimid and Mamlūk periods in Egypt, "robes of honor" no longer needed to have been worn by the caliph or sultan himself, but gifts of expensive robes were integral to granting an individual power within the court or government.[101] Sufi masters likewise materially assisted their students by giving them their own robes, which in turn enabled the student to move to the next spiritual level simply by wearing them.[102] That Sultan al-Malik al-Mu'ayyid had taken on the role of powerful intercessor that was normally associated with Sufi shaykhs becomes apparent when Ibn Taghrībirdī affirmed that the "the vast throng" had faith "in the efficacy of his prayer," and that "from that day the plague began gradually to decrease." The population recognized and accepted the sultan's attempt to don the trappings of spiritual power, albeit temporarily, as did, it would seem, Allah himself, as he took away the plague. Again, however, even if religious minorities are not mentioned in this passage, part of the basis of the prayer's success also derives from the multiplicity of types of participants: various types of Sufis, qadis, and the "vast throng" of people who lent their intercessory power to that of the sultan.[103] Ecological disaster became the factor that forced the Muslim leadership to abandon concerns about religious and gender hierarchies in favor of calling upon all potential spiritual power, whether from the Sufis, women, or non-Muslims. While sultans, amirs, and caliphs had sometimes disregarded hierarchies of gender and religious difference in favor of participating in shared festivals, in these processions to intercede against natural disaster, qadis and scholars, very often the group from which the strongest opponents to such shared rituals came, became part of a sacred community that included women, Jews, and Christians.[104]

Conclusions

Despite the vehement protestations of individuals like Ibn al-Ḥājj, the presence of *all* members of the community, including those normally designated religious outsiders, became an essential component of festivals. In the formally organized intercessory processions, women and non-Muslims were recognized as having access to spiritual power that was necessary for the ritual's success. The need to carefully demarcate difference was temporarily suspended in a liminal moment sparked by crisis. That the government, and certainly members of the religious elite, were sometimes less tolerant of similar mixing in long-standing festivals or prayers at gravesites that were not organized by the authorities represents a fear of chaos—the uncontrolled mixing of genders and religious communities. However, while we cannot explore with certainty the meanings that the large numbers of participants attributed to such mixings at long-standing festivals, building upon Boaz Shoshan's discussion of popular culture in medieval Egypt, I would tentatively suggest that the idea that all needed to be a part of a festival and that all had spiritual power was one that had become inherent in many of these celebrations such as Nawruz and Palm Sunday, and a characteristic which governing authorities borrowed and incorporated into their own rituals at the same time that they attempted to control or condemn such practices elsewhere.

In a society such as the medieval Middle East, in which clothing was already imbued with so much symbolic meaning, both anxieties about difference and power and efforts to expand the definition of community were bound to be reflected in the rhetoric and uses of clothing, as we see. Part of that rhetoric was about the violated gender and religious boundaries that inappropriate clothing at festivals represented. Yet the sacred and simultaneously playful abandonment of difference at religious celebrations in al-Andalus, North Africa, Egypt, and the Levant likewise expressed itself in the festive abandonment of clothing altogether (in baths) or the rules of appropriate, differentiating attire for men, women, Muslims, and *dhimmi*. While this process sometimes became too alarming for Muslim legalists, government leaders, or even Jewish community leaders, during times of uncontrollable ecological crisis that affected men and women, Muslim and *dhimmi* alike, anxieties of difference were deserted in favor of appropriating the intercessory power of *all* members of the community. This appropriation was likewise symbolized by clothing. In the instance of Sultan al-Mu'ayyid, he transformed himself from sultan to "friend of God," the better to intercede before God against the plague. Yet using clothes to create identity or include others in it had begun long before, with the Fāṭimids' use of gifting of robes of honor as a way of generating cohesion and belonging in their court even across religious divisions.

Paula Sanders has noted that the Fāṭimids, drawing from practices and ideologies from North Africa, regarded the *muṣallā* (open prayer ground) rather than the mosque as the most appropriate for festal prayers. The caliph, his retinue, and, eventually, other portions of the populace joined in processions through the city to this created holy space.[105] This reshaping of traditional Muslim festivals along with the Fāṭimids' willingness to tolerate dissenting religious practices—Jewish, Christian, and Sunni—created a set of circumstances which encouraged the mingling of *dhimmi* and Muslim in religious celebrations.[106] Urban processions passed through *dhimmi* neighborhoods, and sometimes Muslim holy spaces were established on or near Christian or Jewish sites.[107] Such acts undoubtedly caused resentment; however, they also incorporated the holy space of the religious other into Muslim sacred space while at the same time retaining its sacral quality to non-Muslims. Processions in and of themselves, something Christians and Jews had long practiced in the context of their own religions, invited the participation of all viewers by the mere fact of being outside.[108] Caliphs, amirs, and later, Mamlūk sultans enjoyed the processions and festivities of Christians and Jews setting a precedent themselves of shared ritual and extended community boundaries. I would suggest that by the time the Mamlūks came to power, many of these shared festivals that regularly took place outdoors had become well ingrained, so much so that they became a matter of course for much of the population, even the sultans themselves. Some of the specifically Isma'ili ideologies involving the *muṣallā* may have dissipated; however, many of the religious festivals, complete with their traditional inclusion of Muslims and non-Muslims, men and women, remained.

While caliphs, amirs, and sultans frequently sponsored even non-Muslim religious festivals, they also regularly took steps to curtail them. That anxiety about defining community and gender boundaries seems to have increased from the eleventh century, and especially after the beginning of the Crusades, reflects consternation about multiple sites of conflict and potential threat that included but was not confined to concerns about the increasing power of Christians, Jews, and women. In Iberia, Muslims faced increasing pressure from Christians attempting to gain control of the entire region and at the same time intense cultural borrowing and interchange between Jews and Muslims especially, but also with Christians. In Egypt and the Levant, tension between Shi'a and Sunni during the Fāṭimid and Ayyūbid periods and between Turk and Arab in Mamlūk society; fear of the Franks, and, later, the Mongols; concern about the sincerity of converts who became Muslims out of fear or to keep their jobs; and, finally, the stress of coping with the plague all increased tension overall. Confronted with such seeming chaos, much of which was beyond their control, political and religious leaders attempted to assert themselves over those boundaries they believed they could control—those of gender and religious difference. As with so many other societies, the increased apprehension about women's behavior and gender boundaries reflected anxieties that extended beyond relations between men and women. The emphasis on clothing, both negative and positive, is also telling. Marjorie Garber argues that anxieties about cross-dressing often have little to do with clothing, or even gender itself, but rather reflect fears about the violation and uncontrollability of other kinds of boundaries—between Protestants and Catholics during the Reformation and Counter-Reformation, for example.[109] At the same time, Johan Huizinga, in his study on the cultural meaning of play, argued that ritual and play, even in their simplest forms are related, indeed different manifestations of the same impulse, and that integral to play is both the abandonment of hierarchy and the adoption of disguise or alternative identities.[110] In festivals from the Fāṭimid through the Mamlūk periods, "play," with its temporary shedding or disguising of identity and hierarchy of all kinds became all the more essential as people faced a growing need for expanding the *communitas* and for creating sacred time and space in the face of ecological, religious, and political confusion and danger. Yet imbedded within play is the potential for unpredictable and uncontrolled freedom and subversion of power structures.[111] Thus these festivals, with their mixing of members of different genders and religious beliefs, also came to symbolically epitomize the very threats and chaos that they were designed to counter. If those in positions of political power seem to have wavered between participation and condemnation, it is because they were caught between the need to encourage *communitas* and its concomitant sacrality, and the need to control the society that they ruled.

Notes

I wish to thank Professors Carol Duncan (Wilfred Laurier University), Fatima Sadiqi (Sidi Mohamed Ben Abdellah University), Laura Nasrallah (Harvard Divinity School), Caroline Johnson Hodge (College of the Holy Cross), Shelly Rambo (Boston University, School of Theology), and Ann Braude (Harvard Divinity School), all of whom read and commented on an earlier draft of this article during the seminar for Women's Studies in Religion Program at Harvard Divinity School. I also wish to thank Professors Ethel S. Wolper (University of New Hampshire) and Indrani Chatterjee (Rutgers University), both of whom also read and commented upon drafts of this article. All work and errors are my own; however, their suggestions have proven invaluable in shaping the final version.

1. لقول النبي "لعن الله اليهود,اتخذوا قبور انبيائهم
   Al-Bukhārī, *Ṣaḥīḥ al-Bukhārī*, trans. Muḥammad Muḥsin Khān (Riyadh: Dār al-Salām, 1997), I.8. 427.
2. ام سلمة ذكرت لرسول الله كنيسة رأتها بأرض الحبشة يقال لها: مارية, فذكرت له ما رأت فيها من الصور, فقال رسول الله: "أولئك قوم اذا مات فيهم العبد الصالح او الرجل الصالح بنوا على قبره مسجدا وصوروا فيه تلك الصور, اولئك شرار الخلق عند الله
   Ibid. I.8. 434.
3. Ibid. I.8. 427.
4. On the early debates about funerary rites and honoring the dead in Islam, see Leor Halevi, *Muhammad's Grave: Death Rites and the Making of Islamic Society* (New York: Columbia University Press, 2007), 14–42, 114–60.

5. Peter Brown, *The Cult of the Saints: Its Rise and Function in Latin Christianity* (Chicago: Chicago University Press, 1981), 26; Maribel Fierro, "The Treatises against Innovations (*kutub al-bida'*)," *Der Islam: Zeitscrhift für Geschichte und Kultur des islamischen Orients* 69 (1992): 204–46; Alexandra Cuffel, "From Practice to Polemic: Shared Saints and Festivals as 'Women's Religion' in the Medieval Mediterranean," *Bulletin of the School of Oriental and African Studies* 68/3 (2005): 401–19; Halevi, *Muhammad's Grave*, 120–42.
6. Brown, *Cult of the Saints*, 25–49, 93–105.
7. Victor Turner, "Death and the Dead in the Pilgrimage Process," in *Blazing the Trail Marks the Way in the Exploration of Symbols*, ed. Edith Turner (Tuscon: University of Arizona Press, 1992), 29–47, esp. 30; Victor and Edith Turner, *Image and Pilgrimage in Christian Culture* (New York: Columbia University Press, 1978), 1–38, 180. The liminality of pilgrimage because of travel would have been diminished considerably for those who were merchants and thus accustomed to travel.
8. Turner, *Image and Pilgrimage*, 250–51.
9. Christopher S. Taylor, *In the Vicinity of the Righteous: Ziyāra and the Veneration of Muslim Saints in Late Medieval Egypt* (Leiden: Brill, 1999), 59–61, 77–79; Josef Meri, *The Cult of the Saints among Muslims and Jews in Medieval Syria* (Oxford: Oxford University Press, 2002), 122–23; Joel Kramer, "A Jewish Cult of the Saints in Fāṭimid Egypt," in *L'Egypte Fatimide son art et son histoire: Actes du colloque organize à Paris les* 28, 29, *et* 30 *mai* 1998, ed. Marianne Barrucand (Paris: Presses de l'Université de Paris-Sorbonne, 1999), 579–601.
10. Bonnie Wheeler's "Models of Pilgrimage: From Communitas to Confluence," *Journal of Ritual Studies* 13/2 (1999): 26–41, in which she critiques Turner and Durkheim and applies more recent anthropological theories to medieval European pilgrimage, is an important exception.
11. Turner, *Image and Pilgrimage*, 252; V. Turner, "The Center Out There: Pilgrim's Goal," *History of Religions* 12/3 (1973): 191–230; V. Turner, *The Ritual Process: Structure and Anti-Structure* (Ithaca, NY: Cornell University Press, 1969), 132; Tim Olaveson, "Collective Effervescence and Communitas: Processual Models of Ritual and Society in Emile Durkheim and Victor Turner," *Dialectical Anthropology* 26 (2001): 89–124; John Eade, "Introduction," in *Contesting the Sacred: The Anthropology of Christian Pilgrimage*, ed. John Eade and Michael Sallnow (Urbana: University of Illinois Press, 2000), ix–xxx.
12. Wheeler, "Models of Pilgrimage"; Eade, "Introduction," John Eade and Michael Sallnow, "Introduction," John Eade, "Order and Power at Lourdes: Lay Helpers and the Organization of a Pilgrimage Shrine," Christopher McKevitt, "San Giovanni Rotondo and the Shrine of Padre Pio," Glenn Bowman, "Christian Ideology and Image of a Holy Land: The Place of Jerusalem Pilgrimage in the Various Christianities," and Michael Sallnow, "Pilgrimage and Cultural Fracture in the Andes," all in *Contesting the Sacred*, ix–xxx, 1–29, 51–76, 77–97, 98–121, 137–53 respectively; Yoram Bilu, "The Inner Limits of Communitas: A Covert Dimension

of Pilgrimage Experience," *Ethos* 16/3 (1988): 302–25; Simon Coleman, "Do You Believe in Pilgrimage? *Communitas*, Contestation and Beyond," *Anthropological Theory* 2 (2002): 355–68; Graham St. John, "Alternative Cultural Heterotopia and the Liminoid Body: Beyond Turner and ConFest," *Australian Journal of Anthropology* 12/1 (2002): 47–66; Frank Korom, "Caste Politics, Ritual, Performance, and Local Religion in a Bengali Village: A Reassessment of Liminality and Communitas," *Acta Ethnographica Hungarica* 47/3–4 (2002): 397–449; and Selva Raj, "Transgressing Boundaries, Transcending Turner: The Pilgrimage Tradition at the Shrine of St. John de Britto," *Journal of Ritual Studies* 16/1 (2002): 4–18.

13. Eade and Sallnow, "Introduction," esp. p. 5. Italics in the original.
14. Olaveson, "Collective Effervescence"; Wheeler, "Models of Pilgrimage"; St. John, "Alternative Cultural Heterotopia"; Andrea Dahlberg, "The Body as a Principle of Holism: Three Pilgrimages to Lourdes," in *Contesting the Sacred*, 30–50; Eade, "Order and Power at Lourdes."
15. The first of these was Abū 'Abd Muḥammad ibn Waḍḍāh al-Qurṭubī, *Kitāb al-bida'*, ed. M. A. Duhmān (Damascus: Matba'at al-I'tidal, 1930). See Fierro, "Treatises against Innovations."
16. Fierro, "Treatises against Innovations"; Cuffel, "From Practice to Polemic"; Yehoshua Frenkel, "Muslim Pilgrimage to Jerusalem during the Mamluk period," in *Pilgrims and Travelers to the Holy Land*, ed. B. F. LeBeau and M. Mor (Omaha: Creighton University Press, 1996), 63–87. Even though Ibn Taymīyya was Ḥanbalī, he was strongly influenced by Mālikī thought. See Niels Henrick Olesen, *Culte des saints et pèlerinages chez Ibn Taymiyya* (Paris: Paul Geuthner, 1991), 16–17, 155.
17. Marie-Thérèse Urvoy, "Aspects de l'hagiographie musulmane," *Bulletin de Litterature Ecclesiastique* 46 (1995): 97–120; Boaz Shoshan, *Popular Culture in Medieval Cairo* (Cambridge: Cambridge University Press, 1993), 12–22; C. Williams, "The Cult of the 'Alid Saints in the Fatimid Monuments of Cairo," *Muqarnas* 3 (1995): 39–60. Aḥmad al-Badawī, who spent most of his life in Egypt, became one of the most popular Sufi figures there. The festivities surrounding his *mawlid* (birth/death day) became especially well known for objectionable practices. See Urvoy, "Aspects," and Shoshan, *Popular Culture*. Catherine Mayeur-Jaouen points out, however, that the earliest accounts of Aḥmad al-Badawī do not include a maghribi origin. Catherine Mayeur-Jaouen, *Histoire d'un pèlerinage légendaire en islam: le mouled de Tantâ du XIIIe. siècle à nos jours* (Paris: Aubier, 2004).
18. Fierro, "Treatises against Innovations."
19. Of the *bida'* treatises identified by Fierro, one of them was composed by a Baghdadi author, Abū al-Faraj 'Abd al-Raḥmān b. 'Alī ibn al-Jawzī (d. 1200 CE), while the rest were written by authors living and working in al-Andalus, the Maghrib, Egypt, and the Levant. Ibn al-Jawzī only occasionally discusses the imitation of non-Muslim religious practices, suggesting that this issue was not as pressing in Baghdad as it was in al-Andalus, the Maghrib, Egypt, and the Levant. See D. S. Margoliouth,

"*Talbis Iblis*," *Islamic Culture; The Hyderabad Quarterly Review* 9/3 (1935): 377–99, esp. pp. 388–99, 10/1 (1936): 20–39, esp. p. 21, 10/2 (1936): 169–92, esp. p. 177. Ṣafī al-Dīn Idrīs b. Baydakīn b. 'Abd Allāh al-Turkumānī (fl. between 14th–15th centuries CE) lived in Mecca as well as Egypt. Fierro also notes an element of anti-Shi'a polemic in these texts. For example, in the case of al-Ṭurṭūshī, he directed his critiques in part to innovations established in N. Africa by the Fāṭimids and sought to ally himself with or encourage the religious reforms of the Almoravids. Fierro, "Treatises against Innovations"; M. J. Viguera, "Las Cartas de al-Gazālī y al-Ṭurṭūshī al soberano almorávid Yūsf b.Tashufīn," *Al-Andalus* 42 (1977): 341–74.

20. Jean Maurice Fiey, *Chrétiens Syriaques sous les Abbassides surtout à Bagdad (749–1258), Corpus Scriptorum Christianorum Orientalum*, vol. 420, subsida tomus 59 (Louvain: Secrétariat du CSCO, 1980), 13.
21. Fiey, *Chrétiens Syriaques sous les Abbassides*, pp. 27–28.
22. For example, in the eleventh century, the Jew Samuel ha-Nagid attained the rank of wazir under Bādīs in Granada and was succeeded by his son Joseph, which eventually resulted in an uprising and sharp polemic about the situation by Muslims and Jews. Eliyahu Ashtor, *The Jews of Moslem Spain*, 3 vols, (Philadelphia: Jewish Publication Society of America, 1992) 2/3: 41–189; Ross Brann, *Power in the Portrayal: Representations of Jews and Muslims in Eleventh- and Twelfth-Century Islamic Spain* (Princeton, NJ: Princeton University Press, 2002), 24–53, 129–39.
23. Mohammed-Tahar Mansouri, "Juifs et Chrétiens dans le Maghreb fatimide (909–69)," in Barrucand, ed., *Egypte Fatimide*, pp. 603–11. Mansouri suggests that Fāṭimids often drew upon *dhimmi* support because they saw *dhimmi* as more trustworthy than the Sunni majority whom the Fāṭimids ruled. For later associations between Fāṭimids, Jews, or other kinds of *dhimmi*, see Ibn Taymīyya, *Majmū 'fatāwā Shaykh al-Islā Aḥmad b. Taymīya*, ed. 'A. al-'Āṣimī, 37 vols. (Riyad: n.p., 1961/2–1966/7; reprinted, S.I.: n.p., 1977) 27: 161, 167, 174–75.
24. Brann, *Power in the Portrayal*; Muḥammad ibn al-Walīd al-Ṭurṭūshī, *Kitāb al-ḥawādith wa-al-bida'*, ed. M. Talbi (Tunis: Imprimerie Officielle, 1959, 139–40).
25. On fear of eastern Christian, especially Coptic, collusion with Crusaders or Byzantines, see Huda Lutfi, "Coptic Festivals of the Nile: Aberrations of the Past?" In *The Mamluks in Egyptian Politics and Society*, ed. Thomas Philipp and Ulrich Haarmann (Cambridge: Cambridge University Press, 1998), 254–82; M. Perlemann, "Notes on Anti-Christian Propaganda in the Mamlūk Empire," *Bulletin of the School of African Studies* 10 (1940–42): 842–61; 'Uthman b. Ibrāhim an-Nāblusi, *Histoires Coptes d'un Cadi medieval, extraits du Kitāb tajrīd Saif al-Himma li'stikhrāj mā fī dhimmat al-dhimma*, ed. Claude Cahen in *Bulletin de l'Institut Français d'Archéologie Orientale* 59 (1960): 133–50, relevant passages on pp. 137, 146–48; Ghāzī ibn Wāsiṭī, "An Answer to the Dhimmis," ed. and trans. Richard Gotteil, *Journal of the American Oriental Society* (1921): 383–457, relevant pages in Arabic pp. 394, 400–2, in English pp. 426–27, 435–38; Ibn Naqqash,

"Fetoua relative à la condition des zimmis, et particulièrement des Chrétiens, en pays Musulmans, depuis l'etablissement de l'Islam jusqu'au milieu du VIIIe siècle de l'hégire," trans. M. Belin in *Journal Asiatique* (1851): 417–516, relevant passages pp. 442, 479–82; Ibn Qayyim al-Jawziyya, *'Aḥkām'ahl al-dhimma*, ed. Subhi al-Salih, part 1 (Damascus: Matb'at Jami'at Dimashq, 1961), 218. A number of these passages deal with a particular incident in which letters to the Franks with sensitive material were found in the house of the Christian advisor, Abu al-Faḍl ibn Dukhān, to al-'Adid (1160–1171). On expectations of a Coptic alliance with Ethiopia, see the following: Adam Knobler, "Missions, Mythologies and the Search for Non-European Allies in Anti-Islamic Holy War, 1291–c. 1540" (Ph.D. diss., University of Cambridge, 1990), 155–71, 194–98, 212–19, especially 161; Taddesse Tamrat, *Church and State in Ethiopia* 1270–1527 (Oxford: Clarendon Press, 1972), 51–58, 250–57; Sawīrus ibn al-Muqaffa', *History of the Patriarchs of the Egyptian Church, Known as the History of the Holy Church*, III/1 (Cairo: Société d'archéologie copte, 1969), Arabic, pp. 56–57, English pp. 34–35 (there the Coptic patriarch plays upon Mamlūk fear of Ethiopian military action to convince the Mamlūk sultan to appoint a new metropolitan who would have more authority than the current one and be more independent of the Coptic patriarch). On employment and resentment of *dhimmi* in government positions, see Tamer el-Leithy, "Coptic Culture and Conversion in Medieval Cairo, 1293–1524 A.D.," 2 vols. (Ph.D. diss., Princeton University, 2005), 1:50–56, 106–7, 123–25, 176–81 (he also discusses Muslim fears of Christians passing military information to crusaders in these pages); Mark R. Cohen, *Under Crescent and Cross: The Jews in the Middle Ages* (Princeton: Princeton University Press, 1994), 65–68; Cohen, *Jewish Self-Government in Medieval Egypt: The Origins of the Office of the Head of the Jews, ca.* 1065–1126 (Princeton, NJ: Princeton University Press, 1980), 219–21; Antoine Fattal, *Le statut légal des non-Musulmans en pays d'Islam* (Beyrouth: Impr. Catholique, 1958), 240–42; Ashtor, *Jews of Moslem Spain*, 2/3:41–189; Linda S. Northrup, "Muslim-Christian Relations During the Reign of the Mamlūk Sultan al-Manṣūr Qalāwūn, A.D. 1278–1290" and Donald P. Little, "Coptic Converts to Islam during the Baḥrī Mamlūk Period," both in *Conversion and Continuity: Indigenous Christian Communities in Islamic Lands Eighth to the Eighteenth Centuries*, ed. Michael Gervers and Ramzi Jibran Bikhazi (Toronto: Pontifical Institute of Medieval Studies, 1990), 253–61, 263–88 respectively; Donald P. Little, "Coptic Conversion to Islam under the Baḥrī Mamlūks, 692–755/1293–1354," *Bulletin of the School of Oriental and African Studies* 39 (1976): 552–69; Donald Richards, "The Coptic Bureaucracy under the Mamlūks," *Colloque International sur l'histoire du Caire* (Cairo: Ministery of Culture, the Arab Republic of Egypt, General Egyptian Book Organization, 1972): 373–81; Paula Sanders, *Ritual, Politics, and the City in Fatimid Cairo* (Albany: State University of New York Press, 1994), 21.

26. El-Leithy, "Coptic Culture and Conversion," 1:52–53, 67–100, 181–98.
27. Sanders, *Ritual, Politics and the City*, 3.

28. Samuel Cohn has argued against identifying the "Black Death" with the bubonic plague. See his *The Black Death Transformed: Disease and Culture in Early Renaissance Europe* (London: Arnold / New York: Oxford University Press, 2003). He focuses primarily on Italy, however, and does not deal with the Middle East. On the plague in the Middle East, see Michael Dols, *The Black Death in the Middle East* (Princeton, NJ: Princeton University Press, 1977); Dols, "The Second Plague Pandemic and Its Recurrences in the Middle East: 1347–1894," *Journal of the Economic and Social History of the Orient* 22 (1979): 162–89; Dols, "Al-Manbiji's 'Report of the Plague': A Treatise of the Plague of 764–65/1362–64," *Papers of the Eleventh Annual Conference of the Center for Medieval and Early Renaissance Studies: The Black Death: The Impact of the Fourteenth-Century Plague*, ed. Daniel Williman (Binghamton, NY, Center for Medieval and Early Renaissance Studies, 1982), 65–75; Dols, "The Comparative Communal Responses to the Black Death in Muslim and Christian Societies," *Viator: Medieval and Renaissance Studies* 5 (1974): 269–87; Dols, "Ibn al-Wardi's Risalah al-Naba' 'an al-Waba, a Translation of a Major Source for the History of the Black Death in the Middle East," in *Near Easter Numismatics, Iconography, Epigraphy and History: Studies in Honor of George C. Miles,* ed. Dickran Kouymjian (Beirut: American University of Beirut, 1974), 443–55; Daniel Panzac, *Quarantaines et lazarets: l'Europe et la peste d'Orient, XVIIe-XXe siècles* (Aix-en-Provence: Edisud, 1986); Panzac, *La peste dans l'Empire Ottoman,* 1700–1850 (Louvain: Peeters, 1985); Stuart Borsch, *The Black Death in Egypt and England: A Comparative Study* (Austin: University of Texas Press, 2005).
29. Borsch, *Black Death in Egypt and England*, 34–54; Dols, *Black Death*, 163–65.
30. Cohen, *Under Crescent and Cross*, 52–74.
31. Ibid., 107–20.
32. This is one of the main arguments of her book; however, see Sanders, *Ritual, Politics, and the City*, 79–82 for the clearest articulation of this thesis. On the political function of festivals in medieval Egypt, also see Shoshan, *Popular Culture*, 70–76.
33. Shoshan, *Popular Culture*, 49–70. Also see el-Leithy, "Coptic Culture and Conversion," 1:121.
34. El-Leithy, "Coptic Culture and Conversion," 1:119–24; Lutfi, "Coptic Festivals."
35. Aḥmad ibn 'Alī al-Maqrīzī, *Kitāb al-mawā'iẓ wa-al-i'tibār: fi-dhikr al-khiṭaṭ wa-al-āthār, al-ma'rūf bi-al-khiṭaṭ al-Maqrīziya*, 2 vols. (Beirut: Dār Sādir, 1970), 1:264. (Henceforth cited as *Khiṭaṭ*.) This section is translated into French in *Patrologia Orientalis*, ed. R. Graffin and F. Nau, trans. I. Kratchkovsky and A. Vasiliev (Paris: Firmin-Didot, 1915), vol. 10, fasc. 4, p. 316. Henceforth, *Patrologia Orientalis* will be abbreviated *PO*.
36. Lutfi, "Coptic Festivals of the Nile."
37. On this, see above.
38. Al-Muqaffa', *History of the Patriarchs*, Arabic, pp. 40–41, English, pp. 48–51. On hostility toward Copts more generally: M. Perlmann, "Notes on anti-Christian

Propaganda in the Mamlūk Empire," *Bulletin of the School of Oriental and African Studies*, University of London 10/4 (1942): 843–61.

39. كل يوم الى ورا بدل البول بالخرا\\\\فزما نا تهودا وزمانا تنصرا\\\\وسيصبو الى المجوس اذا الشيخ عمرا
Abū al-Maḥāsin ibn Taghrībirdī, *al-Nujūm al-zāhira fī mulūk Miṣr wa al-Qāhirah*, 16 vols. (Cairo: al-Hay'ah al-Miṣrīyah al-'Āmmah lil-Ta'līf wa al-Nashr, 1929–72), 14:255–56; ibn Taghrībirdī, *History of Egypt*, 8 vols., trans. William Popper (Berkeley: University of California Press, 1958), part 4, vol. 18:10.

40. The emir of Granada was Badis ibn Habbus al-Himyari (1038–73 CE). Ibn Taghrībirdī identifies the poet as Abu l-Qasim Khalaf al-Ilbiri, known as al-Sumaisir.

41. Aḥmad ibn'Abd al-ḥalim ibn Taymīyya, *Kitāb iqtiḍa' al-ṣirāt al-mustaqīm mukhālafat aṣḥāb al-jaḥīm*, ed. Muḥammad ḥamid al-Fiqī (Cairo, 1979). See his first point of consideration pp. 207–8. English translation: Muhammad Umar Memon, *Ibn Taymiya's Struggle against Popular Religion With an Annotated Translation of his Kitāb iqtiḍa' al-ṣirāt al-mustaqīm mukhālafat aṣḥāb al-jaḥīm* (The Hague: Mouton, 1976), 206–7.

42. Some of the anti-Copt treatises from the period contain a story in which the caliph 'Umar ibn al-Khattab rebukes one Abu Musa for hiring a Christian scribe despite 'Umar's prohibition. Abu Musa replied that the secretary's writing skills interested him, not his religion. Ibn Naqqas, "Fetoua relative à la condition des zimmis," 428; ibn Wāsiṭī, "Answer to the Dhimmis," Arabic p. 388, English p. 419; al-Jawziyya, *'Aḥkām'ahl al-dhimma*, part 1, pp. 210–11. Presumably, those with Abu Musa's attitude in their own period goaded these authors to protest against the employment of *dhimmis*.

43. و كان رسم النصارى فى بيت المقدس جار فى كل عام بحمل شجرة عظيمة من شجر الزيتون فى عيد الشعانين من الكنيسة المعروفة بالعازرية الى كنسة القيامة و بينهما مسافة بعيد و أن يشق بها شوارع المدينة بالقراءة و الصلوات حاملين الصليب مشهورا و يركب والى البلد فى جميع موكبه معهم و يذب عنهم و كان الرسم بمصر و سائر البلاد أيضا أن تزين الكنائس فى العيد بأغصان الزيتون و قلوب النخل و يفرق منها على الناس فى هذا اليوم على سبيل التبريك بها فمنع الحاكم فى هذه السنة أهل بيت المقدس من رسمهم ذلك و أمر أن لا يعمل ذلك فى شئ من أعمال المملكة فى ذلك اليوم و لا يحمل ورقة من أوراق الزيتون و لا من سعف النخل فى كنيسة من سائر الكنائس و لا يلحظ شئ منها فى يد مسلم و لا نصرانى و لا غيرهما من جميع الناس و حظر عليهم أشد تحظير
Yahya ibn Sa'id of Antioch, *History*, in *PO*, vol. 23, fasc. 3, pp. 487–88.

44. Cohen, *Under Crescent and Cross*, 57–64.

45. On al-Hākim's attitude toward *dhimmi* and others, see Sanders, *Ritual, Politics and the City*, 3, 23, 57; S. D. Goitein, *A Mediterranean Society: The Jewish Communities of the Arab World as Portrayed in the Documents of the Cairo Geniza*, 6 vols. (Berkeley: University of California Press, 1967–93), 2:299–300; 5:21; Jean-Michel Mouton, "La presence au Sinaï à l'époque fatimide," *L'Égypte Fatimide: Son art et son histoire: actes du colloque organize à Paris les* 28, 29 *et* 30 *mai* 1998, ed. M. Barrucand (Paris, Presses de l'Université de Paris-Sorbonne, 1999), 613–23.

46. الحاكم فى كثير الآعوام متنكرا و شاهدهمخضرهم
Ibn Sa'id, *History*, 494.

47. فمنع الحاكم الكل فى سنة أربعمائة من جميع ذلك و لا يتعرض أحدا من سائر الناس كافة الى شئ منه فى هذه الليلة و ذلك اليوم و أن يعرض عنه و يصرف عن ذكره و يجرى مجرى سائر الايام و لا يستعد له و لا يحفل به

Ibid.

48. Lutfi, "Coptic Festivals"; al-Maqrīzī, *Khiṭaṭ*, I.69. 266; al-Maqrīzī, *Kitāb al-Sulūk li-ma'rifat duwal al-mulūk*, ed. Muḥammad Muṣṭafā Ziyāda (Cairo: Lajnat al-Talif wa-al-Tarjamah wa-al-Nashr, [1958] 1973), 4:68; Muḥammad b. Aḥmad ibn Iyās, *al-Badā'i'al-zuhūr fi waqā'i'al-duhūr*, ed. Muḥammad Muṣṭafā (Cairo/Wiesbaden: Franz Steiner, [1984] 1992), 1:324, 566.

49. Al-Maqrīzī, *Khiṭaṭ*, I. 266. Of course, al-Maqrīzī may have been attempting to denigrate the Fāṭimid caliph by portraying him as participating in a Christian festival; however, other sources also attest to such behavior by Muslim officials, Fāṭimid or otherwise (see notes above and below).

50. و قد صار كثير من جهال النساء يدخلن أولادهن الى الحمام فى هذا الوقت. و يزعن ان هذا ينفع الولد, و هذا من دين النصارى.

Ibn Taymīyya, *Kitāb iqtiḍa'*, 227; Ibn Taymīyya, *Ibn Taymiya's Struggle*, 222. Compare with Muḥammad ibn Muḥammad Ibn al-Ḥājj,. *Al-Madkhal*, 4 vols. in 2, (Cairo: al-Maṭba'a al-Misrīya, 1929), 2:59; al-Maqrīzī, *Khiṭaṭ*, I. 265–66.

51. See, for example, R. Simon b. Samson in *Oẓar masa'ot. Qoveẓ tiyurim shel nos'im Yehudim be-'Ereẓ Yisra'el, Surya', Miẓrayim ve-arẓot aḥerot. Reshimot 'ole regel le-qivre Avot u-qedoshim 'im mapot, he'arot u-mafteaḥ*, compil. J. D. Eisenstein (New York: sn, 1926; reprint, Tel-Aviv: sn, 1969), 62 and in *Jewish Travellers in the Middle Ages: 19 Firsthand Accounts*, ed. and trans. E. N. Adler (London: Routledge, 1930; reprint, New York: Dover, 1987), 107 (citations from 1987 ed.); Meshullam ben Menahem, da Volterra, *Mas'a Meshulam mi Volterah be-'Ereẓ Yisra'el bi-shenat* 241 *(*1481*)*, ed. A. Yaari (Jerusalem: Mosad Byalik, 1948), 71–72, and Meshullam ben Menahem, da Volterra in *Jewish Travellers*, 188–90; Symon Semeonis, *Itinerarium Symonis Semeonis Ab Hybernia Ad Terram Sanctam*, ed. Mario Esposito, *Scriptores Latini Hiberniae*, vol. 4 (Dublin: Dublin Institute for Advanced Studies, 1960), 80/81–82/83. This is translated in Symon Semeonis, *Western Pilgrims: The Itineraries of Fr. Simon Fitzsimons (1322–23), a Certain Englishman (1344–45), Thomas Brugg (1392)*, trans. Eugene Hoade (Jerusalem: Franciscan Print Press, 1970 reprint), 31. On Jewish pilgrims to the Middle East—both European and local—and their interest in Muslim holy places, see Meri, *Cult of the Saints*, 214–50; Elka Weber, "Sharing Sites: Medieval Jewish Travellers to the Land of Israel," in *Eastward Bound: Travel and Travellers, 1050–1550*, ed. Rosamund Allen (Manchester: Manchester University Press, 2004), 35–52; Cuffel, "From Practice to Polemic." On Western Christian reactions to Muslim veneration of the Virgin Mary in particular, see Cuffel, "'Henceforward All Generations Will Call Me Blessed': Medieval Christian Tales of Non-Christian Marian Veneration," *Mediterranean Studies* 12 (2003): 37–60. The attitudes of medieval and early modern Jews, Christians, and Muslims from both the Christian (Latin Europe and Byzantium) and Muslim

Mediterranean toward shared saints and festivals is the subject of my next book: *Shared Saints and Festivals among Jews, Christians, and Muslims in the Medieval Mediterranean.*

52. Fratris Felicis Fabri, *Evagatorium in Terrae Santae, Arabiae et Egypti peregrinationem*, vol. 3, ed. Konrad Dieterich Hassler (Stuttgart: Societatis litterariae stuttgardiensis, 1849), part 2, vol. 3, 75b, p. 5. There is also a partial French translation: *Voyage en Egypte de Felix Fabri* 1483, 3 vols, trans. Jacques Masson (Cairo: Institut francais d'archéologie orientale du Caire, 1975), 1:371; Symon Semeonis, *Itinerarium Symonis Semeonis*, 80/81–82/83; Symon Semeonis, *Western Pilgrims*, p. 31.

53. و من ذلك ما يفعله بعض المسلمين فى أحد أعياد القبط الذى يسمونه عيد الزيتونة فتخرج النصارى فى ذلك اليوم فى موضع يقال له المطوية الىبئر هناك تسمى بئر البلسم و هى معروفة مشهورة. فيجتمع اليها فى ذلك اليوم فى الغالب جمع كثير من القبط و غيرهم من بلاد كثيرة يأتون اليها للغسل من مائها. ثم أن بعض المسلمين يفعلون ذلك و يهرعون اليه كما تفعل النصارى و يغتسلون كغسلهم و ينكشفون لذلك فى الغالب. و هذا فيه ما تقدم ذكره من كشف العورات و بعظيم مواسم أهل الكتاب كما تقدم. ويزيد هذا أنهم يسافرون اليها من المواضع البعيدة نساء و رجالا و شبانا و يجتمعون هناك و ينهتكون فيه كغيره. و فى اجتماعهم من المفاسد ما تقدم ذكره. لكن فى هذا زياد مفسدة أخرى وهى نظر الذمية الى جسد المسلمة و هو حرام و قد منعه العلماء رحمة الله عليهم . هذا و ان كان الغسل من ذلك الماء مباحا فعله لكن فى غير وقت اجتماعهم و فى التلويح ما يغنى عن التصريح.

Muḥammad ibn Muḥammad ibn al-Ḥājj, *Al-Madkhal*, 4 vols. (Cairo: al-Maṭba'a al-Misrīya, 1929), 2:59–60.

54. A. Cuffel, "Polemicizing Women's Bathing among Medieval and Early Modern Muslims and Christians," in *Nature and Function of Water, Baths, Bathing and Hygiene from Antiquity through the Renaissance*, ed. Cynthia Kosso and Anne Scott (Leiden: Brill, 2009), 171–88.

55. Ibn al-Ḥājj, *Al-Madkhal*, 2:50–51;'Idrīs b. Baydakīn al-Turkumānī, *Kitāb al-luma' fī al-ḥawādīth wa-al-bida'*, 2 vols., ed. Ṣubḥī Labib (Cairo: Qism al-Dirāsāt al-Islāmīya bi-al-Ma'had al-Almānī lil-Āthār / Stuttgart: Franz Steiner, 1986), 1:93; Shoshan, *Popular Culture*, 43, 46; B. Langner, *Untersuchungen zur historischen Volkskunde Ägyptens nach Mamlukischen Quellen* (Berlin: K. Schwarz, 1983), 36.

56. Ibn al-Ḥājj, *Al-Madkhal*, 2:172; al-Ṭurṭūshī, *Kitāb al-ḥawādith wa-al-bida'*, ed. M. Talbi, p. 142; Arabic text and translation also excerpted in *Christians and Moors in Spain*, 3 vols., *Arabic Sources (711–1501)*, ed. and trans. Charles Melville and Ahmad Ubaydli (Warminster, U.K.: Aris and Phillips Ltd., 1992), 3:120–21; Goitein, *Mediterranean Society*, 5:43, 96–99; Cuffel, "Polemicizing Women's Bathing"; Heinz Grozfeld, *Das Bad im Arabisch-Islamischen Mittelalter: eine kulturgeschichtliche Studie* (Wiesbaden: Harrassowitz, 1970), 127; Abraham David, *To Come to the Land: Immigration and Settlement in Sixteenth-Century Eretz-Israel*, trans. Dena Ordan (Tuscaloosa: University of Alabama Press, 1999), 50.

57. Ibn al-Ḥājj, *Al-Madkhal*, 2:46–51; on Sha'bān, 1:312. Also see Lutfi, "Coptic Festivals." The fifteenth of Sha'bān, or Mid-Sha'bān, is thought to be the day in which God decides who will die during the following year. One should fast and pray for the dead; however, often this holiday is also celebrated by preparing

special foods, ostensibly for the dead, and other festive activities. On this festival, see G. E. von Grunebaum, *Muhammadan Festivals* (London: Curzon Press, 1976), 53–54; M. J. Kister, "'Sha'bān Is My Month': A Study of an Early Tradition," *Studia Orientalia momoriae D. H. Beneth dedicate* (Jerusalem: Magnes Press, 1979), 15–37.

58. Aḥmed ibn Yahya Wansharīsī, *Al-Mi'yār al-mu'rib wa-al-jāmi'al-mughrib 'an fātāwā' ahl Ifrīqīya wa-al-Andalus wa-al-Maghrib*, 13 vols. (Ribat: Wizārat al-'awqāf wa-al-shu'ūn al-Islāmīya lil-Mamlaka al-Maghribīya, 1981–), 11:150–52. Also in *Christians and Moors in Spain*, 3:28–31.

59. On restrictions on *dhimmi* behavior, see Cohen, *Under Crescent and Cross*, above.

60. Sanders, *Ritual, Politics and the City*, 48–52.

61. Shoshan, *Popular Culture*, 70–76.

62. و من البدع اجتماع بارض الاندلس على ابتياع الحلوى ليلة سبع و عشرين من رمضان: و كذالك على اقامة ينير بابتياع الفواكه كالعجم: و اقامةالعنصرة و خميس ابريل بشراء المجبنات و الاسفنج و هى من الاطعمة المبتدعة. و خروج الرجال جميعا او اشتاتا مع النساء مختلطين للتفرج, و كذالك يفعلون فى أيام العيد و يخرجون للمصلى. و يقمن فيه الخيم للتفرج لا للصلاة.

al-Ṭurṭūshī, *Kitāb al-ḥawādith wa-al-bida'*, ed. Talbi, 140–41 and in *Christians and Moors in Spain*, 3:120–21. On this passage and its authorship, see *Kitāb al-ḥawādith wa-al-bida'= El libro de las novedades y las innovaciones*, ed. and trans. M. Fierro (Madrid: Consejo Superior de Investigaciones Cientficas, Instituto de Cooperación con el Mundo Arabe, 1993), 134 (2.4.6); F. de la Granja, "Fiestas cristianas en al-Andalus (Materiales para su studio) II Textos de al-Ṭurṭūšī el cadi 'Iyāḍ y Wanšarīsī," *Al-Andalus* 35 (1970): 119–42, esp. 120–24. The Arabic does not specify which Muslim festivals, though the translator of the passage in *Christians and Moors in Spain* fills in the festivals, though leaves out mention of the *muṣallā*. Compare with Ibn al-Ḥājj, *Al-Madkhal*, 1:297–98.

63. TS (Taylor Schechter Collection) 20.117, line 15, published in Simha Assaf, ed., *Texts and Studies in Jewish History* (Jerusalem: Mosad ha-Rav Kuk, 1949), 160–61, citation on 161.

64. Kramer, "Jewish Cult of the Saints," esp. 584; Goitein, *Mediterranean Society*, 2:300–301, 591 n. 4, 5:510 n. 56; for another example, see TS Box K 15.2v, line 7, cited and discussed in Mark Cohen, *Poverty and Charity in the Jewish Community of Medieval Egypt* (Princeton, NJ: Princeton University Press, 2005), 152. Coptic converts to Islam often retained close ties with their old community; this document may indicate similar patterns in the Jewish community. El-Leithy, "Coptic Culture and Conversion," vol. 1 *passim*.

65. TS. 20.117 lines 13–29 in Assaf, *Texts*, 161. Kramer, "Jewish Cult of the Saints"; Goitein, *Mediterranean Society*, 5:20–24; Meri, *Cult of the Saints*, 222–24.

66. Kramer especially points out the similarity of behavior at Dammuh to that at the graves of Muslim saints. The description also resembles the Muslim festival in honor of the prophet Moses celebrated in Jericho and Damascus by Muslims and, sometimes, by Jews and Christians. Joseph Sadan, "Le tombeau de Moïse à Jéricho et à Damas: une competition entre deux lieux saints principalement à l'époque

ottoman," *Revue des Études Islamiques* 49 (1981): 59–99. For unrestrained behavior (and disapproval of it) at gatherings in honor of living and dead saints, also see Boaz, *Popular Culture*, 13, 17.

67. Al-Ṭurṭūshī, *Kitāb al-ḥawādith wa-al-bida'*, ed. 'Abd al-Majīd Turkī (Beirut: Dār al-Gharb al-Islāmī, 1990): nos. 46–51, pp. 118–22. Compare with no. 138, pp. 188–89, in which he seems to compare singing the Qur'an to monks singing scripture in their churches and with nos. 180–81, pp. 219–21, where he objects to the practice of decorating mosques as Christians and Jews do their churches and synagogues.
68. و لا تغتروا بمن ينسب الى العلم و قد اتبع فى طاعة النسوان و الصبيان هواه al-'Azafi, "Fiestas cristianas en al-Andalus (Materiales para su estudio) I: 'al-Durr al-munaẓẓam' de al-'Azafi," *Al-Andalus: Revista de las Escuela de estudios Arabes de Madrid y Granada* 34 (1969): 1–53. The remark is on pp. 19 (Arabic), 33 (Spanish).
69. Cuffel, "From Practice to Polemic."
70. Ibn al-Ḥājj, *Al-Madkhal*, 1:267–70, 290, 312; Cuffel, "From Practice to Polemic"; H. Lufti, "Manners and Customs of Fourteenth-Century Cairene Women: Female Anarchy versus Male Shari'i Order in Muslim Prescriptive Treatises," in *Women in Middle Eastern History: Shifting Boundaries in Sex and Gender*, ed. N. R. Keddie and B. Baron (New Haven, CT: Yale University Press, 1991), 99–121.
71. Aḥmad al-Tīfāshī, *Nuzhat al-Albāb fīmā lā Yūjad fī Kitāb*, ed. Jamāl Jum'a (London: Riyad a-Rayyis lil-Lutub wa-al-Nashr, 1992), 238–41; al-Tīfāshī, *Les Délices des Coeurs, ou ce que l'on ne trouve en aucun livre*, trans. René R. Khawam (Paris: Phébus, 1981), 266–72.
72. Al-Maqrīzī, *Khiṭaṭ* 1:269. For a discussion of this passage and similar ones, see Shoshan, *Popular Culture*, 43, 46, 49, 112 n. 28; Lutfi, "Coptic Festivals," esp. 278–79. On "effeminates," also see E. Rowson, "The Categorization of Gender and Sexual Irregularity in Medieval Arabic Vice Lists," in *Body Guards: The Cultural Politics of Gender Ambiguity*, ed. J. Epstein and K. Straub (New York: Routledge, 1991); Rowson, "The Effeminates in Early Medina," *Journal of the American Oriental Society* 111 (1991): 671–93.
73. צביאן ולא רגל מא צבי לאלא אן יתעלק בה[ם. . . . ואן לא יתעדא אנסאן לא רגול ולא ואמרה אלי [..... TS. 20. 117 lines 20–21. Also see Kramer's discussion in "Jewish Cult of the Saints."
74. Khaled el-Rouayheb, *Before Homosexuality in the Arab-Islamic World*, 1500–1800 (Chicago: University of Chicago Press, 2005), 25–51; J. W. Wright and E. Rowson, eds., *Homoeroticism in Classical Arabic Literature* (New York: Columbia University Press, 1997); Stephen O. Murray and Will Roscoe, *Islamic Homosexualities: Culture, History and Literature* (New York: New York University Press, 1997), 55–96, 142–57; F. Rosenthal, "Ar-Razi on the Hidden Illness," *Bulletin of the History of Medicine* 52 (1978): 45–60. In this last piece and the accompanying primary source, male attraction to other men is treated as a disease with varying hopes of a cure.
75. و يتلذذون بذلك كأنهم فى ذلك اليوم كلهم نساء Ibn al-Ḥājj, *al-Madkhal* 2:52. Also see Lutfi's discussion of this passage in "Coptic Festivals," 280.

76. On this in Ibn al-Ḥājj and other Muslim authors of *bidaʿ* treatises, see Cuffel, "From Practice to Polemic."
77. For Ibn Taymīyya's comment, see above.
78. Kramer," "Jewish Cult of the Saints," esp. 586–87. He is focusing specifically on the customs and objections surrounding the synagogue of Moses at Dammuh; however, his observations may be broadened to include the entire phenomenon. Compare with Taylor, *In the Vicinity of the Righteous*, 59–61; Meri, *Cult of the Saints*, 122–23.
79. Ibn Taghrībirdī, *History of Egypt*, English trans., 13:129, 18:145–49; Ibn Iyas, *Journal d'un Bourgeois du Caire*, ed. and trans. Gaston Wiet, 2 vols. (Paris: Libraire Armand Colin, 1955–60), vol. 1, p. 73.
80. Lutfi, "Coptic Festivals."
81. Lawrence I. Conrad, "A Ninth-Century Muslim Scholar's Discussion of Contagion," in *Contagion: Perspectives from Pre-modern Societies*, ed. Lawrence I. Conrad and Dominik Wujastyk (Aldershot: Ashgate, 2000), 163–77; Dols, *Black Death*, 109–21; Ibn Iyas, *Journal d'un Bourgeois du Caire*, 1:72–74, 277, 280.
82. Ibn Riḍwān, *Medieval Islamic Medicine: Ibn Riḍwān's Treatise "On the Prevention of Bodily Ills in Egypt,"* ed. Adil S. Gamal, trans. and intro. Michael Dols (Berkeley: University of California, 1984); Lutfi, "Coptic Festivals."
83. Ibn Saʿid, *History*, 413.
84. Ibn Iyas, *Journal d'un Bourgeois du Caire*, 1:60, 73–76, 279–82; Prosper Alpini, *Histoire naturelle de l'Egypte*, 1581–1584, trans. R. de Fenoyl, ed. R. de Fenoyl and S. Sauneron, 4 vols. in 2 (Cairo: Institut français d'archéologie orientale du Caire), 1:16; Alpini, *La médicine des egyptiens*, 2 vols., trans. R. de Fenoyl (Cairo: Institut français d'archéologie orientale, 1980), 1:126–35; Jean Coppin, *Voyages en Égypte de Jean Coppin: 1638–1639, 1643–1646*, ed. Serge Sauneron (Cairo: Institut français d'archéologie orientale,1971), 57, 295; Claude Balme, *Observations et réflexions sur les causes, les symptoms et le traitement de la contagion dans différentes maladies et spécialement dans la peste d'Orient et la fièvre jaune* (Paris: Béchet, 1822), 242–43.
85. Mishnah Taʿanit, 3.8; BT Taʿanit 8a, 10a–18b; Midrash Genesis Rabbah 33.3; Midrash Leviticus Rabbah 34.4; *Pesiqta de Rav Kahana ʿal pi ketav yad Oqsford, ṿe-shinuye nusḥaʾot mi-khol kitve ha-yad u-sheride ha-genizah*, 2 vols., ed. J. Mendelbaum (New York: Bet ha-midrash le-Rabanim sheba-Ameriqah, 1962), no. 24:11, 2:358–68; *Pesiḳta de Rab Kahana*, trans. William G. Braude and Israel J. Kapstein (Philadelphia: Jewish Publication Society, 1975), no. 24:11, pp. 371–78; *Midrash Tehillim: ha-mekhuneh Shoḥer ṭov*, ed. S. Buber (Vilna: ha-ʾalmanah ve-ha-ʾaḥim Rom, 1891), Psalms 2, 18, 19, 26, 119, pp. 26, 141–42, 170, 219, 488; *The Midrash on Psalms*, 2 vols., trans. William G. Braude (New Haven, CT: Yale University Press, 1959), Psalms 2, 17 (addendum), 18, 19, 26, 119, 1:38, 223, 241–43, 282, 362–64, 2:246–47; Richard Kalmin, "Holy Men, Rabbis, and Demonic Sages in Late Antiquity," in *Jewish Culture and Society under the Christian Roman Empire*, ed. Richard Kalmin and Seth Schwartz (Leuven: Peeters, 2003), 213–49; Hayim Lapin, "Rabbis and Public Prayers for Rain in Later Roman Palestine," in *Religion*

and Politics in the Ancient Near East, ed. Adele Berlin (Bethesda: University Press of Maryland, 1996), 105–29; Baruch Bosker, "Wonder-Working and the Rabbinic Tradition: The Case of Ḥanina ben Dosa," *JSJ* 16/1 (1985), 42–91; Ephraim Urbach, *The Sages: Their Concepts and Beliefs*, trans. Israel Abrahams (Cambridge, MA: Harvard University Press, 1987), 103, 481; W. S. Green, "Palestinian Holy Men: Charismatic Leadership and Rabbinic Tradition," *Aufstied und Niedergang der römischen Welt* 2, 19/2 (1979): 619–47.

86. ולא יוסתקא מא פי אלסבת אלא מא יושׁ]ב. . . . . TS 20.117 line 25, Assaf, *Texts*, p. 161.
87. Gregory of Tours, *Vita s. Remigius* I; idem, *History of the Franks*, X.1; Johannes Diaconum, *Vita Gregorius Magnus* I.42; Gregory the Great, *Registrum epistolarum*, ed. Dag Ludvig Norberg, 2 vols. (Turnholt: Brepols, 1982–), XI.57.
88. Gregory the Great, *Registrum* II.
89. Al-Bukhārī, *Saḥīḥ*, II.15; al-Mālik, *al-Muwatta'*, book 13. The Jewish writers of the statute of Dammuh clearly saw any intercessory prayers that the congregation or visitors might undertake as part of this Muslim ritual of intercession for rain since the writers employ the verb *istiqa'*.
90. On medieval and early modern Jewish pilgrimage to gravesites to pray for rain, see Pinhas Giller, "Recovering the Sanctity of the Galilee: The Veneration of Sacred Relics in Classical Kabbalah," *Journal of Jewish Thought and Philosophy* 4 (1994): 147–69.
91. Gregory of Tours, *History of the Franks*, X.1.
92. בחוצות אנשים ונשים וטף צועקים אל אלהי הרוחות להשקיט הארץ ולהרגיעה להושיע אדם ובהמה. . . . ואשר יכול הכותב לעשות כי דבר אל העם לקדש צום לקראות עצרה ולצאת אל השדה אל בית הקברות בצום ובכי ומספד. . . . גם מושל העיר עם עושי מלאכת המלך תקעו להם אהלים חוץ למדינה ועד עתה הם [שם]

    TS 18 J 3 f. 9, ed. and trans. in Jacob Mann, *The Jews in Egypt and Palestine under the Fātimid Caliphs: A Contribution to Their Political and Communal History Based Chiefly on Geniza Material Hitherto Unpublished and a Second Supplement to the "The Jews in Egypt and Palestine under the Fatimid Caliphs,"* 2 vols. in 1 (New York: Ktav Publishing House, 1970), 1:156–58, 2: 176–78. Also translated in Goitein, *Mediterranean Society*, 5:63–65, citation on 64. I have presented Goitein's translation of the passage.
93. Rabbinic Jews, like Muslims and Christians, very much believed in the ability of the holy dead to intercede on behalf of the living. Meri, *Cult of the Saints*, 214–50; Goitein, *Mediterranean Society*, 2:162–63, 554 nn. 28–31; 3:2–6; 5:178, 183–86; Elliot Howrowitz, "Speaking to the Dead: Cemetery Prayer in Medieval and Early Modern Jewry," *Journal of Jewish Thought and Philosophy* 8 (1999): 303–17.
94. Benjamin Kedar notes that for groups from differing religious communities of the Middle East to come together at a sacred site or ritual without actually mingling or sharing any religious rites was not unusual. Kedar, "Convergences of Oriental Christian, Muslim and Frankish Worshippers: The Case of Saydnaya and the Knights Templar," in *The Crusades and the Military Orders: Expanding the Frontiers of*

Medieval Latin Christianity, ed. Zsolt Hunyadi and József Laszlovsky (Budapest: Central European University, 2001), 89–100; Kedar, "Convergences of Oriental Christian, Muslim, and Frankish Worshippers: The Case of Saydnaya," in *De Sion exibit lex et verbum domini de Hierusalem: Essays on Medieval Law, Liturgy and Literature in Honour of Amnon Linder*, ed. Yitzhak Hen (Turhout: Brepols, 2001), 59–69.

95. Shoshan, *Popular Culture*, 9–22; Cuffel, "From Practice to Polemic"; Urvoy, "Aspects"; Annemarie Schimmel, "Sufismus und Heiligenverehrung im Spätmittelalterlichen Ägypten," in *Festschrift Werner Caskel zum siebzigsten Geburtstag* 5 *März* 1966, ed. Erwin Gräf (Leiden: Brill, 1968), 274–89.

96. Ibn Taghrībirdī, *History of Egypt*, English trans., 19:137.

97. نودى فى البلد أن يصوم الناس ثلاثة أيام و أن يخرجوا فى اليوم الرابع و هو يوم الجمعة الى عند مسجد القدم يتضرعون الى الله و يسألونه فى رفع الوباء عنهم فصام أكثر الناس و نام الناس فى الجامع و أحيوا الليل كما يفعلون فى شهر رمضان, فلما أصبح الناس يوم الجمعة السابع و العشرين منه خرج الناس يوم الجامعة من كل فج عميق, و اليهود و النصارى و السامرة, و الشيوخ و العجائز و الصبيان, و الفقراء و الامراء و الكبراء و القضاة من بعد صلاة الصبح فما زالوا هنا لك يدعون الله تعالى حتى تعالى النهار جدا, و كان يوم مشهودا.

Ismā 'il ibn 'Umar ibn Kathir, *al-Bidāyah wa al-nihāyah fi al-tārīkh*, vol. 14 (Cairo, n.d.), p. 226; For a slightly different translation and discussion of this passage in the context of the plague, see Dols, *Black Death*, 251.

98. ثم ركب السلطن بعد صلاة الصبح و نزل من قلعة الجبل بغير أبهة الملك بل عليه ملوطة صوف أبيض بغير شد فى وسطه, وعلى كتفيه مئزر صوف مستدل كهيئة الصوفية. . . . فلما وصل السلطان الى مكان الجمع بالصحراء و نزل عن فرسه و قام على قدميه و عن يمينه و شماله الخليفة و القضاة و أهل العلم و من بين يديه و خلفه طوائف من الصوفيه و مشايخ الزوايا. . . . فبسط السلطان يديه و دعا الله. . . . و الجم الغفير يراه و يؤمن على الدعاء, و طال قيامه فى الدعاء و كل أحد يدعو الله تعالى و يتضرع. . . . و أخذ الطاعون من يومئذ فى النقص بالتدريج.

Ibn Taghrībirdī, *Nujūm*, 14:77–80; Ibn Taghrībirdī, *History of Egypt*, English trans., 17:64–66. Also see the discussion of this passage in Dols, *Black Death*, 246–53.

99. The emphasis on the white robe may have developed from the Fāṭimid caliphs' custom of wearing white robes during processions (white was the color of the Fāṭimid caliphate); however, these robes could be made of linen or silk, and thus were not typical Sufi robes which were usually wool. On the Fāṭimid caliphs' donning white robes for processions, see Sanders, *Ritual, Politics and the City*, 31, 61, 71. On Sultan Shaykh al-Malik al-Mu'ayyad's particular relationship with Sufis and Sufism see Schimmel, "Sufismus un Heiligenverehrung." Also compare this incident with Muzaffar al-Dīn Kökbürü's passing out of cloaks from a Sufi retreat to various leaders during the Prophet Muḥammad's *maulid*. (Muzaffar was a brother-in-law of Salaḥ al-Dīn): von Grunebaum, *Muhammadan Festivals*, 75.

100. Dominique Sourdel, "Robes of Honor in 'Abbasid Baghdad during the Eighth to the Eleventh Centuries" and Thomas Allsen, "Robing in the Mongolian Empire," both in *Robes and Honor: The Medieval World of Investiture*, ed. Stewart

Gordon (New York: Palgrave, 2001), 137–45, 305–13 respectively. Thomas Allsen, *Commodity and Exchange in the Mongol Empire: A Cultural History of Islamic Textiles* (Cambridge: Cambridge University Press, 1997).

101. Sanders, *Ritual Politics and the City*, 23–26, 29–31, 47, 78–79; Paula Sanders, "Robes of Honor in Fatimid Egypt" and Carl Petry, "Robing Ceremonials in Late Mamluk Egypt: Hallowed Traditions, Shifting Protocols," both in Gordon, ed., *Robes and Honor*, 225–39, 353–77 respectively.

102. Jamal Elias, "The Sufi Robe (*Khirqa*) as a Vehicle of Spiritual Authority," in Gordon, ed., *Robes and Honor*, 275–89.

103. Compare this passage with a similar description al-Maqrīzī gives in his *Sulūk*. He also emphasizes the Sultan's donning of Sufi robes for the purposes of intercessory procession. Lutfi argues that the fact that al-Maqrīzī did not mention the presence of Jews and Christians is unusual, and she attributes this exclusion to what she believes to be al-Maqrīzī's agenda to disassociate *dhimmi*, especially Coptic, rituals from successful state (Muslim) ritual and history. See her "Coptic Festivals."

104. On extreme crisis as a goad to abandon contested identities and hierarchies at shrines, see Coleman, "Do You Believe in Pilgrimage?"; Glenn Bowman, "Nationalizing the Sacred: Shrines and Shifting Identities in the Israeli-Occupied Territories," *Man* [n.s.] 28 (1993): 431–60.

105. Sanders, *Ritual, Politics and the City*, 45–54.

106. Sanders hints at this process, however, she is primarily focused on the Isma'ili incorporation or tolerance of Sunnis. See *Ritual, Politics and the City*, 52.

107. For example, al-Ḥākim built the Rāshida mosque on the site of a Jacobite church and the place was surrounded by Jewish and Christian graves. Sanders, *Ritual, Politics and the City*, 54. Some sites, such as the Hebron gravesite of the biblical patriarchs, were naturally holy to members of two, or in this case, all three religions.

108. Jews and Christians along with their Muslim compatriots decorated the streets of the procession route for the New Year and Nile celebrations. Sanders, *Ritual, Politics and the City*, 74.

109. Marjorie Garber, *Vested Interests: Cross-Dressing and Cultural Anxiety* (New York: Routledge, 1993), 21–32.

110. Johan Huizinga, *Homo Ludens: A Study of the Element of Play in Culture* (Boston: Beacon Press, 1950), 8–22.

111. Galina Lindquist, "Elusive Play and Its Relations to Power," *Focaal: European Journal of Anthropology* 37 (2001): 13–23.

5

Khiḍr and the Politics of Place

CREATING LANDSCAPES OF CONTINUITY

Ethel Sara Wolper

THIS ESSAY EXAMINES the relationship between Khiḍr, the legendary Muslim figure of rebirth and renewal, and the conversion of major monuments in the Islamic world. It addresses the construction of Khiḍr as a symbol of contact and conversion in the Muslim world. Through an analysis of what motivated Ottoman authors to include accounts of Khiḍr in the transformation of the Hagia Sophia into an Ottoman mosque, the essay traces two major developments in the Ottoman understanding of Khiḍr. The first of these is exemplified by Khiḍr's association with the Umayyad Mosque of Damascus, while the second focuses on Khiḍr as worshiped in a series of smaller shrines in the Anatolian countryside. As this paper argues, different developments in the formation and dissemination of Khiḍr attributes were, like the act of conversion, subject to the changing needs and values of different audiences. The relationship between the polyvalent Khiḍr and the never-ending process of conversion marked many of the major conquests and population transfers of the Middle Ages.

Khiḍr, or al-Khaḍir (the verdant or green man; Khaḍr in Laird's chapter in this volume) and his associated traditions have been aptly described as a "phenomenon" that takes up "a huge space within Muslim traditions and cultures."[1] Known as a prophet or saint, Khiḍr is an immortal being who can travel great distances in short periods of time and has many manifestations.[2] He is linked to the unnamed companion of Moses, identified as the servant of God in the Qur'an (18:60–62), and appears in the exegesis, Hadith (the prophetic tradition), and *Qiṣaṣ al-anbiyā'* (stories of prophets) as well as a large number of Sufi texts and folk traditions.[3] He is also commonly traced to three pre-Islamic traditions: the Jewish legend of Elijah, the Alexander romance, and the Epic of Gilgamesh.[4] Each of these accounts stresses his importance as a figure that holds the secrets of life. As a spiritual guide who is able to take on different forms, Khiḍr performs a series of enigmatic actions and exemplifies both the attainment and possession of esoteric knowledge.

Sites associated with Khiḍr appear throughout the Muslim world.[5] Today, Khiḍr's name and its variants describe a large number of hills, villages, lakes, and mosques in the Middle East and Asia. Khiḍr's visits to a number of mosques, tombs, and dervish lodges are recorded in local legends and usually marked by some architectural features within these buildings. Sometimes, Khiḍr sites were marked by inscriptions that were carved on building portals or in particular sections of buildings. In other cases, it was local legends and literary accounts alone that tied Khiḍr to individual buildings. Large numbers of these sites are clustered along frontier zones. In the Islamic world, major frontier zones were in medieval Anatolia and Syria, and in India. In these regions, mixed Muslim populations came in close contact with diverse populations whether Hindu, Christian, or Jewish. Not only were these frontier zones places where diverse populations came into contact with each other, but they also contained a number of pre-Islamic structures that were modified by Muslim inhabitants.[6]

Literary accounts and archaeological evidence tie Khiḍr to a number of major monuments throughout the Islamic world.[7] At various times, Khiḍr has been found in prayer at the Mosque of Al-Aqṣā, the Umayyad Mosque of Damascus, the Mosque of ʿAmr, the Kaʾba, and the Great Mosque of Tunis.[8] In many cases, accounts of Khiḍr's visits to major monuments cast them in a new series of associations with each other, creating new sacred geographies. In these accounts, the daily prayer circuits of Khiḍr are described. According to the Jerusalem historian Mujīr al-Dīn (d. 1521), every Friday Khiḍr prays in five different mosques—Mecca, Medina, Jerusalem (al-Aqṣā), Quba, and Sinai.[9] As will be shown below, his visits to the Umayyad Mosque of Damascus were recorded in traditions and marked by inscriptions. In each of these places, and during each of these visits, accounts of Khiḍr's visit tie his appearance to the sanctity of a specific site. Because many of these sites, such as the Hagia Sophia, have visible pre-Islamic origins and continue to be places of worship for Christians and Jews, Khiḍr's presence also serves as a way of highlighting how and when various religions and cultures come together.

Because of Khiḍr's complex nature, it has been very easy to misunderstand the functions of this multivalent figure. Islamic folk literature emphasizes his role as a spiritual guide who is able to change form and appear at will. Khiḍr has often been described as a Muslim version of saints George and Theodore with whom he shares the identity of an equestrian military dragon-slayer.[10]

Because of Khiḍr's attainment of immortal life, he is also associated with the Prophet Elijah. Yet, as this paper argues, Khiḍr's role in the construction, conquest, and conversion of the Hagia Sophia compel us to study the Khiḍr cult in Turkey as more than a local adaptation of a Christian saint. Legends about Khiḍr and the Hagia Sophia, while supporting "the symbolic construction of local sanctity," provided a series of links between the Hagia Sophia and other sites.[11] The reason Khiḍr was given pride of place as the architect of the Hagia Sophia was that by the Ottoman period he had become associated with two important traditions that the Ottomans needed to effect the transition of the Hagia Sophia. One, exemplified by the Umayyad Mosque of Damascus, was based on a series of traditions that served to link formative centers in Islamic history. The other tradition was based on a series of associations between universal claims of Turco-Islamic sovereignty, equestrian military saints, and Khiḍr.

The Hagia Sophia/Aya Sofya

Shortly after the Ottoman conquest of Constantinople in 1453, the Ottoman sultan Mehmet II was faced with the task of rebuilding the imperial Byzantine city. Mehmet the Conqueror's biographer, Shemseddin, wrote in 1480 that the sultan found the church of the Hagia Sophia, the great crowning achievement of the Byzantine Empire, in ruins.[12] Transforming this imperial church into the main mosque of the Ottoman Empire was a delicate task that required equal efforts from architects and panegyrists. Ottoman writers read Procopius and other Byzantine panegyrists to study what made the Hagia Sophia so awe-inspiring. In describing the architectural wonders of this monument, Ottoman writers consulted editions and translations of the ninth-century *Diegesi peri tes Hagias Sofias* (Narrative concerning Hagia Sophia) and began writing their own accounts. In these new accounts, the early history of the Greek church was linked to the heroes and prophets of Islam. Yet, although Solomon and a variety of Muslim martyrs were mentioned in these descriptions, it was the multivalent and enigmatic prophet-saint Khiḍr who was given pride of place for his involvement in choosing the location and form of the Hagia Sophia.[13] In Shemseddin's version, Khiḍr had urged the Byzantine emperor Justinian to build the church on the site of an ancient temple to show the triumph of Christianity over paganism. In addition, Shemseddin mentioned that the plan of the great church followed a divinely inspired one revealed to Khiḍr and given to the church's architect.[14] In a move linking Christianity's triumph over paganism with Islam's role as the inheritor of Byzantium, Muslim authors described Khiḍr as the figure who advised the architect to put up the great dome, one of the great wonders of the building, on the prophet's birthday.[15]

One of the best ways to understand what motivated Ottoman authors to include references of Khiḍr in accounts of the construction, conquest, and conversion of the Hagia Sophia is to address some of the controversies surrounding the new Ottoman capital. With such an approach, we can begin to understand the myth-making that accompanies the conversion of such major monuments as the Hagia Sophia/Aya Sofya as a necessary and ongoing process. There was, for example, no direct correlation between the conquest of Constantinople and its choice as the new capital. Although Sultan Mehmed wanted to move the capital to Constantinople, there were large groups of Ottoman elites who wanted to keep the capital at Edirne and saw such a move as a threat to the source of their strength and identity.[16]

At the same time, the special qualities and sacred status of the Hagia Sophia made it a difficult building to transform. The majesty of its formal qualities caused Christian and Muslim authors to attribute the creation of the building to God.[17] The Byzantines had believed that the plan of the Hagia Sophia was divinely inspired and added a series of mosaics in key places that further emphasized the divine nature of the structure. Those walking in through the southwest vestibule, the passage used during official Byzantine processions into the church, passed through a doorway whose lintel was embellished with a tenth-century mosaic depicting the Virgin and Child flanked by Justinian and Constantine. In the image, Constantine holds a model of the city of Constantinople while Justinian offers a miniature Hagia Sophia to the *Theotokos*, the Mother of God. The message underlined by this mosaic depiction of their offerings, both of the imperial city of Byzantium and the Hagia Sophia, was further emphasized as one proceeded into the church. After passing through the narthex, the official entrance to the main church was marked by another mosaic in the lunette above the central door leading from the inner narthex to the nave. This mosaic shows an unnamed emperor bowing before an enthroned Christ.[18] These panels helped celebrate and define the architectural triumph of the Hagia Sophia within a Byzantine vision of the dual triumph of Christianity and Byzantium. They reflect an imperial vision from the tenth and eleventh centuries whereby the church, built after the Nika riots of 532, was as much a triumph of Christianity over paganism as of the continuing glory of Byzantium.[19]

Because the church was heavily laden with the symbolism of the dual triumph of Christianity and Byzantium, the Ottomans needed to incorporate this triumph into their claims of universal Turco-Islamic sovereignty. In stressing Ottoman claims to be the rightful heirs of the Byzantines, they needed a figure that could provide a Turco-Islamic context for their transformation of the Hagia Sophia church into the mosque of Aya Sofya while stressing the existence of a pre-Islamic past. To the Ottoman conquerors, claims of universal Turco-Islamic sovereignty were founded on two related traditions. The first were prophetic traditions about the Muslim capture of Constantinople and the second concerned accounts of the semi-mythical *ghāzī* heroes who fought in the name of Islam against the Byzantines. As historical and literal figures, *ghāzī*s date back to the seventh century when the first Arab believers sought to conquer Constantinople.[20] By the tenth century when Turkish rulers began to redefine the Arab-Byzantine frontier as a Turkish-Byzantine one, Turkish rulers translated Arab *ghāzī* epics into an Anatolian landscape and emphasized these connections through the discovery of the graves of *ghāzī* martyrs in Turkish lands. Sultan Mehmed II's discovery of the grave of Abū Ayyūb al-Anṣārī, a Companion of the Prophet who tried to conquer Constantinople in the year 668–69, helped link the early Arab *ghāzī* fighters who tried and failed in taking Constantinople with the Ottoman Turks who saw themselves as *ghazī*s par excellence.[21] At least two accounts of the conquest of Constantinople describe Sultan Mehmed II's miraculous discovery of Abū Ayyūb al-Anṣārī's grave.[22]

In the elaborate myth-making that began in the decades following the Ottoman conquest of Constantinople, the Ottomans incorporated the Aya Sofya into two symbolic networks that expressed and recontextualized the continuing sanctity of its site and form while connecting the building to Ottoman claims of universal sovereignty. First, they linked Constantinople and the Hagia Sophia to Islam's formative years as a way to redefine the conquest of the Hagia Sophia as a culmination of early Muslim visions. At the same time, as rulers in a newly established Ottoman city that needed to house an Anatolian elite, they looked toward the heroes of a more recent Anatolian past to support their rule. How and why Khiḍr played a major role in this process will be examined in this chapter's next two sections.

Constantinople, Damascus, and Khiḍr

The Umayyad Mosque of Damascus provides an important example of how references to Khiḍr could be used to link central sites in the Islamic world and underline the piety of local places and figures. These links occurred on multiple levels. On the most basic level, accounts of Khiḍr stopping to pray at a building connected it with the other places that he stopped to visit in his daily prayer circuits. Because of Khiḍr's ability to travel great distances in short periods of time, we find daily prayer sites in Jerusalem, Damascus, Mecca, and a number of other early Islamic centers. Medieval Muslim authors, especially compilers of biographical dictionaries and *hadith* collections, gave Khiḍr a role in choosing and linking building sites together in a new sacred geography. No other Muslim saint could travel such distances within a day, nor was their continued appearance assured through the attainment of immortality. On another level, Khiḍr worked as a symbol of prophetic authority further underlining the fact that Damascus and Constantinople were linked by prophetic traditions about the Muslim conquest of Constantinople.[23] Finally, both buildings are among the most important converted buildings in the Islamic world. As such, stories about their conversion had a significance that went far beyond the time and place of their construction.

Written accounts and archaeological evidence describe a Khiḍr place in the Umayyad mosque of Damascus. An eleventh-century tradition states that the Umayyad caliph al-Walīd, wishing to pray during the night, entered the mosque and found Khiḍr at prayer between the Bāb al-Sāʿā and the Bāb al-Khaḍrāʾ.[24] Medieval authors also wrote about this site, calling it either a *zāwiya* (corner of a mosque) or *maqsūra* (cordoned-off area reserved for prayer). Ibn al-ʿAsākir (d. 1176), author of a twelfth-century biographical dictionary on the city of Damascus, wrote that there was a *maqsūra* in the Great Mosque where Khiḍr prayed every day.[25] Another account, by the scholar and pilgrim al-Harawī, mentions a *zāwiya* of al-Khiḍr where Khiḍr is seen to attend prayers.[26] Scholars in more recent years have noted a small inscription referring to a Khiḍr place in the site mentioned in these medieval sources. According to Sourdel-Thomine, Wulzinger recorded an inscription of a *maqsūra* of al-Khiḍr in the Great Mosque.[27] This same site was described by Kriss and Kriss-Heinrich in the mid-twentieth century.[28] In later years, other Khiḍr sites were found in different areas of the mosque.[29]

In the case of the Umayyad mosque of Damascus, Khiḍr's role in making connections between it and the Hagia Sophia also incorporated earlier links between Damascus and Constantinople. Muslims had been trying to capture Constantinople since 669 when the first armies were sent out. The Prophet had even predicted that the Arabs would one day conquer Constantinople. According to this tradition, the prophet had stated: "they will conquer Constantinople. Hail to the prince and the army to whom this is granted."[30]

The Umayyad caliph al-Walīd sent out an expedition in 717 in hopes of conquering the city. According to Flood, al-Walīd's military expeditions coincided with the building of the Umayyad Mosque of Damascus and embodied Umayyad ambitions to fulfill the prophet's prophecy. As Flood argues, when al-Walīd was supervising the building of the Great Mosque, he assumed that the conquest of Constantinople was imminent and sought to create a style that would unite the Great Mosque of Damascus with the Hagia Sophia.[31]

Even without these stylistic similarities, there are a number of significant parallels between the history of the Umayyad Mosque of Damascus and the history of the Hagia Sophia that involve the conquest and conversion of sacred sites. Traditions about these buildings address the importance of their sites, origins, and associations with mythic and historical figures. Both buildings were built on sacred sites that had gone through multiple transformations before they were turned into mosques. The Umayyad Mosque of Damascus was built on a pagan sanctuary that originally contained the Temple of Jupiter in its center. The temple was surrounded by a rectangular enclosure. In the years before the Muslim conquest, the Cathedral of St. John was built on the sanctuary replacing the pagan temple. After the initial Muslim conquest of Damascus, a special area was reserved for Muslim prayer. This area, or *musallā* (Muslim prayer space), was most likely in the southeastern part of the sanctuary outside the church and near the enclosure.[32] Christians and Muslims prayed at this site until al-Walīd's decision to tear down everything within the holy area and devote the entire space to a mosque. Al-Walīd built a triple-aisled prayer-hall against the south wall of the sanctuary. The building was approximately 160 meters long and opened up into a large courtyard. Two towers that survived from the pre-Islamic sanctuary were at the southwestern and southeastern corners of the new enclosure. According to Ibn al-ʿAsākir, during the construction of the mosque al-Walīd chose to keep the most important relic from the church, the head of John the Baptist, in its original site within the newly built mosque. He had the area marked with a special column.[33] This Christian relic within the Great Mosque of Damascus became an important site of veneration for Muslims and Christians alike. It is likely that this column was to the northeast of the central *mihrab* in the eastern part of the prayer-hall. Having a Khiḍr and St. John site within the mosque sanctuary underscored the link between Muslim Damascus and the saintly figures whose presence in Damascus predated the Arab conquest. The proximity of these sites not only allowed St. John and Khiḍr to be worshiped within one sanctuary, but in so doing emphasized a discourse of conversion and continuity; the Khiḍr prayer-place supported the continuation of local sacrality while linking Damascus to crucial periods and places in Islamic history.

Like the Hagia Sophia, the Great Mosque of Damascus's multilayered history and complex religious associations are underlined through a number of references to the legendary prophet Khiḍr. On one level, accounts of Khiḍr prayer-places in the building reinvigorated links between the Umayyad mosque and the Umayyad caliph al-Walīd. The account also lends an extra sanctity to the site while serving as a reminder of the building's multiple histories. It was al-Walīd who had torn down the church and created the Umayyad mosque. Accounts of his meeting with Khiḍr while doing extra night prayers lend an extra sanctity to al-Walīd. At the same time, the association between Khiḍr and the patron who ordered the conversion of a building is echoed in later accounts. By the time of the twelfth-century account of al-Harawī, Khiḍr had become associated with a number of pre-Islamic sites throughout the Islamic world, in general, and, in Syria and Palestine, in particular.[34] Most of these sites had once been Christian structures and Khiḍr's association with them provided a crucial link between a Christian past and an Islamic present.

Khiḍr and Anatolia

Before the Ottoman conquest of Constantinople in 1453, the cult of Khiḍr had also become popular in Anatolia and Rumelia. In a number of steps that began with the Byzantine defeat by the Seljuk Turks at the 1071 Battle of Manzikert, Khiḍr joined and merged with a number of local and regional traditions represented by saints, prophets, *ghāzīs*, and other religious martyrs.[35] To understand these transformations, we need to begin with an examination of the religious landscape of Byzantine Anatolia. By the tenth century, a number of military saints had become popular in Byzantine Anatolia. These saints, often depicted on horseback in the act of slaying a serpent or dragon, roamed the Anatolian countryside in an ongoing battle against evil.[36] St. George's popularity was so great that the first Turkish Islamic dynasty in this region, the Dānishmendids, issued bilingual coins with images of a dragon-slaying figure meant to represent St. George.[37] St. George was a symbol of resurrection and renovation whose festival honored spring.[38] With the Islamization of Anatolia, the mounted Khiḍr, also associated with renewal, became linked to many St. George sites and practices.

Khiḍr's association with the prophet Elijah, with whom he shares immortality, was, like his association with St. George, prominent in Anatolia and the Levant. According to Yerasimos, Khiḍr replaced Elijah on the many high spots in Anatolia and Rumelia that had been devoted to the Jewish prophet. The relationship between these two figures became so intertwined that they are often depicted together in manuscripts. In Anatolia, a composite figure, Khiḍr-Ilyas or Hıdrellez, arose from the joining of Khiḍr and Elijah. The composite Khiḍr-Ilyas is also often associated with other saints. By the fourteenth century, visitors to Turkey wrote that the Turks worshiped St. George in the figure of Khiḍr-Ilyas (Hıdrellez).[39]

It was also in the period between the Islamic conquest and before the Ottoman conquest of Constantinople, that Turkish Islamic rulers patronized manuscripts about the *ghāzī* warriors who fought against Byzantium. Some of these, like Malik Dānishmend in the *Dānishmendnāme*, were legendary Turkish versions of the early Arab *ghāzī*s who had tried to defeat Constantinople. Although the border between the Muslim and non-Muslim worlds had changed, the fight was the same one. In a process of symbiosis, which was common to this period, Khiḍr appeared in these stories and played a major role in offering guidance to these Turkicized *ghāzī*s. In turn, Khiḍr, as one who inhabited the same literary landscape, took on many *ghāzī* attributes. These included great acts of bravery usually performed on horseback, offering aid to travelers in need, and the conversion of Christians to Islam.

As a prophet, legendary figure, and saint, Khiḍr played a crucial role in the reformulation of sacred space that took place in the centuries following the Turkish conquest of Anatolia. The Turkmen groups that began to migrate into Anatolia encountered a landscape dotted with sacred sites associated with Christian saints and Old Testament figures.[40] Although many of these sites were taken over by mystic groups and other Muslim figures, Christians still considered them to be sacred. A large number of these sites, which are often called shared sanctuaries, were associated with Khiḍr (like the village al-Khaḍr discussed by Laird in this volume). By the beginning of the fifteenth century, shrines once dedicated to St. George, St. Theodore, and the prophet Elijah, and now known in Muslim sources as shrines of Khiḍr, formed a new north–south pilgrimage route between Sinope on the Black Sea, passing through Albistan to either Aleppo or Mosul. These sites included a Khiḍr-Ilyas monastery in Sinope, a Khiḍr mountain in Merzifon, a *zāwiya* near Çorum linked to the cult of Khiḍr, and a column in the main mosque of Sivas where people brought sickly children in the hopes of finding a cure.[41] While associations with Khiḍr signified that they were a focal point of Muslim practice, references to local traditions and beliefs were emphasized through the display of Christian and antique building fragments on the outside of these buildings.

By the time of the Ottoman conquest, Anatolia was filled with enough Khiḍr sites to establish certain patterns. For the most part, these were built on Christian sites and in areas with mixed and frequently changing populations. At the same time, many of these buildings displayed Christian fragments. Based on this evidence, we can assume that Khiḍr's connection to buildings was understood by large portions of the Muslim population as an indicator of the building's non-Muslim past. For the Ottomans of the mid-fifteenth century, the most immediate non-Muslim past was a Christian one. In other words, calling a building a Khiḍr mosque, naming a part of a building a Khiḍr *maqām*, and incorporating Khiḍr into myths about a building were ways of expressing the Christian significance of a site. At the same time, Khiḍr was imbued with a variety of heroic qualities that had been developed in stories about the semi-mythical landscape of the Anatolian frontier with Byzantium where *ghāzī* warriors began to take on the heroic qualities and military exploits of Byzantine military saints. These heroic qualities became particularly important in the years immediately following the Muslim conquest of Constantinople when the capital was moved from Edirne. Edirne had long been associated with a series of early and important Ottoman victories. Khiḍr's role as a sort of patron saint of Edirne made the need to link him to Constantinople and the attempted conquests by the Prophet's Companions and followers even greater.

Khiḍr and the Ottoman Transformation of the Hagia Sophia

The transformation of the Hagia Sophia church into the Aya Sofya mosque, like that of many converted monuments, was an elaborate process that took place over a number of centuries. Initial acts of prayer and building were not enough to answer all the questions raised by such a dramatic act as the conversion of a major monument. According to Ottoman sources, "Sultan Mehmet, the father of the conquest, after conquering this House of Arts (Constantinople) had it (the church of St. Sophia) cleaned within and without, added a minbar, and performed his first prayer there on Friday."[42] In the following years, panegyrists created an Islamic framework for the church's most obvious features—its plan and dome. Ottoman authors replaced the angel whom the Byzantines had believed provided the church's divinely inspired plan with Khiḍr, thereby invoking a series of associations between itinerant dragon slayers who roam the Anatolian countryside, fighting evil and performing miracles, and the early heroes of Islam. Some of these figures were the martyr saints of Christianity, while others had a history in Anatolia and, especially, Edirne, where they brought armies and the righteous to victory. In this way, Khiḍr's presence underlined the sacred nature of a site and allowed local populations a way to comprehend the conversion of religious buildings. In the case of the Hagia Sophia and its imperial associations, the challenge was a process that involved multiple written and visual sources. The Ottomans used these to construct the transformation of the Hagia Sophia as a crucial link in their ambitions of universal sovereignty.

Notes

1. Irfan A. Omar, " 'Reflecting Divine Light': *al-Khidr* as an Embodiment of God's Mercy (raḥma)," in *Gotteserlebnis und Gotteslehre: Christliche und Islamische Mystik im Orient*, ed. Tamcke Martin. (Wiesbaden: Harrassowitz, 2010), 167.
2. In recent years, a number of excellent studies of the figure have been published. Some of the most relevant to this discussion are: A. J. Wensinck, "al-Khadir," in the *Encyclopedia of Islam*, 2nd ed. (Leiden: Brill, 1990), 902–5; Françoise Aubaile-Sallenave, "Al-Khidr, 'L'Homme au Manteau Vert' en pays Musulmans: Ses fonctions, ses caractéres, sa diffusion," *Res Orientales* 14 (2002): 11–36; the extensive study by Patrick Franke, *Begegnung Mit Khidr: Quellenstudien Zum Imaginären im Traditionallen Islam* (Stuttgart: Steiner, 2000); and Franke, "Khidr in Istanbul: Observations on the Symbolic Construction of Sacred Spaces in Traditional Islam," in *On Archaeology of Sainthood and Local Spirituality in Islam: Past and Present Crossroad of Events and Ideas*, ed. George Stauth, Yearbook of the Sociology of Islam 5 (Bielefeld: Verlag, 2004), 36–56 (Among other things, Franke brings many of Wensinck's conclusions up to date). For a recent discussion of Khiḍr as a literary figure, see Theo Maarten van Lint, "The Gift of Poetry. Khidr and John the Baptist as Patron Saints of Muslim and Armenian 'Āšıqs-Ašułs," *Redefining Christian Identity*, ed. J. J. Van Ginkel and H. L. Murre-Van der Berg (Leuvain: Peeters 2005), 361. Scholarly treatments of more specific aspects of Khiḍr will be discussed below.
3. Omar, "Reflecting Divine Light," 167.
4. On his relationship to Alexander, see I. Friedlander, *Die Chadirlegende und die Alexander Sage* (Leipzig: J.C. Hinrichs, 1913). For information about the special qualities of Khiḍr and Khiḍr-Ilyās (Hızır-İlyas) in the Turkish world, see Pertev Boratav, "Türklerde Hızır" *İslām Ansiklopedisi*, vol. 5, part 1 (Istanbul Türkiye Diyanet Vakfı, 1987), 462–71. On the relationship between Khiḍr and Elijah, see Joseph W. Meri, "Re-appropriating Sacred Space: Medieval Jews and Muslims Seeking Elijah and Al-Khadir," *Medieval Encounters* 5, no. 3 (1999): 237–64. One of the most important early studies on this topic is Massignon's, "Elie et son role transhistorique, Khadiriya en Islam," *Opera minora I* (1963): 142–61.

5. Although it is beyond the scope of this essay, it is important to note the large and growing number of Khiḍr sites in Europe and the Americas. He also has a growing presence in cyberspace and at least one internet site devoted to him (www.khidr.org). Khiḍr is also worshipped at a number of Christian sites in the Middle East. The most famous medieval site is the monastery of Mar Behnam in Iraq.
6. For more on the complex relationship between Khiḍr sites and frontier regions, see Ethel Sara Wolper, "Khiḍr and the Changing Frontiers of the Medieval World," *Medieval Encounters* 17 (2011): 120–46. In her dissertation on Damascus in the Umayyad period, Nancy Khalek describes Syria as a type of liminal space. See Nancy A. Khalek, "From Byzantine to early Islam: Studies on Damascus in the Umayyad Era," (PhD diss., Princeton University, 2006).
7. Franke makes the argument that Khiḍr sacralizes space in two ways: Khiḍr's "cyclical appearances" at certain sites and his being incorporated into building foundation myths. For one of the earliest references to Khiḍr's role in foundation myths, Franke cites Ibn Ḥajar al-ʿAsqalānī's reference to a passage from the *Kitāb Makka* of al-Fākihī (d. 885), which describes an encounter between the fifth Shi'i Imam and Khiḍr on the origin of the Ka'ba. In this encounter, as in later ones, Khiḍr either describes or affirms a site's sacred status. See Franke, "Khidr in Istanbul," 52.
8. Franke, *Begegnung mit Khidr*, 114–24 and "Khidr in Istanbul."
9. Some of the earliest accounts of this circuit (Mecca, Medina, Jerusalem, Quba, and Mt. Sinai) are found in the tradition of Shahr ibn Ḥawshab (d. 718) and appear in a variety of sources. See Franke, *Begegnung mit Khidr*, 115 and below.
10. This correlation is especially strong in Syria and Palestine to the extent that Tawfik Canaan and other authors describe them as one in the same. Canaan writes on page 120 that he "shall close this section with a study of the shrines of el-Hader (St. George), the most renowned saint physician for nervous and mental troubles. This man of God, who is honored by all creeds in Palestine, possesses many sanctuaries." See his *Mohammedan Saints and Sanctuaries in Palestine* (London: Luzac & Co., 1927). Likewise, Meri makes the same attribution in Syria but focuses on Elijah and not St. George, "Re-appropriating," 238.
11. Unlike Franke, who is primarily concerned with how Khiḍr sacralizes profane space, this study views the formerly Christian and Jewish sites associated with Khiḍr as "liminal" spaces where the Christian significance is highlighted through a number of material and literary artifacts that remain legible to local populations. Franke, "Observations on the Symbolic," 52.
12. Stephane Yerasimos has made a study of the large number of texts on the Hagia Sophia written before the sixteenth century. See his *Legéndes d'empire: la fondation de Constantinople et de Sainte-Sophie dans les traditions turques* (Paris: Institut Français D'Études Anatoliennes D'Istanbul et Jean Maisonneuve, 1990). Yerasimos' translation is from an Ottoman chronicle in 1491 and is based on Friedrich Giese,

Die altosmanischen anonymen Chroniken Tewārīh-I Āl-I'Osmān, part 1: *Text und Variantenverzeichnis* (Breslau: Selbstverlage, 1922), 71–111. For information about the Ottoman production of texts on the Hagia Sophia, see Gülru Necipoğlu, "The Life of an Imperial Monument," in *Hagia Sophia from the Age of Justinian to the Present*, ed. Robert Mark and Ahmet Ş. Çakmak (Cambridge: Cambridge University, 1992), 198–99. According to Necipoğlu, the original Greek text (1474) is published in Théodor Preger, *Scriptores Originum Constantinopolitanarum*, 2 vols. (Leipzig: B.G. Teubner, 1901–7); it is translated into French and analyzed by Gilbert Dagron, *Constantinople imaginaire: Études sur le recueil des Patria* (Paris: Presses universitaires de France, 1984), 191–314. For the early Ottoman texts on the Hagia Sophia by Yusuf bin Musa (1479) and Shemseddin (1480), see Felix Tauer, "Notice sur les versions persanes de la legénde de l'Edification d'Ayasofya," in *Fuat Köprülü Armağanı* (Istanbul: Osman Yalcin, 1953), 487–94. For a discussion of the conversion of the Hagia Sophia and other churches, see Süleyman Kinimtayif, *Converted Byzantine Churches in Istanbul: Their Transformation into Mosques and Masjids* (Istanbul: Ege Yayinları, 2001).

13. Muslim martyrs associated with early Muslim attempts to conquer Constantinople, like Abū Ayyūb al-Anṣārī (whose tomb was discovered by Mehmed II outside the city walls) and Sayyid Baṭṭāl, were reported to have prayed in the Hagia Sophia; see Necipoğlu, "Life of an Imperial Monument," 200. For more on al-Anṣārī, see Nancy Khalek, "Dreams of Hagia Sophia: The Muslim Siege of Constantinople in 674 CE, Abū Ayyūb al-Anṣārī, and the Medieval Islamic Imagination," in *The Islamic Scholarly Tradition: Studies in History, Law and Thought in Honor of Professor Michael Allan Cook*, ed. Asad Q. Ahmed, Behnam Sadeghi, and Michael Bonner (Leiden: Brill, 2011), 131–46 and below. I would like to thank Dr. Khalek for generously sharing a draft of the article.
14. Yerasimos, *Légendes*, 121–22. For a more extensive description of Khiḍr's role in the building and renovation of the Hagia Sophia, see Evliya Efendi's *Narrative of Travels in Europe, Asia, and Africa*, trans. Joseph Von Hammer-Purgstall (New York: Johnson Reprint Corp., 1968). Evliya Efendi and other Ottoman sources are discussed in Franke's extensive appendix which includes excerpts from Evliya Efendi and other Ottoman sources. See *Begegnung mit Khidr*.
15. The collapse of its eastern semi-dome had occurred on the night of the Prophet's birth and, according to various accounts, it was Muhammad himself who had sanctioned its rebuilding with mortar made from Meccan earth. See Necipoğlu, "Life of an Imperial Monument," 198, Cyril Mango, "Byzantine Writers on the Fabric of Hagia Sophia," in *Hagia Sophia from the Age of Justinian to the Present*, ed. Mark and Çakmak, 41–56 and Mango, *Hagia Sophia: A Vision for Empires* (Istanbul: Ertuğ & Kocabıyık, 1997), lii. According to legend, the mortar was mixed with the prophet's saliva and water. For more on these accounts, see Franke, "Khidr in Istanbul," 42–3.

16. Çiğdem Kafescioğlu, *Constantinopolis/Istanbul: Cultural Encounter, Imperial Vision, and the Construction of the Ottoman Capital* (University Park: Pennsylvania State University Press, 2009), 6. See, also, Yerasimos, *Légendes*, 203–10 and Franke, "Khidr in Istanbul." Khiḍr has long been linked to the city of Edirne. The most important site is the station of Khiḍr (Hızırlık).
17. For a discussion of the myth of the divine origins of the church and its incorporation into Ottoman accounts, see Yerasimos, *Légendes*, 120 and Franke, "Khidr in Istanbul." Many of the Hagia Sophia's Christian mosaics were not covered until decades after the conquest. Cyril Mango thinks it was not until the Ottoman repairs of 1607–9 that the figure of Christ at the center of the dome was removed. Mango, *Hagia Sophia*, l. According to Hasluck, other mosaics were not obscured until as late as 1717. See Frederick Hasluck, *Christianity and Islam under the Sultans* (Oxford: Clarendon Press, 1929), 9–11. There is an extensive amount of material on these mosaics. See, especially, Cyril Mango, *Materials for the Study of the Mosaics of St. Sophia in Istanbul* (Washington, D.C.: Dumbarton Oaks, 1962), 87–91 and Robert Nelson, *Hagia Sophia, 1850–1950: Holy Wisdom Modern Monument* (Chicago: University of Chicago Press, 1989), 19–20.
18. Although the emperor is commonly identified as Leo VI (886–912), Mango believes that the figure could just as well be Basil I (867–86) who also did major work on the Hagia Sophia; Mango, *Hagia Sophia*, xlix.
19. Mango, *Hagia Sophia*, 14.
20. *Ghāzī* is literally translated as "one who engages in raids against infidels." The term took on a variety of meanings during the Ottoman period and became a controversial term in the formation of Ottoman history. For a study of some of the definitions and implications of the term in Ottoman history, see Cemal Kafadar, *Between Two Worlds* (Berkeley: University of California Press, 1995). For the role of these *ghāzīs* in the Arab-Byzantine encounters of the seventh to tenth centuries, see Marius Canard, "Les expeditions des arabes contre Constantinople dans l'histoire et dans la légende," *Journal Asiatique* 208 (1926): 61–121.
21. For medieval accounts of these graves, see Nadia Maria El-Cheikh, "Byzantium through the Islamic prism," in *The Crusades from the Perspective of Byzantium and the Muslim World* (Washington, D.C.: Dumbarton Oaks, 2000), ed. by Angeliki E. Laiou and Roy Parviz Mottahedeh 53–70 and Khalek, "Dreams of the Hagia Sophia."
22. Yerasimos, *Légendes*, ch. 6 and Khalek, "Dreams of Hagia Sophia."
23. Khiḍr's significance as an apocalyptic figure played a major role in linking some of these sites. For an excellent study that touches upon the relationship between Khiḍr and the role of Jerusalem at the end of time, see Gülru Necipoğlu, "The Dome of the Rock as Palimpsest: ʿAbd al-Malik's Grand Narrative and Sultan Süleyman's Glosses," *Muqarnas* 25 (2008): 17–105. I would like to express my gratitude for the author's generosity in sharing this text.

24. Nikita Elisséeff, *La description de Damas d'Ibn ʿAsākir* (Damascus: Institute Français de Damas, 1959), 20. Flood argues that al-Walīd found Khiḍr in the central *mihrab*. See Finbarr Barry Flood, *The Great Mosque of Damascus: Studies on the Making of an Umayyad Visual Culture*, Islamic History and Civilization, Studies and Texts 33, ed. Wadad Kadi (Leiden: Brill, 2001), 120–21 (n. 38).
25. Elisséeff, *La description*, 20.
26. ʿAlī ibn Abī Bakr al-Harawī, *A Lonely Wayfarer's Guide to Pilgrimage: ʿAlī ibn Abīi Bakr al-Harawī's Kitāb al-Ishārāt ilā Maʿrifat al-Ziyārāt*, trans. and intro. Josef W. Meri (Princeton, NJ: Darwin, 2004), 59.
27. Cited in al-Harawī, *Lonely Wayfarer*, 59.
28. Rudolf Kriss and Hubert Kriss-Heinrich, *Volksglaube im Bereich des Islam* (Wiesbaden: Otto Harrassowitz, 1960), 1:213.
29. Aubaille-Sallenave, "Al-Khidr, 'L'Homme au Manteau Vert,'" 26.
30. There are a number of traditions about the conquest of Constantinople. Many of these are apocalyptic in nature and are discussed in Yerasimos, *Légendes*, ch. 6 and Necipoğlu, "Life of an Imperial Monument," 199.
31. The argument is usually made for the many formal associations between the Umayyad Mosque of Damascus, the Mosque of Al-Aqṣā and al-Walīd's restorations to the Prophet's Mosque in Medina. Flood argues for the incorporation of Constantinople models and cites criticisms against al-Walīd for making the Great Mosque of Damascus look too much like a church. See Flood, *Great Mosque of Damascus*, ch. 1. Nancy Khalek, who examines Damascus and the Umayyad Mosque within a network of Eastern Mediterranean cities and other building activity in Syria, focuses much more on the negotiations between Christian and Muslim tradition and identity in the seventh and eighth centuries. See Khalek, *Damascus after the Muslim Conquest: Text and Image in Early Islam* (New York: Oxford University Press, 2010) and "From Byzantium to Early Islam," Introduction.
32. Flood, *Great Mosque of Damascus*, 2; Jean Sauvaget, "Le plan antique de Damas," *Syria* 26 (1949): 314–19.
33. An eleventh-century legend, picked up and transmitted by Ibn ʿAsākir and Ibn Jubayr, states that the Church of St. John was divided between Muslims and Christians. Other accounts suggest that Muslims and Christians prayed within the same pagan enclosure but not within the church proper, for example Elisséeff, *La description*, 32–33. The early history of the Great Mosque of Damascus is still a subject of controversy. For an early overview, see K. A. C. Creswell, *A Short Account of Early Muslim Architecture* (Beirut: Libraire du Liban, 1968), 44–81. Although the question of the use of the space after the initial Muslim conquest is beyond the scope of this inquiry, it needs to be addressed through the much more difficult question of how early Muslims distinguished themselves from Christians and Jews. For more on this, see Fred Donner, "From Believers to Muslims: Confessional Self-Identity in the Early Islamic Community," *Al-Abḥāth* 50–51 (2002–3): 9–52 and S. Bashear, "Qibla Musharriqa and Early Muslim Prayer in Churches," *Muslim World*

81, nos. 3–4 (1991): 267–82 and Khalek, "From Byzantium to Early Islam." A fascinating study of the Islamization of the cult of John the Baptist is found in Khalek, *Damascus after the Muslim Conquest*, 117–20.

34. Khiḍr sites are found in a number of places that went through extensive conversions and were inhabited by a mixture of Muslims and Christians. Some of these sites, such as the former cathedral of St. George, make explicit connections to Khiḍr through inscriptions. See G. Jerphanion, "Le lieu du combat de Saint Georges a Beyrouth," *Mélanges de l'université Saint-Joseph*, vol. 2 (Beyrouth: Imprimerie Catholique, 1927), 251–65. For sites in Palestine, see Tewfik Canaan, *Mohammedan Saints and Sanctuaries in Palestine* (1927 reprint from *Journal of the Palestine Oriental Society*; Jerusalem: Ariel Publishing House, 1970) and, more specifically, A. Augistinoviç, *El-Khadr and the Prophet Elijah* (Jerusalem: Franciscan Printing Press, 1972).

35. For more on this process, see Ethel Sara Wolper, "Khidr, Elvan Çelebi and the Conversion of Sacred Sanctuaries in Anatolia," *Muslim World* 90 (2000): 309–22 and Oya Pancaraoğlu, "The Itinerant Dragon Slayer: Forging Paths of Image and Identity in Medieval Anatolia," in *Encounters with Islam: The Medieval Mediterranean Experience*, ed. Robert Ousterhout and D. Fairchild Ruggles, *Gesta* 4/2 (2004): 151–64.

36. For more information on the uses of saints George and Theodore in Anatolia, see Christopher Walter, *The Warrior Saints in Byzantine Art and Tradition* (Aldershot: Ashgate, 2003) and, more specifically, Speros Vryonis Jr., *The Decline of Medieval Hellenism in Asia Minor* (Berkeley: University of California Press, 1971), 34–42, 197, 440, 474, 485. Matt Immerzeel has written a series of articles on depictions of warrior saints in Syria and Jordan; see, for example, "Divine Cavalry: Mounted Saints in Middle Eastern Christian Art," *East and West in the Crusader States: Contexts-Contacts-Confirmations*, ed. Krijnie Ciggaar and Herman Teule (Dudley, MA: Leuven, 2003), 265–86.

37. These coins have attracted a great deal of scholarly attention. For two fascinating studies of St. George in the world of twelfth-century numismatics, see Nicholas Lowick, "The Religious, the Royal and the Popular in the Figural Coinage of the Jazīra," in *The Art of Syria and the Jazīra 1100–1250*, Oxford Studies in Islamic Art 1, ed. Julian Raby (Oxford: Oxford University Press, 1985), 159–74 and Rustam Shukurov, "Christian Elements in the Identity of the Anatolian Turkmen," in *Cristianità d'Occidente e cristianità d'Oriente*, 2 vols. (Spoleto: La Sade della Fondazione, 2004), 1:707–64. I would like to thank Tom Sinclair for his generosity in bringing this article to my attention.

38. For more on St. George and the "Georgic" Cults, see H. S. Haddad, "Georgic" Cults and Saints of the Levant," *Numen* 16 (April 1969): 21–39.

39. John Cantacuzenas (1347–54) wrote that the Turks worshiped St. George in the figure of Khiḍr-Elias According to local tradition, Hıdrellez. See Vryonis, *Decline of Medieval Hellenism*, 485.

40. A number of ancient and Christian sites in central and northern Anatolia can be found in Franz Cumont, *Studia Pontica* 1–3 (Bruxelles: H. Lamertin, 1903–10).
41. These sites are summarized in Ahmet Yaşar Ocak, *Islām-Türk Inançlarında Hızır Yahut Hızır Ilyas Kültü* (Ankara: Ankara Üniversitesi Basimevi, 1958), 128–29. Although some of Ocak's information comes from Evliya Çelebi [*Evliya Çelebi Seyahatnamesi* (Istanbul, 1314–50) 2:188], I have only included sites discussed by medieval authors in this route.
For more on the monastery in Sinope, see Ibn Battuta, *Travels in Asia and Africa, 1325–1354*, tr. H. A. R. Gibb (London: Hakluyt Society, 1962), 466. Gibb translates *ribāṭ* as hermitage. There is a discussion of a Khiḍirlik mountain, a Khiḍr tomb in Çorum, and the Sivas Ulu Cami column in Hikmet Tanyu, *Ankara ve Çevresinde Adak ve Adak Yerleri* (Ankara: Ankara Üniversitesi Basimevi, 1967), 165, 190, and 281.
Also of significance in linking these sites to other pilgrimage routes is a Khiḍr site in Kayseri that has been active since 1241. See Tahsın Özgüç and Mahmut Akok, "Alayhan, Öresun Han ve Hızırilyas Köşkü," *Belleten* 21/81 (1957): 139–48.
42. Suleyman Kirimtayif citing Ayvansaray. See Kirimtayif, *Converted Byzantine Churches in Istanbul: Their Transformation into Mosques and Masjids* (Istanbul: Ege Yayinlari, 2001), 11.

6

Foundational Legends, Shrines, and Ismāʿīlī Identity in Gorno-Badakhshan, Tajikistan

Jo-Ann Gross

> Each of the kings (*mīrs*) of Shughnān[1] and noble *sayyids* of Kuhistān records his line of descent (*silsila-yi ansāb*) in a book with the genealogy (*nasab-nāma*) continuously transmitted orally from his ancestors, [including] where they came from, [how] they became established in Kuhistān, what kind of rank they achieved and how they took [them], such as the rank of shaykh and *mullā* and *rāʾis-i qawm* [clan leader], and [their] teaching (*taʿlīm*) and guidance (*hidāyat*), and the likes of those [who] came from Khurāsān accomplished their activities in this province and passed from the transitory world.[2]

MĪRZĀ FAZL ʿALĪ Beg Surkh Afsar, the author of three supplements to Mīrzā Sang Muḥammad Badakhshī's history of Badakhshan, *Taʾrīkh-i Badakhshān*, wrote this passage in 1907.[3] He emphasizes here and several times in his text the importance of oral tradition in Badakhshan, his own primary source of knowledge.[4] Local foundational narratives, which continue to inform the communal and religious identity of Ismāʿīlīs in Badakhshan today, trace the ancestry of the rulers, *pīrs*, *khalīfas*, and *shaykhs* of Shughnan and the surrounding regions to several foundational figures, who are believed to have arrived in the valley in the eleventh and twelfth centuries.[5] The purpose of this study is to explore the geography of sacred knowledge in the Pamir through such foundational traditions and discuss their relationship to the present-day sacred landscape of shrine networks in the regions of Shughnan (Shughnon), Rosht-qalʿa (Roshtkala), Ishkāshīm (Ishkoshim), and Wakhān (Vakhon).

Using oral narratives, genealogies, and historical literature, we will discuss how local traditions and networks of shrines intersect in ways that express Ismāʿīlī religious legitimacy and communal identity and map a sacred Islamic history that links local and distant cultural geographies and regional and universal traditions. We will focus on two interrelated themes: first, foundational narratives of Ismāʿīlism in Gorno-Badakhshan, based on nineteenth- and twentieth-century written sources that are largely oral in origin, and second, stories linked with a network of shrines in Shughnan, Rosht-qalʿa, and along the Panj River in the Wakhan region close to the Afghanistan border. Of particular importance to this study are shrines and oral traditions that authenticate links to the family of the Prophet Muḥammad (*ahl al-bayt*) through ʿAlī b. Ḥusayn (known as Zayn al-ʿĀbidīn; d. 680/714), the third Ismāʿīlī Imām and son of Imām al-Ḥusayn (d. 680), Muḥammad al-Bāqir (d. ca. 732), the fourth Ismāʿīlī Imam and son of ʿAlī b. Ḥusayn, and Muslim foundational figures and local religious figures in Badakhshan.[6] As will be shown, shrines associated with these bringers of Islam serve both as spiritual markers of the Islamic sanctification of the community and as links with the origins of the Ismāʿīlī Imamate. Finally, it is hoped that this study will provide a useful approach to the local landscape of sacred shrines in Central Eurasia, but not one defined by a Great Tradition/Little Tradition perspective. My main theoretical interests concern the relationship between foundational narratives, genealogical traditions, and the construction of sacred space, particularly the role of oral history and memory and the geography of sacred knowledge. Specifically, I am interested in the ways in which narrative traditions about religious progenitors in Badakhshan contribute to the genesis of Ismāʿīlī communal identity, and how those traditions are linked with shrines where sacred power is localized.[7]

The spread of Nizārī Ismāʿīlī Shīʿism to Badakhshan took place through the activities of individual *dāʿīs* or missionaries.[8] Ismāʿīlīs belong to the Shīʿa branch of Islam and recognize seven Imams or spiritual leaders as rightful successors to Muḥammad, based on descent from ʿAlī b. Abī Ṭālib, Muḥammad's cousin and son-in-law and the fourth caliph in Sunnī Islam, and Fāṭima, Muḥammad's daughter and ʿAlī's wife.[9] Following the death in 765 of Jaʿfar al-Ṣādiq, the fifth Ismāʿīlī Imam, there was a split over the succession since Jaʿfar al-Ṣādiq's son, Ismāʿīl b. Jaʿfar, died before he did. Ismāʿīlīs accept Jaʿfar al-Sādiq's son as his successor, whereas Twelver Shīʿīs reject him and instead accept Ismāʿīl's younger brother, Mūsā al-Kāẓim, as the true Imam. Ismāʿīlīs believe in the concept of ongoing revelation through the guidance of the *Imām al-qāʾim* (the living Imam). The authority to interpret the inner meaning (*bāṭin*) of the Qur'ān lies solely with the Imam as the direct descendant of ʿAlī. The Ismāʿīlīs of Badakhshan belong to the Nizārī community, whose members follow the Aga Khan; the present and 49th Imam is Prince Karim al-Ḥusseini Aga Khan IV.[10]

In his study of the Pamiri Ismāʿīlī Ṣūfī, Mubārak-i Wakhānī, Abdulmamad Iloliev identifies two periods in the development of Ismāʿīlism in Badakhshan, that of the *Daʿwat-i Nāṣir* (Mission of Nāṣir-i Khusraw) and that of the *Panj-Tanī* (The Fivers).[11] The earliest propagation of Ismāʿīlism to Badakhshan is commonly ascribed to the celebrated Ismāʿīlī poet-philosopher and *ḥujjat* (chief *dāʿī*) of Khurasan, Nāṣir-i Khusraw (1004–ca. 1077).[12] After his conversion to Ismāʿīlism in the Fāṭimid capital of Cairo, he established close relations with the Fāṭimid caliph, al-Mustanṣir bi'llāh (d. 1095), who appointed him to the position of *ḥujjat* as the Imam's representative in Khurasan. Nāṣir-i Khusraw returned to Balkh in 1052 to spread the faith. He was forced to flee in 1060 due to his controversial writings and missionary activities, and settled in the remote valley of Yumgān in present-day Badakhshan in Afghanistan, where he remained until his death.[13] Following the defeat of Alamūt in 1256, when the Mongols destroyed the fortress of the Ismāʿīlīs in the Alborz Mountains, local *pir*s apparently exerted more autonomy, especially in more remote areas such as the Pamir.[14] Many Ismāʿīlīs took refuge by fleeing to regions such as Badakhshan. "Hence, the process of Islamisation or rather the indigenization of Islam in the region was strongly influenced by and increasingly active during the asylum-seeking movement of the post-Alamūt period."[15] Local traditions in Badakhshan, moreover, trace the process of Islamization, and its implicit connection with the family of the Prophet, to a series of divinely inspired missionaries who are described as having arrived in the twelfth century, the interim period between Nāṣir-i Khusraw and the Alamūt defeat.[16]

The political fate of the Ismāʿīlī populations in the Pamir regions of present-day Tajikistan and Afghanistan is tied to the period of British imperial expansion into India and the resultant competition between Russia and Britain, known as "The Great Game." Since 1895, when the Pamir Agreement was established by an Anglo-Russian Commission, the Panj River, the upper course of the Amu Darya, divided the previously culturally contiguous regions of present-day Afghanistan and Tajikistan Badakhshan (Gorno-Badakhshan). The establishment of the Wakhan Corridor was intended to create a neutral zone between the British and Russians, who had long been engaged in competition for land and influence. Jonah Steinberg summarizes the situation:

> It was at the end of this period that national boundaries were formed; these boundaries are crucial for our discussion of the local experience of geopolitics. Until the 1870's, the valleys of the Pamir (as well as some of those in what is now Pakistan and Afghanistan) constituted a number of small.... principalities who maintained allegiance and paid tribute only to the Mir of Badakhshan. In 1877 and 1878 the Emirate of Bukhara seized Darwaz in the Pamir. Remaining adjacent areas stayed under the control of the Afghan Emir through an agreement dating from 1873 that had allocated to them Wakhan, Shughnan, and Rushan. The Afghans seized Shughnan in 1883 as a response to the Russian advance... A number of conflicts followed, until the Emir of Afghanistan finally settled on the river as the border in 1893 and made it part of an accord that established the Wakhan corridor as a buffer zone between the Russian and British Empires.[17]

In 1920, Soviet rule was imposed on the right side of the Panj River, and in 1925 the Autonomous Region of Gorno-Badakhshan (GBAO) was created and attached to the Tajik Autonomous Soviet Republic of Tajikistan within the Uzbek Soviet Socialist Republic; in 1929 it was added to the newly created Tajik Soviet Socialist Republic (Tajik SSR).[18] Following the breakup of the Soviet Union in 1991, Tajikistan became independent, but due to regional and ethnic tensions, civil war broke out in 1992. From 1923 until the Tajik Civil War in 1992, particularly from 1936 when the Soviets closed the border between Afghanistan and Tajikistan, the Ismāʿīlī community in Badakhshan was isolated from the wider world community and their religious practices were severely limited.[19] Despite severe restrictions imposed on them by Soviet authorities, dynastic *pir*s and *khalifa*s retained their prestige among the Nizārī Ismāʿīlī communities, and residents continued to be guided by them in family matters.[20] The Soviet-Afghan War (1979–89) was a difficult period for Pamiris, since Soviet troops occupied Afghan Wakhan, and the Afghan regions of Ishkashim and Shughnan served as the base for Aḥmad Shāh Masʿūd, the Tajik *mujahedīn* leader known as the Lion of the Panjshīr Valley. Soviets were thus suspicious of Pamiris on both sides of the Panj River.

The Tajik Civil War (1992–97) that erupted following the breakup of the Soviet Union brought immense suffering to Tajiks throughout the county and a humanitarian disaster in GBAO, especially when coupled with the economic collapse that ensued.[21] Beginning in 1993, the Aga Khan Development Network (AKDN) provided aid that saved many Pamiris from starvation. Since that time, the AKDN has been very active in the region, focusing on economic and cultural development, education, institution building, infrastructure projects, and health care, among other programs. The Ismāʿīlī Tarīqah Boards, reopening of relations with the international Ismāʿīlī community, and direct contact with the Aga Khan himself through his visits to Gorno-Badakhshan have had a significant impact on social and religious institutions, politics, education, and culture in Badakhshan.[22]

Shāh Khāmōsh and Ismāʿīlī Foundational Narratives

Ismāʿīlī foundational narratives and genealogical charters dating from the nineteenth century to the present map an Islamic topography that traces the introduction of Islam to the region and connects the Imamate to Ismāʿīlī figures, Sufi *shaykhs*, and shrines. Fazl ʿAlī Beg, in his 1907 supplement to the eighteenth-century history, the *Taʾrīkh-i Badakhshān*, lists four ancestors of the *qawm-i Kuhistān-i Badakhshān*: Shāh(-i) Khāmōsh (Shoh Khomūsh), Shāh Kāshān (Shoh Koshon), Shāh Malang (Shoh Malang), and Bābā ʿUmār Yumgī (Bobo ʿUmor Yumg).[23] Two other local sources dating from the early twentieth century trace a similar foundational narrative that maps an Islamic topography through the family of the Prophet, the Ismāʿīlī Imams and a group of divinely inspired *sayyids* who arrive in the Shughnan valley in the twelfth century, namely the *Taʾrīkh-i Mulk-i Shughnān* (Taj. Taʾrīkhi Mulki Shughnon) of Sayyid Haydarshāh Mubārakshāhzāda and the *Taʾrīkh-i Badakhshān* of Qurbān Muḥammadzāda Ākhun[d]-Sulaymān and Maḥabbat Shāhzāda Sayyid Fuṭūrshāh. In contrast to Fazl ʿAlī Beg's history, the latter sources exclude Bābā ʿUmār Yumgī and list Shāh Burhān Valī (Shoh Burhon) instead.[24] Qurbān Muḥammadzāda Ākhun-Sulaymān and Maḥabbat Shāhzāda Sayyid Fuṭūr-Shāh describe the four men as *qalandars*, brothers who emigrated from Isfahan. Other important sources include the historical and ethnographic studies of Russian scholars such as A. Bobrinksoi, V. Ivanov, M. Andreev, and A. Semenov, among others, as well as European travel narratives such as those of Thomas Gordon, Ole Olufsen, and Aurel Stein.[25]

Fazl ʿAlī Beg's history is notable because he highlights the prominent role of Sayyid Mīr Ḥasan Khāmōsh (1066–1136), a Sufi and *sayyid* whom he describes as the primordial ancestor of the shahs and *pirs* of Shughnan and the spiritual link between them and the family of the Prophet Muḥammad.[26]

> To this day the lineage [*nisbat*] of the great *shāhzādas* [descendants of shahs] of Kuhistān is from Shāh Khāmōsh. Each branch [*shuʿbat*] pos-

sesses a mountain or castle. Some of them have positions of rulership, while others are *pirs* and *murshids* [spiritual advisors] occupied with the guidance and teaching of religion.[27]

According to the author, Shāh Khāmōsh was a descendant of Imām Ḥusayn, the son of Sayyid Ḥaydar Isfahānī, and was born in Isfāhān in 1066.[28] His miraculous abilities became apparent at the age of twelve, when he foresaw the birth of the Hanbalite scholar, *sayyid*, and eponym of the Qādirīya Sufi order, ʿAbd al-Qādir Jīlānī (1077/8–1166).[29] Fazl ʿAlī Beg notes that Shāh Khāmōsh was *walī* on his mother's side and *walī Uwaysī*[30] on his father's side, and that the mothers of ʿAbd al-Qādir Jīlānī and Shāh Khāmōsh were sisters, both being daughters of Sayyid ʿAbdullāh Sawmaʿī.[31] Shāh Khāmōsh studied with his father until the age of 21, when he left for Baghdad to further his study of spiritual experience and esoteric science (*ʿilm-i ḥāl va ʿilm-i bāṭin niz kāmil*).[32]

According to the pilgrimage narrative related by Fazl ʿAlī Beg, within four days of his arrival, Shāh Khāmōsh met with ʿAbd al-Qādir Jīlānī, who was living in Baghdad, and they then set out for pilgrimage to Mecca to circumambulate the Kaʿba (*bayt al-muqaddas*) and to Medina to visit the tomb of the Prophet Muḥammad.[33] The author's account, as summarized below, authenticates the divine mission Shāh Khāmōsh was destined to carry out, establishes a lineage of sanctity that further strengthens his link to the *ahl al-bayt*, and documents his spiritual tie to the early Sufi master, Junayd al-Baghdādī (830–910).[34]

While Shāh Khāmōsh was absorbed in the contemplation and witnessing of the divine essence (*murāqaba va mushāhada*), the voice of Muḥammad suddenly called out from his tomb, but Shāh Khāmōsh did not respond. Muḥammad called, "I commanded Wārith Junayd to be selected to be the one."[35] Abū'l Qāsim al-Junayd al-Baghdādī was an important and influential Sufi of the Baghdad school who was known as the "Master of the Sect" (*Sayyid al-ṭāʾifa*). Junayd al-Baghdādī and ʿAbd al-Qādir Jīlānī appeared and completed the circumambulation of the Kaʿba. Junayd called Shāh Khāmōsh three times and told him to cease his contemplation, but Shāh Khāmōsh did not hear.[36] Junayd called, "We are the great *khalīfa* and there is a key to the treasury of the secrets of Divine unity (*ganjīna-ye asrār-i tawḥīd*)." Junayd then bestowed the key on Shāh Khāmōsh and ʿAbd al-Qādir Jīlānī and transmitted his spiritual knowledge to them.[37]

Junayd also commanded Shāh Khāmōsh to travel to Khuttalān (Khatlon)[38] to propagate Islam. Shāh Khāmōsh traveled with three companions, Shāh Malang, Shāh Kāshān, and Bābā ʿUmār Yumgī.[39] He arrived in Shughnan, which was then ruled by the princes of Kashgar, and turned his attention to the religious instruction of the populace (*taʿlīm-i ʿilm-i dīn va āmīn*).[40] He proved his spiritual abilities by curing Gulshakar, the ill 14-year-old daughter of the ruler of Shughnan. In gratitude, the governor offered her to Shāh Khāmōsh in marriage, the first of three marriages he made to the daughters of local rulers in Badakhshan and Khuttalan.[41] His marriage to Gulshakar established Shāh Khāmōsh as "the ancestor of the amirs and shahs of Shughnan (*awlād-i amīrān o shāhān-i Shughnān*)."

To fulfill the mission commanded of him by Junayd, Shāh Khāmōsh journeyed to Khuttalan (Khatlon) by way of Vanj, converting the population to Islam and intermarrying with local ruling families. He married the daughter of the ruler in Vanj, who bore him a son named Abū Yūsuf Shāh, and in Kulāb (Kulob) he married the daughter of Sayyid ʿAlī Shāh Valī.[42] When Sayyid ʿAlī Shāh Valī heard that Shāh Khāmōsh had arrived in Muʿminābād (Muminobod) he came out to meet him and presented him with a horse, and after some days he gave one of his three daughters to Shāh Khāmōsh in marriage. They resided in the village of Dara-yi Turkīya in the region of Kulab, where he also ordered Sayyid ʿAlī Shāh Valī to reside. In Fazl's ʿAlī Beg's time, the village was known as Langar-i Shāh Khāmōsh (Langari Shohi Khomush near Muminobod), where his shrine (fig. 6.1) and a recently renovated mosque are located.[43]

FIGURE 6.1 Entrance to the *mazār* of Shāh Khāmōsh, Langar-i Shāh Khāmōsh, Muʿminābād. © Jo-Ann Gross.

The travel narrative of Sir Thomas Edward Gordon, published in 1876,[44] contrasts with the above account in interesting ways. It includes an account of Shāh Khāmōsh's Islamizing role, which was related to him by his travel companion, Captain H. R. E. Trotter, whose assistant surveyor met with Yūsuf ʿAlī Shāh, the ruler and *pir* of Shughnan and Rushan at the time.[45]

> According to Shighni accounts, the family of the Shah of Shighnon originally came from Persia, and the first arrival from that country (said to have been between 500 and 700 years ago) was the Shah-i Khamosh, who was a Syud and a Fakir. The country was at that time in the hands of the Zardushtis (ancient Guebers—fire-worshippers), a powerful and learned race. The Shah-i Khamosh commenced to teach these people the Koran. There were already at this time Musulmans in the neighboring country of Darwaz, and many of them flocked into Shighnan as followers of Shah-i Khamosh. In about ten years he had converted large numbers of the people, and a religious war commenced, which ended in this leader wresting the kingdom from Kahakah, the ruler of Shighnan and Roshan under the Zardushtis, the seat of whose government was then at Balkh. After this the teaching of the people continued, and in ten years more all had been converted to the Shiah form of the Muhammadan faith.[46]

Gordon thus describes Shāh Khāmōsh as a Shīʿī Islamizer and *faqīr* (Sufi) who wrested control of Shughnan from the Zoroastrian ruler Qah-qaha (Kah-kaha), succeeded in converting the populace to Shīʿism, and established an ancestral line of descent for the local Muslim rulers.[47]

The *Taʾrīkhi Mulki Shughnon* of Sayyid Haydarshāh Mubārakshāhzāda, which is based on his own knowledge and the oral accounts he collected from those with whom he was acquainted, includes a narrative about the victory of Shāh Malang (Shoh Malang), whom he describes as a dervish, over Zoroastrianism, and the subsequent arrival in Shughnan of Shāh Khāmōsh. He writes,

> After Chinese rule, a fire-worshipper named Riv-i Farhād was the ruler of Shughnan in Ver. He called for the people to practice Zoroastrianism until Shāh Darvīsh—Sayyid Shāh Malang—removed the *farr* [divine glory] of Riv-i Farhād with his miraculous *duʿa* [supplication] and he followed the dervish path for five years. After that, Shāh Khāmōsh came from Shiraz to Sheva by way of Afghanistan and while he was

> asleep a pigeon received the divine command to nest in his cap and in his sleep he received a revelation that that very pigeon would not fly until its offspring took flight, and Shāh Malang stayed for five years. After that, they say he came to Shughnan and ruled for six years. After that he left and one of his *murīds* [disciples], Sayyid Shāh Malang ʿAbd al-Muḥammad, came to the throne.[48]

A 1992 publication in Tajik of a selection of oral narratives contains a similar narrative about Shāh Malang and Shāh Khāmōsh, including Shāh Malang's banishment of Riv-i Farhad with his miraculous invocation (*duʿā*) and the story of the pigeon and Shāh Khāmōsh. However, the latter tradition adds,

> Shoh Khomush remained in Shughnon for six years and then traveled to Kulob by way of Darvoz. In Kulob, Shoh Khomush lived in the village of Muminobod. Many people in Shughnon converted to Islam, and because of that many khalifas were brought there from Shughnon. The mazor of Shoh Khomush is located in Kulob, and many people make the pilgrimage [*ziyorat*].[49]

The accounts described above illustrate a continuous narrative tradition that delineates the transmission of Islam to Shughnan and Khuttalan and traces the genealogical link between the rulers and religious authorities in Badakhshan and the family of the Prophet Muḥammad through Shāh Khāmōsh and Shāh Malang. The *sayyid* and Sufi status of Shāh Khāmōsh as well as the transmission of *maʿrifa* (spiritual knowledge) and the secrets of *tawḥīd* (unity of God) to him by Junayd al-Baghdādī, as chosen by the Prophet, incorporates the Prophet into the history of Badakhshan. The physical concretization of this narrative framework in the sacred landscape and the process of its broader incorporation of the Ismāʿīlī Imamate is the subject of the balance of this study, through a discussion of Ismāʿīlī shrine networks in the present-day regions of Shughnan (Shughnon), Rosht-qalʿa (Roshtkala), Ishkashim (Ishkoshim) and Wakhan (Vakhon).

Shrine Networks, Sacred Space, and the Motif of the Cave

The Central Eurasian shrine landscape is diverse and is associated with Sufi figures, early Islamic figures, Shīʿī Imams, political rulers, and local village elders. The study of Islamic shrines in Central Eurasia, where they are so ubiquitous a part of the sacred landscape, includes architectural, archaeological, historical, religious, and ethnographic works that focus on a variety of social, economic, and political aspects, including shrine administration and shrine families, communal identity, assimilation and conversion, concepts of sainthood, political roles, patronage and endowment, hagiographical traditions, shrines and communal identity, ritual and practice, and pilgrimage. Western scholarship on shrines in early modern Central Eurasia, the majority of which concern urban Sufi shrines, is dominated by historians and, secondarily, by art and architectural historians.[50] Soviet-era studies of shrines, in contrast, are comprised mostly of archaeological and architectural works that focus on the structural development, decorative techniques, and styles as well as the function of various Central Eurasian shrines.

The Islamic shrines of Tajikistan remain largely unstudied by Western scholars, due to the limited access to them until recently and to the prevailing preference for the study of well-documented, urban shrines. Although there has been a notable shift over the past several decades, the two-tiered Great Tradition/Little Tradition, normative Islam/popular Islam conceptual framework, which relegates local shrines to the domain of folk culture and privileges the urban over the rural periphery, is still operative in some scholarly works, especially in reference to shrines situated in remote regions such as Badakhshan (fig. 6.2).[51] Until recently, Soviet-era archaeological, ethnographic, and architectural studies formed the bulk of scholarship on shrines

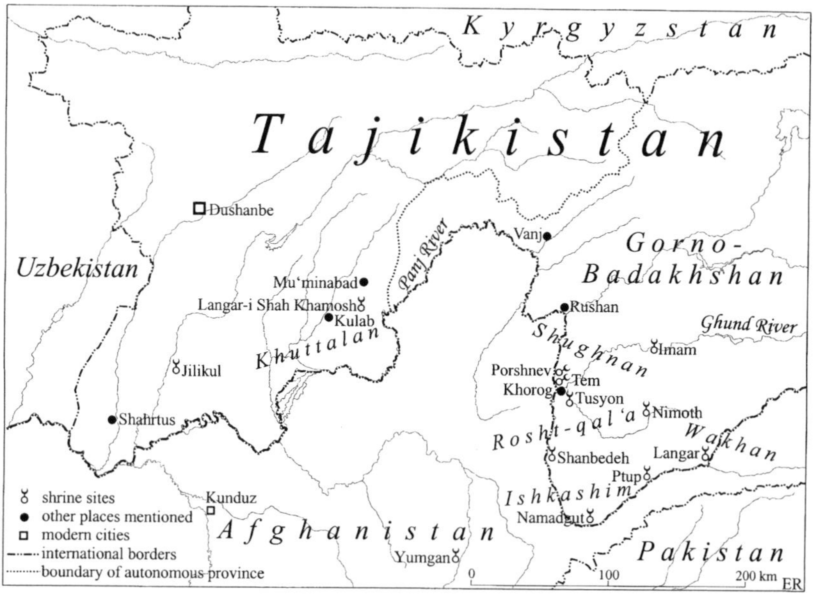

FIGURE 6.2 Map of Gorno-Badakhshan with shrine locations. © Eric Ross.

in Tajikistan.[52] Following the Tajikistan Civil War and with the revival of Islamic identity and the post-Soviet nation-building process, a new focus of interest on the history and culture of Islamic shrines emerged.[53]

When this author visited the *āstān* (oston) of Shāh Burhān (Shohi Burhon) in 2005, located in Shambedeh in the district of Ishkashim, Shogunbek Bozor, then 82 years old, related the following tradition that establishes Zayn al-ʿĀbidīn (Zaynulobiddin) (d. 714), the third Nizārī Ismāʿīlī Imam and son of Imām al-Ḥusayn,[54] as the primordial founder of the Ismāʿīlī community and links him to Shāh Khāmōsh (Shoh Khomush) and Shāh Burhān (Shohi Burhon).

> I can tell you what I have learned from my ancestors and the great ones of our region about the *mazor* of Shohi Burhon. Shohi Burhon and other famous religious people came to Badakhshon to spread Islam and show the people the right path. Three religious figures came from Khuroson in Iran. First came Zaynulobiddin, then Shohi Burhon, and then Sayyid Khomush. They came through Zebak.[55] They taught people about Ḥazrati Muḥammad and the Ismāʿīlī doctrine. When they came to Badakhshon they asked people about their lives and problems. They spoke Arabic. There were learned men [*donishmandon*] among our people who could translate. They brought the true faith and spread it among the people. Shohi Burhon went from village to village and met with people and solved their problems. For example, when he came to our village, the people had many problems. One was that they had no water and were suffering because of it. He made a big canal and solved their problems. It was very difficult work, but Shohi Burhon accomplished it with the help of God, and people believed in him. He had followers [*muridon*] in every village. Sometimes they went to the villages together. The main residence of Shohi Burhon was in Roshtkala [District] in the village of Tusyon. The *mazor* of Shohi Burhon is in our village [Shanbedeh].

Shogunbek Bozor's account maps a broad spiritual geography that unites the Hijaz, Khurasan, and Badakhshan through a commonly defined Islamic genealogy that extends over a sacralized time from the eighth century to the present.

Sayyid Shohikalon Shohzodamuhammad (b. 1921), a prominent *pir*, descendant of Shāh Malang, and resident of the village of Porshnev in Shughnan District, recounted a tradition involving a network of four shrines sacralized by a cave into which Zayn al-ʿĀbidīn entered and exited (fig. 6.3).[56] The first cave marks the *gumbaz* of Zayn al-ʿĀbidīn in the village of Tem in the district of Shughnan.[57] The second cave marks the *qadamgāh* of Muḥammad al-Bāqir (Imom Bokir), the son of Zayn al-ʿĀbidīn (Zaynulobiddin), in Imām (Imom) village in the Ghund valley of Shughnan. The third cave marks the shrine of Shāh ʿAbdāl (Shoh Abdol, i.e., Imām Muḥammad al-Bāqir) in Nimoth, located on the Ghund River in Rosht-qalʿa District, and the fourth cave marks the *mazār* of the Sufi traveler, Shāh Qambār-i Āftāb (Shoh Kambari Oftob) in Langar in Wakhan.[58]

> Zaynuloboddin was the Imom of the Time after Imom Ḥusayn. He came here from Medina. After all, imoms travel everywhere. He came to the gumbaz that is in Tem village [in Shughnon]. That is where he moved. Inside the gumbaz is a big stone, and in front of the stone is a cave. He entered this cave and came out in Ghund, where Imom Muḥammad Bokir was. That is why the name of the village became Imom. From Ghund he entered the cave again and came out in Shakhdara [Valley, in which Nimoth is located] and again entered there and came out in the Vakhon Valley [in Langar, the location of the shrine of Shoh Kambar] in the district of Ishkoshim and then he disappeared. It is unknown where he went from there.

Karim Karimov, the 67-year-old caretaker (*mutavallī*) of the *mazār* of Shāh ʿIsām al-Dīn (Shoh Isomiddin) in the village of Ptup in Wakhan continued the story of Shāh Qambār-i Āftāb (Shoh Kambari Oftob), the last link in the cave story of Sayyid Shohikalon Shohzodamuhammad. He related the following account (fig. 6.4), which was handed down to him from his grandfa-

FIGURE 6.3 Cave narrative of Sayyid Shohikalon Shohzodamuhammad. © Jo-Ann Gross.

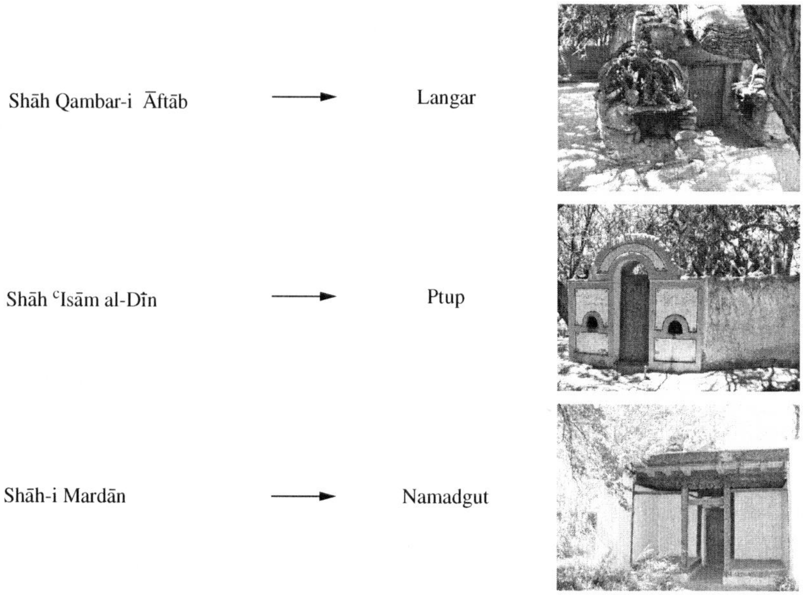

FIGURE 6.4 Narrative of Karim Karimov (Ptup, Wakhān). © Jo-Ann Gross.

ther, linking Shāh Qambār-i Āftāb to two other foundational figures, Shāh ʿIsām al-Dīn (Shoh Isomiddin) and Shāh-i Mardān (Shohi Mardon).[59]

> Between twelve to fourteen centuries ago, Shoh Isomiddin came to Badakhshan and settled in our village of Ptup. His grave is inside this mazor. In my mind, these great men never die. They are always in the heart of the *orifon* (*ʿārifān*) [friends of God].[60] Shoh Isomiddin's house and his walking stick are inside this mazor. Shoh Isomiddin put his stick in the ground and a tree grew from it. He came to Badakhshan with seven men. One of them was Shoh Kambar, who settled in the village of Langar. Another was Shohi Mardon, who settled in Namadgut. And a third, Shoh Isomiddin, settled here in Ptup. Our people had strong faith in Shoh Isomiddin and saved this mazor. Except for his grave, his stick and the stone with the *chiroghdon*[61] are inside this mazor.

Through their physical presence, the shrines of the foundational figures, Shāh Qambār-i Āftāb, Shāh-i Mardān and Shāh ʿIsām al-Dīn, all of which are located along the Panj River in Wakhan, chart a spiritual geography that marks the Islamic identity of the three communities. Shāh ʿIsām al-Dīn's

FIGURE 6.5 Sacred tree. *Mazār* of Shāh ʿIsām al-Dīn (Ptup, Wakhān). © Jo-Ann Gross.

miraculous creation of a tree (fig. 6.5) from his stick is symbolic of the genesis and propagation of Islam centuries ago as well as the *pir*'s own miraculous abilities.

Conclusion

The shrines of Zayn al-ʿĀbidīn, Muḥammad al-Bāqir, Shāh Qambār-i Āftāb, Shāh ʿIsām al-Dīn, and Shāh-i Mardān, and the oral traditions attached to them, reflect a sacred temporal and spatial continuum that links a universal Islamic history with local Ismāʿīlī identity. Fazl ʿAlī Beg identifies Sayyid Mīr Ḥasan Shāh Khāmōsh as the primordial ancestor of the rulers and religious authorities of Shughnan and the spiritual link between them and the family of the Prophet Muḥammad, as authenticated through genealogies and traditions passed to him. The shrines of Badakhshan examined in this paper are authenticated through narrative claims linked to Mecca and Medina and lineages of sanctity tied to the family of the Prophet Muḥammad and the Imamate. They serve as visual and spiritual markers of the Islamic sanctification of the communities in which they are found and reflect an implicit relationship between the emergence of the Ismāʿīlī community in Badakhshan and the sacred landscape of shrines. Two primary foundational narratives trace this emergence. One narrative hagiographical framework set in the eighth century involves the appearance in Badakhshan of the third and fourth Ismāʿīlī Imams of Medina, Zayn al-ʿĀbidīn and Muḥammad al-Bāqir. The other narrative framework is set in the twelfth century and involves Shāh Khāmōsh, whose spiritual knowledge and divine mission to spread Islam in Khuttalan (Khatlon) was transmitted to him by Junayd al-Baghdādī as chosen by Muḥammad. Despite the lack of certitude regarding the actual religious and sectarian identities of Shāh Khāmōsh and his fellow travelers, they are accepted as an integral part of the Ismāʿīlī *daʿwa* and the formation of the indigenous *Panj-Tanī* (Fiver) faith in Badakshan. In the case of Shāh Khāmōsh, the sacred history persists through the continuation of dynastic families of *mīr*s, *khalifa*s, and *pir*s who trace their descent to these figures.

The foundational narrative passed down through the family of Shogunbek Bozor of Shanbedeh village begins with Zayn al-ʿĀbidīn (d. 714), the third Ismāʿīlī Imām and son of Imām al-Ḥusayn (d. 680; grandson of the Prophet), whom he links with the migratory *pir*s, Shāh Burhān and Shāh Khāmōsh. The cave narrative of Sayyid Shohikalon Shohzodamuhammad also begins with Zayn al-ʿĀbidīn, who descends into a series of caves and emerges at three places where key Ismāʿīlī Islamizing figures are located. The first cave from which he emerges is the location of the *qadamgah* of Zayn al-ʿĀbidīn's son, Muḥammad al-Bāqir (d. ca. 732), the fourth Ismāʿīlī Imam; the third cave from which he emerges is the location of the shrine of Shāh Abdāl (Shoh Abdol, i.e. Imām Muḥammad al-Bāqir) in Nimoth (Roshtkala District), and the fourth cave is that of Shāh Qambar-i Āftāb in Langar (Ishkashim District in Wakhan). A shrine thus marks the location of each cave from which Zayn al-ʿĀbidīn emerged, each of which is a pilgrimage site as well as a marker of sacred history rooted in Medina and the family of the Prophet and linked to local identity in the regions of Shughnan, Rosht-qalʿa, and Ishkashim. A second network of shrines, recounted through the oral narrative of Karim Karimov, includes Shāh Qambār-i Āftāb and extends the spiritual geography to include two other Islamizing figures whose shrines are situated along the Panj River in Wakhan, bordering Afghanistan: that of Shāh-i Mardān (ʿAlī) in Namadgut and Shāh ʿIsām al-Dīn in Ptup.

Furthermore, the ubiquitous presence of shrine culture in the local and urban cultures of Central Eurasia, and the social, religious, economic, and spiritual networks associated with them, offers a wealth of interdisciplinary possibilities for an integrative approach to the study of sacred geography, religious identity, architecture, oral narrative, sociopolitical relations, and spiritual practice. With regard to the oral narratives and Ismāʿīlī shrines discussed in this essay, this study demonstrates first, that the sacred landscape of shrines as it unfolds over time and space reveals a continuum of multiple narrative links to Islamic sacred history, local religiosity, foundational legends, and eminent religious figures; second, that the sacred geographies mapped in oral narratives and marked through the physical presence of shrines authenticate local expressions of Muslim identity and, at times, bind them to universal Islamic traditions.[62] Oral narratives play a pivotal role by, in Nile Green's words, "anchoring Islam to their local territory."[63] Finally, this study demonstrates the comparable importance of the written and oral traditions of rural shrines to the written traditions of urban shrines in Central Eurasia (not to imply that urban settings lack oral traditions). The relationship between orality and texuality in the written texts poses historiographical questions that we ought to consider when studying shrine culture in Central Eurasia. Finally, despite their central role as charters of Islamic identity and expressions of local Muslim piety, the social, cultural, and architectural history of rural shrines in Central Eurasia remains largely understudied. Such shrines are too often dismissed as examples of folk tradition upon which an Islamic glaze is painted, thus relegating them to the sidelines rather than considering them within the broad tradition of Islam. If we are to fully understand Islam in Central Eurasia, it is incumbent upon us to consider the urban and rural sacred landscapes as well as the connections between them.

Notes

Research for this article was supported by grants from IREX (International Research and Exchanged Board) with funds provided by the U.S. Department of State through the Title VIII Program. Neither of these organizations is responsible for the views expressed herein.

This study is based on fieldwork conducted in Gorno-Badakhshan in 2004, 2005, and 2008 and archival research conducted in Dushanbe between 2004–10. I am grateful to Umed Mamadsherzodshoev for making his private library in Khorog available and sharing his knowledge, and for his and Sabohat Dunayorova's generous assistance during the course of my field research in Badakhshan. This work could not have been accomplished without the many hospitable people in Badakhshan who so kindly agreed to be interviewed during the course of my research. I am especially appreciative of Sayyid Shohikalon Shohzodamuhammad of Porshnev, with whom I spent a number of memorable afternoons. I also wish to thank Habib Borjian for his editorial review.

1. Prior to 1928 in the region of present-day Tajikistan, Persian was written in Perso-Arabic script; it was changed to Latin in 1928 and then to Cyrillic in 1940. Persian and Arabic forms of place names, terms, and proper names will be used in this paper, followed by the current Tajiki forms in parentheses when appropriate. Tajiki forms of proper names, terms, and place names will be used alone when they refer to present-day persons or places or when quoting direct speech from subjects. Persian and Arabic place names and terms will include diacritical marks the first time they are mentioned; Persian and Arabic proper names and names of publications will include diacritical marks throughout the chapter. Unless otherwise indicated, all dates mentioned will be given as Common Era dates.
2. Mīrzā Fazl ʿAlī Beg Surkh Afsar, *Tatamma-i Taʾrīkh-i Badakhshān* [hereafter TTB], in Mīrzā Sang Muḥammad Badakhshī's *Taʾrikh-i Badakhshān (Istoriia Badakhshana)* [hereafter TB], Russian trans. A. N. Boldyrev, notes and appendix S.E. Grigor'ev (Moscow: Vostochnaia literatura RAN, 1997), fol. 118a. The title of *sayyid* is used for those men who claim descent from the Prophet through his grandson Ḥusayn, the son of ʿAlī b. Abū Ṭālib and Fāṭima. The geographical name of Kuhistan refers here to the western Pāmīr region. *Mullā* refers to a local religious leader.
3. For the historiography of the manuscript, see the introduction (in Russian) by A. N. Boldyrev and S.E. Grigor'ev, 8–24. The *Taʾrīkh-i Badakhshān* was written by two authors. Mīrzā Sang Muḥammad wrote the chronicle, which covers events between 1657–1809. Fazl ʿAlī Beg Surkh Afshar, who refers to himself as the second author of the book, added three supplements to Sang Muḥammad's text and covers subsequent events up to 1907. Sang Muḥammad came from Afghanistan and spent almost fifteen years as a scribe and historian at the court of the ruler of Badakhshan, Muḥammad-Shāh (r. 1792–1822). Fazl ʿAlī Beg came to Badakhshan from tsarist Central Eurasia in the early twentieth century and remained there until 1914. The first edition of TB was published in Leningrad in 1959 by A. Boldyrev. A more recent Persian edition, edited by Manuchehr Sutūda with introductory chapters and notes, was published in Tehran in 1367/1988. Unless otherwise noted, all references cited in this study are to the 1997 Moscow edition, which includes a Persian facsimile of the manuscript, a Russian translation of the text, and a partial translation of the supplements (fols. 114b–127b).
4. Fazl ʿAlī Beg states in TB on fol. 119a that he based his biography of Sayyid Shāh Khāmōsh on the oral traditions (*naql*) contained in the *Kitāb-i Shajarat al-Sākināt*

(Genealogy Book of the Residents). On fol. 114a he writes, "This book was composed by Mīrzā Sang Muḥammad and this insignificant servant began from the place of the first author, supplementing it with his own collection (of information) and relating the events that passed in days long ago over [a period of] 120 years, based on what [I] heard from the upright residents who saw these events with their own eyes and experienced them." Other important local sources on the history of Badakhshan, and Shughnan in particular, are as follows: Qurbān Muḥammadzāda Akhund-Sulaymān (Muhammadzoda Akhundsulaymon) and Maḥabbat Shāhzāda Sayyid Fuṭur-Shāh (Mahabbat Shohzoda Sayyid Futurshoh), *Taʾrīkh-i Badakhshān*, ed. and notes A. A. Yegani, intro. B. I. Iskandarova (Moscow: Idārah-i Intishārāt-i Dānish, 1973). These two teacher-scholars from Khorog wrote their history in the late 1930s. Sayyid Haydar Shāh Mubārakshāhzāda (Sayyid Haydarshoh Muborakshohzoda), *Taʾrīkhi Mulk-i Shughnān* [Tajik translation], ed. Nazardod Jonboboev and Ato Mirkhoja (Khorog: Pomir, 1992). This work was published by A. A. Semenov in the original Persian in 1912. See Semenov, "Iz oblasti religioznykh verovaniia shughnanskikh ismailitov" (Religious Beliefs of the Shughnan Ismāʿīlīs), *Mir Islama* 14 (1912): 523–61; *Istoriia Shughnana. S persidskogo perevel i premchaniiami snabdil* [author of Persian text is Sayyid Haydar Shāh Mubārakshāhzāda] (Tashkent, 1912). See also Umed Mamadsherzodshoev, "Hayot va osori Shohzodamuhammad" (The Life and Work of Shohzodamuhammad, Risolai diplomī (Dushanbe, 1990). In his article on saints and shrines in Wakhan, Abdulmamad Iloliev mentions three additional manuscripts from the St. Petersburg Institute of Oriental Studies, which he describes as having been found in Wakhan at the beginning of the last century and written by unknown authors: *Kitābcha-yi Avval* (First Notebook) and *Kitābcha-yi Duvvum* (Second Notebook), which contain folklore and sayings, and a third work entitled, *Qissa-yi Qah-qaha* (the Story of Qah-qaha*)*. See Abdulmamad Iloliev, "Popular Culture and Religious Metaphor: Saints and Shrines in Wakhan Region of Tajikistan," *Central Asian Survey* 27, no. 1 (2008): 60 and Iloliev, *The Ismāʿīlī-Sufi Sage of Pamir: Mubārak-i Wākhānī and the Esoteric Tradition of Pamiri Muslims* (New York: Cambria Press, 2008), 30 and nn. 13, 48.

5. In contrast to the majority Sunnī population of Tajikistan, Pamiris of Gorno-Badakhshan are followers of the Ismāʿīlī branch of Shīʿī Islam and speak a variety of Pamir languages belonging to the southeastern branch of the Iranian language family. For a recent study of Pamiri ethnic identity in Tajikistan, see Suhrobsho Davlatshoev, "The Formation and Consolidation of Pamiri Ethnic Identity in Tajikistan" (MA thesis, Department of Eurasian Studies, Middle East Technical University, Ankara, 2006). On languages of the Pamir, see I. M. Steblin-Kaminskij, "Central Asia xiii. Iranian Languages," *Encyclopaedia Iranica*, vol. 5, Eisenbrauns (1992): 223–26.
6. For a discussion of Muḥammad al-Bāqir's birth date, see W. Madelung, "Bāqer, Abū Jaʿfar Moḥammad. The Fifth Imam of the Twelver Shiʿites (7th–8th Century)," *Encyclopaedia Iranica*, vol. 3, Eisenbrauns (1988): 725–26.

7. In conceptualizing this project, I have found the work of Nile Green and Devin DeWeese to be particularly helpful. In his study of the Sufi shrines of Aurangabad in the Deccan, Nile Green reminds us that the memory of saints, through narrative and ritual practice, "stands at once in both the present and past, entwining the details of their own highly located careers with grander episodes in the history of the Deccan at large." Green, "Stories of Saints and Sultans: Re-membering History at the Sufi Shrines of Aurangabad," *Modern Asian Studies* 38, no. 2 (2005): 426, 444. Devin DeWeese, in his study of the shrine of Aḥmad Yasavī, discusses the ways in which a shrine can mediate between Islamic and non-Islamic, or Islamizing communities. He concludes, "The shrine of Ahmad Yasavi served as a 'register,' a sanctified and publicly accessible place at which narratives associated with the saint could be 'written' in the memories of shrine attendants and pilgrims alike, and 'storied' in the specific sites and objects that concretized the stories for particular ritual and devotional uses" and that it also served as a "'narrative' lens which at any given time gathered and focused hagiographical narratives circulating among a variety of constituencies, and provided a framework for the constantly shifting patterns of meaning found in those narratives by a wide range of pilgrims to the shrine." DeWeese, "Sacred Places and 'Public' Narratives: The Shrine of Ahmad Yasavi in Hagiographical Traditions of the Yasavi Sufi Order, 16th–17th Centuries," *Muslim World* 90, no. 3–4 (2000): 376.
8. Our understanding of Ismāʿīlism in Badakhshan has significantly broadened over the past decade due to the recent work of scholars in Khorog and Dushanbe such as K. El'chibekov, N. Emil'ianova, Ilban Hajjibikoff, Sh. P. Iusufbekov, T. S. Kalandarov, Omid Shahzada-Mohammad (elsewhere referred to as Umed Mamadsherzodshoev), Nisormamad Shakarmamadov, and Abdulmamad Iloliev, among others. See, for example, K. El'chibekov, "Ismailizm na Pamire [Ismaʿilism in the Pamir]," in Sh. P. Iusufbekov et al., *Istoriia Gorno-badakhshanskoi avtonomnoi oblasti* (Dushanbe: In-t istorii, arkheologii i ėtnografii AN Respubliki Tadzhikistan, 2005), 1: 452–87; Ilban Hajjibikoff, "Sonnat-e 'daʿvat-e baqa' dar Badakhshan [The Tradition of *Daʿwat-i Baqa* in Badakhshan]," *Rudaki* (Dushanbe) 7, no. 10 (2006): 23–36; Iloliev, *Ismāʿīlī-Sufi Sage* and "Popular Culture and Religious Metaphor," 59–73; T. Kalandarov, "Ismailizm na Pamire: poisk novykh putei i reshenii [Ismaʿilism in the Pamir: The Quest for New Paths and Solutions]," *Rasy i naraody* 32 (2006): 180–96; T. Kalandarov, "Religiia v zhizni Pamirtsev xx veka [Religion in the Life of the Pamir People in the Twentieth Century]," in Nadezhda M. Emel'ianova, ed., *Pamirskaia ekspeditsiia (stat'i i materially polevykh issledovanii)* [The Pamir Expedition (Articles and Field Materials)] (Moscow: Institut vostokovedeniia RAN, 2006); Omed Shahzade-Mohammad, "Sunnat-i 'charāgh-rawshan-kunī'-yi Ismāʿīlīān-i Aasyaa-yi markazī [The Custom of Chirāghrawshān-kunī of the Ismāʿīlīs of Central Eurasia]," *Rudaki* 7, no. 10 (2006): 43–52; U. Mamadsherzodshoev [Omed Shahzade-Mohammad], *Manobei sunnati Charogh-Ravshan* (Dushanbe: Merosi Ajam 2009); N. Jonboboev and Omid Shahzade-Mohammad, *Durdonahoi Badakhshon (Asotir va rivoyatho)* [Oral Traditions of Badakhshan] (Khorog, 1992); Nisormamad

Shakarmamadov, *Folklori Pomir* [The Oral Tradition of the Pamir] 2: *Asotir, rivoiat va naqlho* [Myths, Legends, and Narratives] (Dushanbe: Imperial-Grupp, 2005). Earlier scholarship was dominated by Russian orientalists and ethnographers whose research laid the groundwork for the study of Pamiri culture and Ismāʿīlism. See, for example, M. S. Andreev, *Tadzhiki doliny Khuf* [Tajiks of the Khuf Valley] (Stalinabad, 1953), fasc. 2; A. Bobrinskoi, "Sekta Ismailiia v russkikh i bukharskikh predeleakh Srednei Azii: Geograficheskoe rasprostranenie i organizaciia," *Etnograficheskoe obozrenie* no. 2 (Moscow, 1902): 1–20; V. Ivanov, *Sufism and Ismailism: Chirāgh-nāma. Majalla-yi mardumshināsī* [*Revue Iranian d'Anthropologie*] 3 (1959): 13–17; 60–70; V. Ivanov, "An Ismaili Interpretation of the Gulshani Raz," *Journal of the Bombay Branch of the Royal Asiatic Society* 8 (1932): 69–78; V. Ivanov, "A Forgotten Branch of the Ismailis," *Journal of the Royal Asiatic Society of Great Britain and Ireland* (1938): 57–79; A. A. Semenov, "Iz oblasti religioz'nykh verovaniia Shugnanskikh Ismailitov," *Mir Islama* 14 (1912): 523–56 and *K dogmataika pamirskogo ismailizma* [The Dogma of Pamiri Ismailism] (Tashkent, 1926).

For works on Ismāʿīlī literature, see A. Bertels and M. Bakoev, *Alfavitny katalog rukopisei, obnaruzhenykh v gorno-badakhshanskoi avtonomoi oblasti ekspeditsii 1959–1963* (Moscow: Nauka, 1967); Daftary Farhad, *Ismaili Literature: A Bibliography of Sources and Studies* (London: I.B. Tauris, 2004); V.A. Ivanov, *Ismailitskaia rukoposi aziatskogo muzeia (Sobranie I. Zarubina)* (Petrograd: Izvestiia Akademii Nauk, Belletin de l'Academie des sciences, 1917), 359–86; V. V. Ivanov, *Ismaili Literature. A Biographical Survey*, (Tehran: Ismaili Society, 1963); A. A. Semenov, "Opisanie ismailitskich rukopisei, sobrannykh A. A. Semenovym," *Izvestiiia Rossiiskoi Akademii nauk* 12 (Petrograd, 1918): 2171–202; and Kutub Kassam, Hermann Landolt, Samira Sheikh, eds., *An Anthology of Ismaili Literature* (London: I.B. Tauris, 2008).

9. This is in contrast to Sunnī Muslims, the majority of the world's Muslim population, who believe in the caliphate rather than the Imamate. In Sunnī Islam, four "rightly guided" caliphs were successors to the Prophet Muḥammad. The first three caliphs were Muḥammad's close companions and the fourth was ʿAlī, the cousin and son-in-law of the Prophet Muḥammad. The standard western source for the history of Ismāʿīlism is Farhad Daftary's *The Ismāʿīlīs: Their History and Doctrines* (Cambridge: Cambridge University Press, 1990).
10. For a discussion of the concept of *qiyāma* and the *imām-qāʾim* in Nizārī Ismāʿīlism of the Alamūt period, see Daftary, *Ismāʿīlīs*, 388–412.
11. The Panj-Tanī, or "Fivers," recognize five pure persons of the family of the Prophet, namely Muḥammad, ʿAlī, Fāṭima, Ḥasan, and Ḥusayn. See Abdulmamad Iloliev, *Ismāʿīlī-Sufi Sage*, 6.
12. Daftary, *Ismāʿīlīs*, 435–36. Ḥasan-i Ṣabbāh's headquarters was located in the high mountain fortress of Alamūt in Daylamān in the Alburz mountains of Iran. For an overview of the Alamūt period (1094–1258), see ch. 6, "Nizārī Ismāʿīlism of the Alamūt Period," 324–434. For studies of Nāṣir Khusraw, see Nozir Arabzoda, *Nosiri Khusrav* (Dushanbe: Maorif, 1994); A. E. Bertels, *Nasir-i Khosrov i ismailizm*

(Moscow: Izd-vo vostochnoi lit-ry, 1959); Alice C. Hunsberger, *Nasir Khusraw, The Ruby of Badakhshan* (London: I.B. Tauris, 2000); A. A. Semenov, "Shugnanko-ismailitskaiia redaksiia 'Kniga Sveta' Nāṣir-i Khusrsaw," *Zapiski kollegii vostokovedov pri Aziatskom Muzee Akademii Nauk SSSR* 5 (1930): 589–610. Nāṣir-i Khusraw is a highly venerated figure in Tajikistan Badakhshan. In 2003 the Institute of Ismāʿīlī Studies (IIS) and the Ismāʿīlī Religious Education Committee in Tajikistan (ITREC) organized a 3-day international conference in Khorog, Badakhshan to commemorate the 1000th anniversary of his birth. For an analysis of the millennial conference, see Jonah Steinberg, "The Anatomy of the Transnation: The Globalization of the Isma'ili Muslim Community," (Ph.D. diss., University of Pennsylvania, 2006), 151–57.

13. The *qadamgāh* of Nāṣir-i Khusraw (Piri Sho Nosir) is located in Shughnan in the village of Porshnev in a place known as Midenshor, while his burial site (*ziyāratgāh*) is located in the village of Ḥazrat Sayyid in the valley of Yumgan, Afghanistan. On the shrine of Nāṣir-i Khusraw in Yumgan, see the study of Marcus Schadl, "The Shrine of Nasir Khusraw: Imprisoned Deep in the Valley of Yumgan," *Muqarnas: An Annual on the Visual Cultures of the Islamic World* 26 (2009): 63–94. *Qadamgāh* (stepping place) is the term used for a shrine that marks the place where a holy person walked or visited. *Qadamgāh* are often imaginary shrines that locate eminent Shīʿī figures or Sufis in the region. Daftary bases the date of Nāṣir-i Khusraw's exile on when he completed his philosophical treatise, *Zād al-musāfirīn*. Daftary, *Ismāʿīlīs*, 217–18. See also Khalilullah Khalili, "Yamgān," *Aryana* 33, no. 2 (1354/1935): 1–22. Iloliev's suggestion that Nāṣir-i Khusaw's ideas were "popularized and their interpretations harmonized with the beliefs, rituals and practices of the indigenous people" supports the findings of our study. Iloliev, *Ismāʿīlī-Sufi Sage*, 7.
14. Daftary, *Ismāʿīlīs*, 456–62.
15. Iloliev, *Ismāʿīlī-Sufi Sage*, 7. It was during this second period of the *Panj-Tanī* that missionaries infused Ismāʿīlism with beliefs associated with Sufism as well as Twelver Shīʿism. Thus, according to Iloliev, ".... the *Panj-Tanī* faith is understood as a combination of certain elements of the pre-Islamic rituals, imbued with Islamic meanings, the Fāṭimid *daʿwa* (Naṣir-i Khusraw's teachings) and post-Alamūt *taqiyya* ideas." Iloliev, 6–7. The practice of *taqīyya* is the concealment of one's true faith or beliefs when under threat. Iloliev rightly points out that scholars have not adequately focused on the relationship between Sufism and Pamiri Ismāʿīlism and his study of Mubārak-i Wakhān is an important step in that direction. In V. Ivanow's 1932 study of the *Gulshani Raz*, he uses the terms "Islamised Sufis" and "Suficised Ismailism" in reference to this Ismāʿīlī manuscript that is so infused with Sufi concepts. See W. Ivanow, "An Ismaili Interpretation of the Gulshani Raz," *Journal of the Bombay Branch of the Royal Asiatic Society*, 8 (1932): 69. The relationship between Sufism and Ismaʿīlīsm in the context of the foundational narratives discussed in this paper is beyond the scope of this study and will be taken up elsewhere.

16. Iloliev notes, based on Sayyid Jalāāl-i Badakhshī's *Bahr al-Akhbār*, "As indigenous tradition believes, in his missionary travels, Pīr Nāsir-i Khusraw was accompanied by several pious devotees coming from the local people, some of whom become saints, such as Bābā Umar-i Yumgī and Sayyid Suhrāb-i Valī." According to Iloliev, Sayyid Suhrāāb-i Valī lived in the fifteenth century AD. Iloliev, "Popular Culture and Religious Metaphor," 63.
17. Steinberg, "Anatomy of the Transnation," 94. Also see TB and Sayyid Haydarsho Muborakshohzoda, *Ta'rikhi Mulki Shughnon* (Khorog: Pomir, 1992) for the local history of Badakhshan and Shughnan in the late nineteenth and early twentieth centuries. Today, Tajik Wakhan is a part of Gorno-Badakhshan.
18. On the formation of the Republic of Tajikistan and Tajik national identity, see Paul Bergne, *The Birth of Tajikistan: National Identity and the Origins of the Republic* (London, I.B. Tauris, 2007).
19. While the high plains of the eastern Pamir region are inhabited mostly by Kirghiz, the valleys of the western Pamir region, the focus of this study, are inhabited by Iranian peoples who, for the most part, are Nizārī Ismāʿīlīs.
20. Some fled to Afghanistan, however. For a discussion of the situation of *khalifas* during the Soviet period and the impact of the border closing, see V. I. Bushkov and T. S. Kalandarov, "Le passé et le présent des populations du Pamir occidental [The Past and Present of the Populations of the Western Pamir]," *Cahiers d'Asie Centrale* 11–12 (2003): 103–18 and T. Kalandarov, "Ismailizm na Pamire," *Rasy i narody*, 180–96. Bushkov and Kalandarov note, "From 1930–1960 when the war against religion was particularly virulent, Arabic works found in the homes of Ismāʿīlīs served as a pretext for the accusation of anti-Soviet behavior." To avoid this they hid their books and religious manuscripts in the villages, some of which have only recently come to light. Bushkov and Kalandarov, "Le passé et le present," 112–13.
21. During the Civil War, Pamiris of Badakhshan were often deemed suspect due to their involvement in opposition movements, including the Lale Badakhshan Society (The Rubies of Badakhshan) and the Islamic Revival Party (IRP). When the former declared the independence of Gorno-Badakhshan in 1992, the Dushanbe government imposed a 2-year blockade that led to widespread famine. On the Tajik Civil War, see Stéphane Dudoignon, *Communal Solidarity and Social Conflicts in Late 20th-Century Central Eurasia: The Case of the Tajik Civil War*, Islamic Area Studies Working Paper no. 7 (Tokyo: Islamic Area Studies Project, 1998); S. Dudoignon and Guissou Jahangiri, eds., "Le Tajikistan existe-t-il? Destins politiques d'une 'nation imparfaite,'" *Cahiers d'études sur la Mediterranée orientale et le monde turkco-iranien* 18 (1994); Nassim Jawad, *Tajikistan: A Forgotten Civil War* (London: The Minority Rights Group, 1995); Frederic Grare, Shirin Akiner, and Mohammad-Rexa Djalili, eds., *Tajikistan: The Trials of Independence* (London: St. Martins Press, 1998); John Schoeberlein-Engel, "Conflict in Tājikistān and Central Eurasia: The Myth of Ethnic Animosity," *Harvard Middle Eastern and Islamic Review* 1–2 (1994): 1–55.

22. See Steinberg, "Anatomy of the Transnation," 142–209 for an analysis of the Aga Khan Development Network (AKDN) in Tajikistan Badakhshan. Steinberg discusses how the Ismāʿīlī Tariqah Boards have put into question certain traditional (pre-Islamic) Pamiri practices and rituals associated with shrines, such as *chirāghrawshān* (candle-lighting), in their efforts to regulate and standardize Ismāʿīlism. Stéphane Dudoignon notes that the influx of Khoja missionaries (locally referred to as *panj-bahayis*) from the Indian subcontinent has created tensions with traditional *pirs*, which has led some authors in Khorog to produce "apologetic publications on vernacular religious traditions and on the heritage of Nasir-i Khusraw" and others to conveniently ignore the tensions. Stéphane Dudoignon, ed., *Central Eurasia Reader: A Biennial Journal of Critical Bibliography and Epistemology of Central Eurasian Studies* 1 (2008): 338–40; El'chibekov, "Ismailizm na Pamire," *Istoriia Gorno-Badakhshanskoi avtonomnoi oblasti*. On the subject of change and the role of AKDN, also see Hafizullah Emadi, "Politics of Transformation and Ismailis in Gorno-Badakhshan, Tajikistan," *Internationales Asienforum* 29, no. 1–2 (1998): 16–21.
23. TTB, fol. 118b. Bābā ʿUmār Yumgī was evidently the name taken by the ruler of Yumgān, Malik Jahān Shāh, after he converted to Islam and became a deputy of Naṣir-i Khusraw. In his discussion of the spread of Ismāʿīlism to Badakhshan, Iloliev, following A. Bobrinksoi, suggests that political reasons connected to the oppression of Ismāʿīlism in the post-Alamūt period likely was as strong a motivating factor as religious conviction for their migration to Badakhshan. Iloliev, *Ismāʿīlī-Sufi Sage*, 36. See A. Bobrinskoi, "Gortsi verkhoviia Pyandja (*Vaskhsansti i ishkashimtsi*)," (Moscow, 1908), 40, also cited by Iloliev *Ismāʿīlī-Sufi Sage*, p. 36. According to Bobrinskoi's interview with Sayyid Yūsuf ʿAlī Shāh, Shāh Khāmōsh's brother was Shāh Malang, but the term may not have been used to refer to biological kinship.
24. *Taʾrīkh-i Badakhshān* by Qurbān Muḥammadzāda Akhund-Sulaymān and Maḥabbat Shāhzāda Sayyid Fuṭūr-Shāh (1869–1912), fol. 2 and the *Taʾrikh-i Mulk-i Shughnon* by Sayyid Ḥaydarshāh Mubārakshāhzāda, 6–8 and nn. 7–8, 22. Iloliev mentions another local Pamiri manuscript by Sayyid Farukhshah entitled *Sarā-yi Dilrabā* (Attractive Mansion), which this author has not seen, based on a reference of B. Iskandarov, which dates their arrival in Badakhshan to the late sixteenth century. See Iloliev, "Popular Culture and Religious Metaphor," 63. Iloliev later argues that Shāh Khāmōsh and Shāh Malang must have migrated to the Pamir region in the post-Alamūt period since the terms *pir* and *murid* were not yet in use in the earlier period. Iloliev, 38. The Islamization process in Badakhshan was undoubtedly a long-term and continuous one that took place over many centuries. Given the limited sources at our disposal, the construction of an accurate history of this process is impossible and not the subject of this study.
25. See Thomas Edward Gordon, *The Roof of the World: Being a Narrative of a Journey over the High Plateau of Tibet to the Russian Frontier and the Oxus Sources on Pamir* (Edinburgh, 1876); Thomas Gordon, William Conway, and George Curzon,

"Journeyings in the Pamirs and Central Eurasia: Discussions," *The Geographical Journal* 2 (1893): 398–401; Ole Olufsen, *Through the Unknown Pamirs: The Second Danish Pamir Expedition* 1898–1899 (New York: Greenwood Press, 1969) and Aurel Stein, *On Ancient Central-Asian Tracks: A Brief Narrative of the Three Expeditions in Innermost Asia and Northwestern China* (New York: Pantheon Books, 1964). See note 51 for a list of Soviet-era publications. For an excellent review of nineteenth-century scientific exploration, nineteenth-twentieth Russian expeditions, and British and other adventurers and explorers, including maps, see John Middleton and Huw Thomas, *Tajikistan and the High Pamirs* (Hong Kong: Odyssey, 2008), 331–513.

26. TTB, fol. 118a. In his biography Mīrzā Abū'l Fazl refers to him by his epithet (*laqab*) Shāh Khāmōsh as well as by his full name, Sayyid Mīr Ḥasan Shāh, fol. 120b. He also refers to him as *mīr* on fol. 121b.
27. See TTB, fol. 125.
28. TB, fol. 120b.
29. Jīlānī left for Baghdad at the age of eighteen. W. Braune, "ʿAbd al-Kādir al-Djīlānī," *Encyclopaedia of Islam*, 2nd ed. [Henceforth cited as EI².]
30. *Walī* or "friend" [of God] indicates his Sufi status. Uwaysī refers to the disciple who receives spiritual instruction from the spirit of a deceased rather than a living saint. TTB, fol. 121a. According to the story, as described below by Fazl ʿAlī Beg, Shāh Khāmōsh received instruction from the spirit of Junayd al-Baghdādī, thus continuing the Uwaysī tradition.
31. Ibid., fol. 122a.
32. Ibid., fol. 121a.
33. Ibid., fol. 122b.
34. For translated excerpts from Junayd's writings on the concepts of *tawḥīd* (affirmation of divine unity) and *fanāʿ* (annhilation), see Michael Sells, *Early Islamic Mysticism: Sufi, Qur'an, Miʿraj and Theological Writings* (New York: Paulist Press, 1996), 251–65.
35. TTB, fol. 123a. *Wārith* is a title meaning heir or master. In this case, the term refers to Junayd as the inheritor of the tradition of the Prophet.
36. His silence is the origin of his epithet (*laqab*) "Khāmōsh" (silent).
37. TTB, fol. 123a. The spirit of the Prophet appeared, and Junayd taught Shāh Khāmōsh and Jīlānī the spiritual knowledge of *qāl* and *ḥāl*.
38. Khuttalan refers to the region on the right bank of the upper Amu Darya, between the Vakhsh and Panj Rivers, today called Khatlon. See C.E. Bosworth, "Khuttalān," EI².
39. Fol. 124a. See fols. 124a–124b for details about the journey. Shāh Khāmōsh also met with Mir Sayyid Jalāl al-Dīn Guldasta in Muʿminābād. According to the tradition related to A. A. Bobrinskoi by Yusūf ʿAlī Shāh, twelve generations earlier, Shāh Malang came to Kuhistan from Sabzabar and Khurasan with three *pir*s from Isfahan and Hamadan: Shāh Burhān, Shāh Khāmōsh, and Shāh Kāshān. See A. Bobrinskoi,

"Sekta Ismailiia v russkikh i bukharskikh predeleakh Srednei Azii," *Etnograficheskoe obozrenie* 1 (1902), 4–5. According to Qurbān Muḥammadzāda Akhund-Sulaymān and Maḥabbat Shāhzāda Sayyid Fuṭur-Shāh, four *qalandars* (Sufis) came from Isfahan and Kashan by way of Sheva to Shughnan: first, Sayyid Muḥammad Isfahānī, who was known as Shāh Kāshān; second, Sayyid Shāh Malang; third, Sayyid Shāh Khāmōsh; and fourth, Shāh Burḥān Valī. Akhund-Sulaymān and Fuṭur-Shāh, *Ta'rīkh-i Badakhshān*.

40. TTB, fol. 124b. In Shīʿī Islam, the understanding of religion must be based on "the teaching (*tāʿlīm*) of proper authorities; authorities or true imāms, who, according to the Shīʿa, are designated by divine ordinance and not by human choice or reasoning, as in the case of the Prophet himself." In the Alamūt period, Ḥasan-i Ṣabāḥ "reformulated the Shīʿī authority as resting with the Ismāʿīlī imam, and in his absence, with his *ḥujja* (representative)". Daftary, *Ismāʿīlīs*, 369–70.

41. TTB, fol. 124b. Fazl ʿAlī Beg dates the marriage to AH 490 (1056 CE).

42. Sayyid ʿAlī Shāh Valī had three sons: Sayyid Shāh Ṭaher, Sayyid Shāh Jaʿfar, and Sayyid Shāh ʿAdil. TTB, fols. 126a–126b. Fazl ʿAlī Beg states, "Several hundred people exist from among the descendants and celebrated ones of the grandsons and offspring of those three abundantly blessed people." TTB, fol. 126b.

43. On the shrine of Shāh Khāmōsh, see Pavel Samoilik and Yusufsho Yakubov, "Istoriia izuchenie mavzoleiia Shakhi Khomush," in *Akhbori osorkhonai millii jumhurii Tojikiston ba nomi Kamoliddin Bekhzod*, no. 6 (2005), 20–35, Golib Goibov, "Mazori Shohi Khomūsh," in *Chahordah Mazor* [Fourteen Mazars], bilingual ed. in Tajiki with Persian summary, ed. Hamza Kamol (Dushanbe: n.p., 2001), 124–36, and Muhammadali Muzaffari, Hamza Kamol, and Zainuddin Nabotzoda, *Joyhoi mukaddasi Tojikiston* [Sacred Places of Tajikistan], bilingual ed. in Tajik and English (Dushanbe: Devashticg, 2007), 152–55.

44. Gordon, *Roof of the World*. See also Captain H. R. E. Trotter, "On the Geographical Results of the Mission to Kashgar under Sir T. Douglas Forsyth in 1873–65," *Journal of the Royal Geographical Society* 48 (1878): 173–234. The reference to the fortress of Qah-Qaha, the ruins of which are located in the village of Namadgūt, recalls a local tradition that the cousin and son-in-law of the Prophet Muḥammad came to Wakhan to fight against the infidel ruler Qah-Qaha, and as a result the populace converted and became followers of the *ahl al-bayt*. In *Ismāʿīlī-Sufi Sage* Iloliev notes this story and cites Andrei Snesarev's article which discusses the tradition, "Religiia i obichaia gortse zapadnogo Pamira," *Turkestankie vedomosti* 90 (1904): 412. The shrine of Shāh Mardān (the title of ʿAlī), known as Ostoni Shohi Mardon, is located not far from the fortress in Namadgut. The word *oston* is derived from the Persian word *āstān*, which means threshold or resting place. In Tajikistan and other regions of Iran and Central Eurasia, the term may be used to refer to the sacred burial place of a holy person, or a place where a holy person stopped to rest.

45. Gordon, *Roof of the World*, 139.

46. Ibid., 141.

47. It is impossible to know for certain whether Qah-Qaha actually was Zoroastrian, since our sources are limited and rituals such as fire worship were not specifically confined to Zoroastrianism in this region. See Iloliev, *Ismāʿīlī-Sufi Sage*, p. 30 and Richard Foltz, "When Was Central Eurasia Zoroastrian?" *Mankind Quarterly* 38, no. 3 (1998): 189–200 (cited by Iloliev, p. 30).
48. Sayyid Haydarshāh Mubārakshāhzāda [Sayyid Haydarshoh Muborakshohzoda], *Ta'rikhi Mulki Shugnon* [in Tajik], trans. Hazardod Jonboboev and Ato Mirkhoja (Khorog: Pomir, 1992), 7. The author continues to list the subsequent rulers of Shughnan. The original text was written in Persian and was obtained by the Russian orientalist A. Semenov in 1912 when he visited the valley.
49. N. Jonboboev and Sherzod Muhammadsherzodshoev, *Durdonakhoi Badakhshon: asotir va rivoyatho* (Khorog, 1992), 36.
50. The work of Robert McChesney has brought scholarly attention to the social, economic, and political significance of Central Eurasian shrines. Robert D. McChesney, *Waqf in Central Asia: Four Hundred Years in the History of a Muslim Shrine, 1480–1889* (Princeton, NJ: Princeton University Press, 1991); "Society and Community: Shrines and Dynastic Families in Central Eurasia," in R. D. McChesney, *Central Asia: Foundations of Change* (Princeton, NJ: Darwin Press, 1996), 69–116; "Architecture and Narrative: The Khwaja Abu Nasr Parsa Shrine. Part 1: Constructing the Complex and its Meaning, 1469–1696," *Muqarnas* 18 (2001): 94–119; and "Architecture and Narrative: The Khwaja Abu Nasr Parsa Shrine. Part 2: Representing the Complex in Word and Image, 1696–1998," *Muqarnas* 19 (2002): 78–108. Other important studies of shrines include Terry Allen, *A Catalogue of the Toponymns and Monuments of Timurid Herat*, Studies in Islamic Architecture, no. 1, (Cambridge, MA: Aga Khan Program for Islamic Architecture at Harvard University and the Massachusetts Institute of Technology, 1981); Devin DeWeese, "Sacred History for a Central Eurasian Town: Saints, Shrines, and Legends of Origin in Histories of Sayrām, 18th–19th Centuries," *Revue des mondes musulmans et de la Méditerranée* (1999): 245–95; "Sacred Places and 'Public' Narratives: The Shrine of Aḥmad Yasavī in Hagiographical Traditions of the Yasavī Sufi Order, 16th–17th Centuries," *Muslim World* 90, no. 3–4 (2000): 353–76; Lisa Golombek, "The Cult of Saints and Shrine Architecture in the Fourteenth Century," in *Near Eastern Numismatics, Iconography, Epigraphy and History: Studies in Honor of George C. Miles*, ed. Dickran K. Kouymjian, (Beirut: American University of Beirut, 1974), 419–30 and *The Timurid Shrine at Gazur Gah*, Royal Ontario Museum of Art and Archaeology Occasional Paper 15 (Toronto: Royal Ontario Museum of Art and Archaeology, 1969); and Maria Eva Subtelny, "Of Saints and Scribes: the Timurid Shrine as a Vehicle for Agromanagement," in M. E. Subtelny, *Timurids in Transition: Turko-Persian Politics and Acculturation in Medieval Iran* (Leiden: Brill, 2007), 192–234.
51. Joseph Castagné, who gathered his data on shrines during the 1920s, is one exception. See Joseph Castagné, "Le culte des lieux saints de l'Islam au Turkestan," *L'Ethnographie* 46 (1951): 46–124. For discussions of this issue as related to Sufism

and indigenous religion in Central Eurasia, see Devin DeWeese, *Islamization and Native Religion in the Golden Horde: Baba Tükles and Conversion to Islam in Historical and Epic Tradition* (University Park: Pennsylvania State University, 1994), 17–66 and Ahmet T. Karamustafa, *God's Unruly Friends, Dervish Groups in the Islamic Later Middle Period* 1200–1550 (Salt Lake City: University of Utah Press, 1994), 1–12. A cursory glance at western surveys of Islamic architecture reveals little consideration of the local shrine landscape.

52. Soviet-era studies provide an important foundation for the study of *mazārs* and valuable information regarding their physical features, locations, and epigraphic and documentary records. Notable studies were carried out by scholars such as N. Negmatov, Ahror Mukhtarov, A. Egani, O. D. Chekhovich, S. Z. Khmel'nitskii, R. S. Mukimov, and M. S. Mamajanova. Soviet-era studies that include material on the shrines of Tajikistan include: E. A. Davidovich and A. Mukhtarov, *Stranitsii istorii Gissara* (Dushanbe: Irfon, 1969); E. A. Davidovich and B. A. Litvinskii, *Arkheologicheskii ocherk Isfarinskovo raiona* (Moscow, 1955); E. A. Egani and O. D. Chekhovich, *Pis'mennye pamiatniki vostoka* (Dushanbe, 1974); S. Z. Khmel'nitski, *Isledovanie arkhitekurnie pamiatnikov v Ura-Tube* (Dushanbe, 1971), *Khodja Mashad* (Berlin/Riga, 2001); S. Mahmadjonova and P. Mukimov, *Ensiklopediia pamiatnikov sredny vekovo zodchestva* (Dushanbe, 1993); A. Mukhtorov, *Ocherki ta'rikhii mulki Ūroteppa dar asri XIX* (Dushanbe, 1964), *Sirri Mazorkho* (Dushanbe, 1964), *Epigraficheskie namiatniki Kuhistana* (Dushanbe, 1978), *Arkhiteckturnoe naledie Khudjanda* (Dushanbe, 1993); N. Negmatov, P. Pulatov, and S. Khmel'nitskii, *Urtakurgan i Tirizaktepa* (Dushanbe, 1973); N. Negmatov, *Isledovaniie po istorii i kulture Leninabada* (Dushanbe, 1986).

53. The recent work of Golib Goibov, Abdullojon Mirboev, Hamza Kamol and Abdulmamad Iloliev demonstrate the renewed interest of scholars of Tajikistan in the study of local shrines and sacred places in the post-Soviet period. See A. Alizoda, *Khoja Ishoki Khatloni* (Dushanbe, 2002); Golib Goibov, *Mazorkhoi Mavlono Tojiddini Dashti Kuloki va Shaikh Shakiki Balkhi dar nokhiyai Dangara* (Dushanbe, 1998); Iloliev, "Popular Culture and Religious Metaphor," 59–73; Hamza Kamol, ed., *Chahordah Mazor* (Dushanbe, 2001) and "Istoriia mazarov severnogo Tadjikistana," *Avtoreferat, Candidata Istorii Nauk* (Dushanbe, 2002); S. Z. Khmel'nitski, *Khodja Mashhad* (Berlin/Riga, 2001), A. K. Mirbabaev, *Istoriia madrasa Tadjikistana* (Dushabe, 1994); A. Mukhtarov, *Sang khon dile dorad* (Dushanbe, 1999), *Mazari Tajikistana* (Dushanbe, 1995); Muhammadalī Muzaffarī, Hamza Kamol, and Zainuddin Nabotzoda, *Joyhoi muqaddasi Tojikiston* [Sacred Places of Tajikistan], bilingual edition (Dushanbe, 2007); 1986. A volume by Meera Alexseevna Bubnova incorporates the most recent research on ancient monuments from the eighteenth to twentieth century. Bubnova, *An Archaeological Map of Gorno-Badakhshan Autonomous Oblast: The Western Pamirs*, The University of Central Eurasia and A. Donish Institute of History, Archaeology and Ethnography, Academy of Sciences of Tajikistan (Dushanbe, 2008).

54. Shrines dedicated to the family of the Prophet and the ʿAlīd family are scattered across the sacred landscape of Tajikistan. Among them are two shrines associated with Zayn al-ʿĀbidīn (Zaynulobidin), neither of which actually claim to house his body. One is a *gumbaz* located in the village of Tem in Shughnan and the other is in Jilikul near Shahrtus in southwestern Tajikistan, not far from the Afghan border to the south and the Uzbek border to the east. Shrines and sacred places in Badakhshan associated with ʿAlī include the *qadamgāh* of Ḥazrati ʿAli in Langar and the *qadamgāh* of Shāh-i Mardān (Shohi Mardon, meaning ʿAli) in Namadgut. While the *mazār* of Zayn al-ʿĀbidīn in Jilikul, an ethnically diverse region comprised today of Turkmen, Tajiks, and Uzbeks, is associated with reverence for the family of the Prophet Muḥammad, the *gumbaz* in Tem is associated with the Islamizing tradition of Ismāʿīlī Shīʿism in Badakhshan. For a discussion of the *qadamgāh* of Shāh-i Mardān, see Iloliev, "Popular Culture and Religious Metaphor," 65–67.
55. Zebak is located in the Wakhan region of Afghan Badakhshan, not far from the border of Tajikistan.
56. Sayyid Shāhkalān b. Shāhzāda Muḥammad (Sayyid Shohikalon Shohzodamuhammad) is the son of Shāhzāda Muḥammad, who is the brother of Sayyid Yūsuf ʿAlī Shāh, the *Pir-i Rūhānī-yi Mardum-i Shughnān*. Nāṣir-i Khusraw, the highly revered eleventh-century Ismāʿīlī poet, philosopher, and missionary of Khurasan who fled to Badakhshan to escape persecution for his ideas, lived in exile in the remote valley of Yumgān in present-day Afghanistan Badakhshan, where, according to local tradition, he lived in a cave. Sayyid Shohikalon Shohzodamuhammad recalled a similar cave theme in his account concerning Nāṣir Khusraw's death and burial in Yumgan. The use of caves as signifiers of holy places is common in many cultural traditions. Two poignant examples from the Islamic tradition are the cave of Mount Hira, where Muḥammad meditated and received his first revelation, and the cave in which Muḥammad and Abū Bakr took refuge during the *hijra* from Mecca to Medina in 622, which marks the first year of the Muslim calendar. In his study of the conversion narratives of Baba Tukles, Devin DeWeese discusses the "theme of enclosure and emergence" common in origin myths among the Turks and Mongols and in Islamic tradition; DeWeese, *Islamization and Native Religion in the Golden Horde*, pp. 273–90. For a study of the cave tradition connected to Nāṣir-i Khusraw, see Jo-Ann Gross, "The Motif of the Cave and the Funerary Narratives of Nāṣir-i Khusraw," in *Orality and Textuality in the Iranian World*, ed. Julia Rubanovich and Shaul Shaked (Leiden, forthcoming [2012]).
57. The Persian term *gumbaz* (or *gonbad*), meaning "dome," usually refers to a domed tomb, and perhaps there was one at some point in time.
58. For local traditions associated with Shāh Qambar-i Āftāb, see Nisormamad Shakharmamadov and Shohnazar Mirzoev, *Fol'klor Pamira* (in Tajik), vol. 2, *Mify, legendy i skazaniia* [*The Folkore of Pamir*, vol, 2: *Myths, Legends and Stories*], 242–44.

59. Shāh-i Mardān is one of the names of ʿAlī ibn Abī Tālib, the cousin and son-in-law of the Prophet Muḥammad and first Imam in Shīʿism. According to local tradition. ʿAlī came to Badakhshan to defeat the infidel king, Qah-Qaha; the ruins of the fortress of Qah-Qaha are located near Namadgut in Wakhan. For oral traditions associated with Shāh-i Mardān and the battle of Qah-Qaha, see Shakharmamadov and Mirzoev, *Fol'klor Pamira*, 2:76–83. For a discussion of the narrative about the battle of ʿAlī and Qah-Qaha and the recent architectural changes to the *qadamqāh* of Shāh-i Mardān, including the building of a museum, see Iloliev, "Popular Culture and Religious Metaphor," 65–67.
60. The *ʿārifān* are those who are knowers of *maʿrifa* or true knowledge of God (in contrast to *ʿilm* or science).
61. The *chiroghdan* (*chirāghdān*) is a contained space or vessel for the burning of candles and herbs used in certain Ismāʿīlī rituals performed at shrines, rooted in Zoroastrian ritual traditions. Shoh Isomiddin is also known as Shoh Hasan Medina, indicating his origins in the Hijaz.
62. The example of the sacred history of Sayrām is a poignant example, as discussed by DeWeese in his "Sacred History for a Central Eurasian Town."
63. Green, "Stories of Saints and Sultans," 424.

7

Monks and Their Daughters

MONASTERIES AS MUSLIM-CHRISTIAN BOUNDARIES

Thomas Sizgorich

Introduction

IN 1993, EDWARD Said suggested something that probably should have been obvious at the time. Said argued in his *Culture and Imperialism* that cultural forms produced within societies subsumed in imperial or colonial projects, and particularly those that treat relations between imperialist and imperialized subjects, are often most profitably read with close attention to the larger political and cultural circumstances in which they were produced. Said further suggested that such texts may in turn shed considerable light upon the historical circumstances in which they were produced.[1] The publication of *Culture and Imperialism*, like the publication fifteen years earlier of Said's *Orientalism*, sparked much discussion, imitation, and critique.[2] One outpost of the academic world has remained all but untouched by Said's admonition and the many responses to it, however. Those scholars whose focus of inquiry is the literature produced by Muslim and Christian authors in the decades and centuries after the first/seventh century *futūḥ*, or "openings" of formerly Roman and Persian imperial lands in Syria, Egypt, and Mesopotamia, have but infrequently viewed this literature through the analytical prism Said suggested in *Culture and Imperialism*, and indeed seem scarcely aware of it or the long list of other works that have examined the tight interconnections between culture and imperial systems of power and knowledge.

In some ways, this is understandable. Certain figures that perform quite prominently in the analyses of Said, Anne McClintock, or Mary Louise Pratt—those of "nation" and "European modernity," for example—are of course figures "native" to the academic domain of the Modernist, and so are largely assumed to be unavailable for service in analyses of the early Middle

Ages.[3] Perhaps more seriously, European- and American-trained scholars of Arabic language and literature, or Islamic history and religion, may be forgiven for feeling a bit queasy at the first invocation of "Orientalism"; while it is a term scarcely uttered without a sneer in most academic circles, it is still the term of choice for many in our field to denote our discipline. Nor is this a simple problem of awkward semantics; the history of the field itself, many of its founding figures, and many of its crucial scholarly resources bear what some postcolonial critics would insist is an indelible moral stain testifying to the discipline's guilty history of complicity with European colonialism.[4] Indeed, it is one thing to read a highly elaborated discourse of moral outrage over the abuses of European colonialism, riding the swells of that outrage in satisfied camaraderie, and quite another to understand that outrage as aimed, directly or indirectly, at what one does.

Still, the neglect of Said's admonition is unfortunate, to say the least. The *dār al-Islām* ("Abode of Islam") within which early medieval Muslim and Christian authors imagined and wrote was a world created by an explosive process of imperial conquest during which vast non-Muslim populations were taken under the control of a very small Muslim Arab minority.[5] Most of the earliest Muslim histories, legal works, and collections of Qur'ānic exegesis ruminate in whole or in part upon on the origins of the Muslim empire and the dilemmas and challenges of empire.[6] Moreover, in many examples of the *adab* literature of a slightly later period, a highly elaborated imperial Muslim fantasy life emerges in lush narratives of encounter, mimesis, and seduction.[7] Meanwhile, Christian authors living under Muslim rule also found themselves captivated by questions of conquest, empire, and subjection to "foreign" domination. Intriguingly, Christian authors, like their Muslim peers, very often centered these imaginings in what I have, for want of a better term, called "monastic space." By "monastic space," I of course mean Christian monasteries, which loomed large in the fantasies of both Muslims and Christians of this period, but also the distinctive space that was understood by Muslim and Christian authors alike to abide around Christian practitioners of ascetic renunciation. This was an imaginative space that was imbued with the complicated consequences of a highly elaborated mythology concerning monks as bearers of ancient strains of prophetic knowledge and numinous power, a mythology crucial by the second/eighth century at the latest to both Muslim and Christian communal histories.[8] More specifically for our purposes, monastic space was also an imagined space inhabited by idealized and abstracted Christian figures, figures that were suitable, as we shall see, for service as metonyms for an essentialized Christianity and essentialized Christian subjects.

In the first centuries after the *futūḥ*, Christian monastic space provided Christian and Muslim authors a venue in which to fantasize about the relationship of each community with the other. For Muslims, this involved the process of understanding Islam and the Muslim *umma* as integral parts of a much older world and history of prophecy, revelation, and empire. Central to this history in the imaginations of early Muslims were the figure of the monk and the institutions in which monks resided. Monastic space was, early Muslims believed, where Christians were most Christian; it was Christian monasteries, for example, in which true Christianity (or that form of Christianity that most closely reflected the teachings of ʿĪsā, son of Mary) had abided long after its corruption within Roman society.[9] Accordingly, monastic space was a natural environment in which to imagine encounters between Muslims and essentialized representatives of Christianness, and so in which to elaborate imperial fantasies of encounter, seduction, conversion, and domination.

One animating desire of the imperial fantasies so articulated in early Muslim texts is what reads very much as a longing for recognition and acceptance by the conquered Christian subject population. This took the form, on the one hand, of tales told of Muḥammad's recognition by a Christian monk at the earliest stage of his prophetic career, the recognition of Muslim warriors during the conquest by a Christian ascetic as essentially like himself, stories of collegial relations between Christian monks and Muslim pietists, in which those Muslims are made the heirs of a much older pietist tradition, and, finally, the sexual seduction of Christian women and men during Muslim-Christian exchanges in and around monasteries. These stories are remarkable in part because they represent the fantasies of two mutually opposed segments of Muslim society, those of strict pietists on the one hand, and those of privileged power and wealth elites on the other.[10] However much these two groups may have disapproved of the behaviors of the other, each group found in monastic space an ideal venue for the iteration of imperial fantasies crafted in accordance with the specifics of their intra-communal identities.

For the Christians, on the other hand, monastic space provided a venue in which to dream the dreams of a once dominant population now subjected to a "foreign" power. These were fantasies of control, or at the very least powerful acts of subversion and "sly civility" as the postcolonial theorist Homi Bhabha has called it.[11] In these texts, powerful members of the dominant population often find themselves at the mercy of the subject Christian population because the subject population, despite its political dependence and subservience, still possesses individuals who maintain direct relations with the divine, and who can mobilize these relations to serve the ends of their communities. Less often, the power of the Christians manifested in monastic space is less the fearsome power of the prophet and more the wily slipperiness of the trickster who uses the complacency or imperial conceits of the dominant group against it as a means to his/her own ends. These, of course, were familiar tropes in very old Christian narratives; the empires may have changed, but Christianity's organizing narratives had long described precisely these sorts of relations between Christian communities and the powerful of the present world, and indeed understood the capacity of disempowered Christians and Christian communities to operate in this way as a sign of the power of the faith itself.

In what follows, I shall examine the ways in which monastic space was employed by Muslim and Christian authors working in several different literary genres. This will necessarily entail rather rapid movement from one genre to another in order to craft as complete an image as possible of the relations Muslim and Christian authors envisioned in this monastic space. Toward this end, we shall begin with the forms of late antique Christian writing in which monks and monastic space were first crafted, and in which they took on the forms and functions that they would carry into later Christian and Muslim texts.

I

From the fourth century of the Common Era on, Christian monastic space had been a space of definitions and distinctions. In the fourth century, monastic institutions and their ascetic inmates entered the late ancient cultural imaginary as figures inextricably linked to the circumscription of proper Christian belief, behavior, and praxis, and to the institution of communal boundaries that set one "community of God" in stark opposition to those communities alienated from God, whether through the worship of lesser, "pagan" spiritual beings, or through mistaken or erroneous Christological or theological belief.[12] The archetypical monk, Antony, was written into the imaginations of Christians throughout the Mediterranean in this context, as the bishop Athanasius of Alexandria (d. 373 CE) struggled with the leaders of other Christian communities, principally the Arians and Melitians, over the question of which community was the one, true community of God.[13] In the hagiographical works of the succeeding centuries, we consistently encounter monasteries and monastic men and women as figures deeply implicated in intercommunal controversies at whose root were questions of identity, legitimacy, and the authenticity of the truths around which opposed faith communities had cohered.[14]

In practice, however, monastic institutions were never the pristine centers of "orthodox" belief (whatever that was taken to mean in any specific time and place) elite authors like Athanasius made them out to be, nor were the inmates of such institutions necessarily strident champions of one or another theological or Christological position. Instead, as James Goehring has demonstrated, monastic institutions from a very early period seem to have been venues in which ascetics of a variety of theological opinions and representing often opposed communities dwelled in close proximity to one another, and presumably in some sort of practice-based communion with one another, despite whatever specifics of belief might have otherwise divided them. Goehring has suggested convincingly that the basis for participation in these monastic communities was not specific theological belief, as the patristic authors would often have us believe, but rather enthusiasm for a mode of worship based upon renunciation and ascetic rigor.[15]

Similarly, although Christian monks are frequently presented in Christian texts as champions against ancient local religious practice and practitioners, and as fervent destroyers of idols and confounders of the magical practices associated with those idols, archaeological evidence has also shown that in addition to "orthodox" tracts and canonical texts, monastic inmates also possessed considerable libraries of decidedly heterodox reading, including magical pamphlets and detailed instructions for spell-casting.[16] Thus, although monastic space marked crucial boundaries between opposed identity groups, it also seems to have often afforded connections between the very things it was meant to segregate. Indeed, much recent scholarship originating in the fields of anthropology and sociology has suggested that this is frequently the fate of such boundaries and boundary markers. Whether taking the form of front yard fences or ritualized combat, the structures upon which communities depend to impose a readily legible and dependable grammar of demarcation between "us" and "them" tend to bind and join as well as separate and divide. Moreover, according to the cultural anthropologist Fredrick Barth, such boundary markers often have the effect of positively encouraging or facilitating exchange across the boundaries they mark and preserve.[17]

Most often, this function of boundaries is a kind of surplus unintended or unforeseen by those who put such structures in place or who depend upon them as markers of limits, whether these limits are in character geographic, behavioral, doctrinal, political, or otherwise. In the case of monastic space in late antiquity, it was in part the epic scale of the power acknowledged by all Christian communities to reside in ascetic praxis and traditions that engendered this surplus. As an almost universally recognizable sign for the numinous truths upon which bitterly divided communities staked their respective claims to authenticity, monastic space also became for pre-Islamic Christians a site upon which members of opposed communities converged, drawn like moths to what they perceived as the homes of blazing truths in the inky black of the present world, truths whose brilliance blotted out what became by comparison much smaller questions of specific doctrine and dogma.

II

Not surprisingly, with the advent of Islam, very early Muslim authors seized upon the figure of the monk and his sanctuary as a means not only of asserting the defining truths of their own religion, but also as a means of simultaneously declaring a privileged affinity with Christianity.[18] One very early and widely repeated cluster of stories concerning the emergence of Muḥammad as a prophet of God has a young Muḥammad first recognized as a prophet by Christian monks. In the most common variant of these stories, to be found in Ibn Isḥāq's second/eighth century *Sīrat rasūl Allāh*, for example, this monk is a Syrian anchorite named Baḥīrā.[19] In early Muslim Baḥīrā stories, it is often made clear that Baḥīrā is to be understood as a possessor of ancient, arcane knowledge concerning the Abrahamic line of prophets, an inheritance that in some traditions is represented by his possession of ancient texts full of numinous truths. In al-Balādhurī's third/ninth century *Ansāb al-ashrāf*, Baḥīrā is described as one of "the *'ulamā'* of the monks."[20] Accordingly, his recognition of the young Muḥammad as a prophet from the lineage of Abraham, Moses, and Jesus helps to locate both Islam and its prophet within a much older narrative of prophecy and revelation, and so works to authorize Muḥammad and his community as inheritors of true revelation. This, in turn, legitimates Islam as a true community of God.

Similarly, one of the very earliest historical texts we possess for the conquest of Syria, the *Ta'rīkh futūḥ al-Shām* of al-Azdī, contains the following scene. When the Roman army first encountered the Muslim army in Syria, al-Azdī wrote, a Christian Arab ascetic traveling with the Romans was sent into the Muslim camp to ascertain their character. When he returned, he reported to the Roman commander that the invaders were,

> A people staying up through the night praying, and remaining abstinent during the day, commanding the right and forbidding the wrong, monks by night, lions by day. Should their king steal, they cut off his hand, and if he commits adultery they stone him.[21]

Here we have another scene in which a precious form of recognition is granted to the early Muslim community by an ascetic witness, a witness that is who carries the powerful charge accorded to practitioners of ascetic forms of renunciation within the late ancient cultural and religious milieu. The Christian ascetic who enters the Muslim camp recognizes in the founding members of the Muslim communities outside of Arabia a kindred devotion to God, and, accordingly, a brand of piety that marks these men as likely agents of the same God revered by the Christian holy man dispatched by the Roman commander as a spy in the camp of the Muslims. Perhaps not surprisingly, other early Muslim texts recalled some particularly prominent Muslim individuals to have received similar forms of recognition from Christian ascetics. In one third/ninth century text, for example, a Christian monk in Jerusalem is made to tell of the outstanding piety of the caliph ʿUmar II. ʿUmar would frequently stay with the monk, we learn, and the monk recalls that one night, when ʿUmar was sleeping on the roof of his dwelling, water began to drip down on the monk's chest as he tried to sleep. The monk thought this odd, particularly since there was no rain that night, and so he investigated. He soon discovered that the source of the water running down from his roof was the copious weeping of ʿUmar as he performed his prayers.[22]

This borrowing of the Christian ascetic's gaze in the service of very early Muslim imperial fantasy is crucial for contextualizing the campaigns of conquest in which the Muslims are embroiled. Because they are recognized as being "like monks" by a Christian ascetic, for example, and as men whose piety is of a familiar type because it is expressed in familiar ways, the Arab Muslim *mujāhidūn* imagined by al-Azdī are legible not simply as Bedouin raiders, but as agents of God acting in service of authentic revelation. Indeed, one subtext within this work, as Lawrence Conrad and Nadia Maria El Cheikh have noted, is the moral imperative with which the corrupt Romans were driven from the lands of Syria, and replaced with rulers whose piety was recognized first and foremost by the Christian ascetic conjured here.[23] As dreamed by al-Azdī and his sources, it is through this Christian ascetic's eyes that we first glimpse the new rulers of this ancient land, and articulated in this Christian ascetic's words is the basis for Muslim claim upon the legitimate rule of these lands as it emerges in early Muslim imperial discourse.

In these second/eighth and third/ninth century Muslim texts, then, two crucial foundational events in the history of the Muslim *umma*, the emergence of Muḥammad as a prophet, and the conquests of what would become the Muslim empire were cast in the gaze of Christian ascetics for the purpose of locating both events within much longer and older narratives of revelation and empire. In both cases, monastic space was the habitat of Christian figures who could serve as indisputable witnesses to the legitimacy of Islam because they served as metonyms, as they so frequently did for members of Christian communities themselves, for true Christianity as a tradition and real Christians as a community.

These moves on the part of early Muslim authors should be understood as manifestations of one particularly pronounced tendency in Muslim writings of the second/eighth century. In accordance with this tendency, the advent of Islam was cast as but one episode within a much longer history of revelation and empire in the Mediterranean and Middle East. This trend manifested itself in, for example, the inclination of some producers of Qur'ānic exegesis to cast the Persian-Roman wars of the early seventh century as but another front in a larger war of polytheism against monotheism in which Muḥammad's besieged community in Arabia was also embroiled, and which climaxed as, on the same day, the Muslims triumphed at Badr and the Roman forces under Heraclius finally defeated the Persian shah on a faraway battlefield.[24] Elsewhere, such early Muslim authors as Wahb b. Munabbih (d. 110/728) also drew upon the themes, plots, and characters of Jewish and Christian prophetic traditions as a means of situating Muḥammad within the current of sacred history as it was imagined in late antiquity. In one tradition attributed to Wahb and a group of former Christians and/or Jews, for example, the lineage of the prophets is traced from Adam through Abraham and the family of David to Jesus, who would be the last prophet of the Children of Israel.[25] Elisha prophesized Jesus's mission, Wahb reported, as he also prophesized the appearance of Muḥammad. In so doing, he enjoined the commandments of both prophets upon the sons of Israel. "He said, 'He will come to you riding a donkey,' meaning 'Īsā [Jesus] (Peace be upon him), 'and then, after him, one riding a camel (*ṣāḥib al-gamal*) will come to you' meaning Muḥammad (may God bless him and grant him peace)."[26]

In addition to the recognition claimed by Muslim authors for their community in the gaze of Christian ascetics, the emperor Heraclius was also enlisted by such very early authors as al-Azdī as a witness to the piety and legitimacy of Islam's claims to rule what was to become its imperial domain.[27] In time, however, the imperial system for which Heraclius served so ably as a metonym would recede to a rather different stature in the imaginations of most Muslims, and the Roman Empire, while still crucial to Muslim eschatology and political ambitions, would become a figure tinged with the foreign and exotic.[28] By contrast, the subject Christian communities for which monastic space served such a crucial representative function would remain an integral part of the caliphal empire under the Umayyads and the Abbasids. Accordingly, it was upon the stage afforded by monastic space that early Muslim authors continued to bring to life imperial fantasies in which an idealized Christian gaze remained crucial for the articulation of evolving projects of Muslim self-fashioning.

III

One of the genres of early medieval Islamic literature within which this tendency becomes particularly visible is known as *diyārāt* ("monasteries") literature.[29] *Diyārāt* works frequently narrate meetings between Muslims and Christians within the confines of Christian monasteries, which are in turn crafted by the authors of these works as paradisiacal garden spots, surrounded by lush vegetation, nourished by running water and overflowing wine bowls, and populated with desirable young Christian men and women whose seduction by Muslim men frequently provides the culmination of the exoticizing tendencies of such texts.[30]

Consider, for example, the following narrative, which is attributed to the *Kitāb al-diyārāt* of Abū l-Faraj al-Iṣbahānī (d. 967), a text that now only exists in fragments preserved in Abū l-Faraj's other works, or in the texts of later authors. The narrator of this story, a Muslim man named Abū Bakr Muḥammad b. Qāsim al-Anbārī, recalls how he had been a visitor at the monastery of al-Anwār, near the town of ʿAmmūriyya in the territory of the Romans.[31] It seems that he was tasked with traveling to ʿAmmūriyya on some sort of mission, perhaps diplomatic in nature. During his visit to the monastery, he had been treated with great hospitality by one ʿAbd al-Masīḥ ("Servant of the Messiah"), who was archimandrite of the monastery. Before he left the monastery, he notes, he was deeply impressed with the strivings and religious observances of the monks.

A year later, the Muslim performed the Ḥajj, and encountered ʿAbd al-Masīḥ while circumambulating *al-bayt al-sharīf.* When he recognized the old man as a monk, and so as an individual who had no business in Mecca, he asked him, "Aren't you ʿAbd al-Masīḥ the monk? (*anta ʿAbd al-Masīḥ al-rāhib*?)" to which the ascetic formerly known as ʿAbd al-Masīḥ replied, "Nay, rather I am ʿAbd Allāh the desirer of God's pardon (*bal ana ʿAbd Allāh rāghib fī ʿafw Allāh*)"; note the rhyme between *rāhib* and *rāghib*. When he discovered that the former monk had accepted Islam, al-Anbārī was overjoyed and asked to hear how the conversion came about. The former monk then told the following story.

A wandering band of Muslim ascetics (*zuhhād*) had come into the vicinity of the town of ʿAmmūriyya, and dispatched one of its members into the town to get food for the group. Upon arriving in the town, the Muslim ascetic cast eyes upon a Christian slave girl (*jāriyya*) with whom he immediately fell in love. Catching himself coveting the girl, the ascetic slapped himself in the face so hard he lost consciousness for a time. When he recovered himself, he returned to his fellow ascetics, and told them to go on without him; he was staying. His fellows exhorted him, chided him, and finally washed their hands of him, and he returned to the village. There, he sat on the stoop of the shop in which the girl worked, staring into her face. When she asked him what his business was there, he told her, and she tried to get rid of him. The now-former ascetic refused to move, however, and continued to gaze upon the object of his desire.

The girl told her family and neighbors. A deputation of neighborhood youths was given the task of dealing with the amorous Muslim. When they found him, they beat him with rocks until they badly injured his head and destroyed his face. When he was still not dissuaded, the townspeople decided to kill him. One of the townsmen alerted the monk, who came and retrieved the Muslim and nursed him back to health. When he could walk again, the Muslim returned to the front step of the shop in which the slave girl worked. She came to him then and said that she would take mercy on him, and asked him to convert so that they could marry. The idea appalled the Muslim, and he refused just in time to be set upon by the neighborhood gang again. After this second beating, the monk once again tried to nurse him, but this time the beating was too severe and the Muslim died. Before he expired, however, he prayed that he and the girl should be reunited in paradise.

Late that night, the Christian girl let out a great scream as she lay in her bed. The people of the village rushed to her aid, and she told them that the Muslim man had come to her in a dream, and had led her to the gates of heaven, but explained that the kingdom within was forbidden to unbelievers. Accordingly, she converted by his hand, and he led her through a tour of heavenly delights. Finally, they arrived at a castle, and he explained that this castle was for the two of them, and that he would not enter the castle with anyone but her. He then assured her that she would be with him in the castle in five nights, God willing. Then he picked two apples from the trees of the castle, and gave her one and told her to eat it. He then gave her the other, and told her to keep it so that the monks could see it. He then took her back to her house.

When she had finished her story, the young Christian woman pulled the second apple from her pocket, and her neighbors marveled at its beauty as it shone like a star in the darkness of the night. Then they took the girl to the monastery. The monks took the apple and shared it out among themselves to taste it. It was sweeter than any fruit they had known. Perhaps this was a trick by the devil designed to lure this girl from her religion, they said. The villagers took her back to the village, where she ceased to eat and drink for five days. Finally, she went out from her home, laid herself on the grave of the Muslim, and died. In the morning, two Muslim men and two Muslim women, all dressed in clothes of hair, showed up at the village and announced that a Muslim woman had died, and that they were there to bury her. The Christian villagers disputed this, and claimed the dead woman as their own. An argument ensued, and one of the old Muslims suggested summoning the monks from the monastery. If they could remove the body from the grave, then the woman had died a Christian. If the Muslims succeeded in moving the body, on the other hand, then the woman had died a Muslim.

Forty monks, including the archimandrite ʿAbd al-Masīḥ, came and tried desperately to move the body, but they could not. Then the two Muslim men easily removed her body, and carried it to a cave where they and the Muslim women performed purification rites over the body, washing it and praying. Then they buried the woman's body next to that of the Muslim. The monks and the people of the village, having witnessed this, accepted Islam and moved into "the Jazīra" seeking Muslims knowledgeable in Islamic law and praxis to instruct them in their new religion.[32]

While it takes place mostly outside of the monastery itself, the story attributed here to Abū Bakr Muḥammad b. Qāsim al-Anbārī contains several elements that are typical of *diyārāt* literature, and that are particularly indicative of the imperial circumstances under which this literature was produced. Narrated by a former monk, the story tells of the desire of a Muslim man for a Christian woman, a desire that is finally fulfilled not only with the union of two individuals, but with the recognition by the woman, the monk, and the Christian community of ʿAmmūriyya of the defining truth around which the Muslim *umma* as a community is based. One means of measuring the intentions of this story is to consider for a moment some other ways in which it might have unfolded. In the period during which this story takes place, a Christian servant girl residing in *bilad al-Rūm* ("the lands of the Romans") need not have been pursued by a Muslim man in the manner described in this story. Under Muslim law, it would have been fully permissible for a Muslim man to abduct this Christian woman from the *dār al-ḥarb* ("Abode of War," i.e., the lands of the enemy infidel) and to make her his by force.[33]

This is not a story of abduction or rape, however, and the only violence suffered in it is the violence visited upon the Muslim by the Christian inhabitants of ʿAmmūriyya. Rather, this is a story in which, through persuasion and miraculous proofs, the hearts of a Christian community are won to the truth of Islam. It is, moreover, a story in which the desire of the Muslim for his love object is finally returned, and returned in recognition of his gentleness, patience, and the validity of the transcendent truths to which he is a bridge. It is a story, in short, about the winning of hearts and minds by an empire whose rule proceeds from its moral superiority, and from its possession of revealed truths whose power obligates all human beings, but forcibly compels no one.

In another story from Abū l-Faraj's *diyārāt* text, the caliph Mutawakkil (d. 279/892), traveling in Syria, encounters the daughter of a monk while visiting a monastery. The girl, whose name was Saʿānīn, charms the caliph with her fine looks and exquisite manners, but drives him to rapture by reciting Arabic poetry in his presence. The caliph begs the girl to spend the day with him, and she agrees. They feast together and drink wine. Finally, the girl sings for him one of the songs of her people, and his heart is captured. Meanwhile, the girl has been falling for the caliph, and their mutual passion mounts. The story is brought to a rather abrupt ending, as the narrator states, "Then al-Mutawakkil kindled her interest [in his religion]. She accepted Islam, and he married her. She remained a favorite with him until he died. She was in his palace [when it happened]."[34]

In other stories, we encounter similar tales of Muslim-Christian seduction, not all of which necessarily end with the conversion of the Christian. In one such story, for example, a Muslim becomes infatuated with a beautiful young monk and eventually seduces him. When this comes to the attention of the other monks, however, and they plan to throw him from the heights of the monastery, the amorous Muslim beats a hasty retreat from the monastery.[35] As an imperial literature, the *diyārāt* genre enlists the monastery and its inhabitants as handy representatives of the subject Christian population as a whole. These representatives can then be cast in fantasy relationships with Muslim figures, like the caliph himself, who themselves emerge as metaphorical representations of Islam and the Muslim *umma*. In these plays of imperial fantasy, the objects of the desirous Muslim imperial gaze return that desire, and in so doing may often be understood to accept and indeed confirm the communal truths of the Muslims. Conversion is a neat conclusion to such encounters, but it is not necessary; rather, the idealized Christians who inhabit the monasteries and other outposts of Christian ascetic space fulfill their roles in such texts merely by returning the desire of their imperial masters, and, in so doing, affirming the organizing tenets of early medieval Muslim imperial discourse.

IV

The question of seduction and conversion was also very clearly a concern for Christians writing under Muslim imperial rule. In the passion of Michael the Sabaïte, for example, Michael is approached in the marketplace by a eunuch in the service of one of the caliph's wives, and convinced to return with the eunuch to the palace. There, the wife of the caliph is taken with a burning passion for him, much as the Muslim *zāhid* is overcome with desire for the Christian girl in the *diyārāt* text we examined above.[36] Michael resists her attempts to seduce him, however, and is whipped and sent to the caliph with a demand from the wife that she be given power of life or death over the young monk. Intriguingly, in this text the theme of desire between Muslim ruler and Christian subject seems to have carried across confessional boundaries, and to have taken up residence in the literature of the Christian subject population as well as in that of the dominant Muslim group. Once again, moreover, we find that there abides around the figure of the Christian ascetic, in this case the young monk Michael, a space in which Christian and Muslim authors alike could fantasize about the dynamics of empire and power, and could do so in accordance with a shared semiotic vocabulary.

Within this space, Christian authors living under Muslim rule elaborated on very old Christian genres and topoi to articulate certain tenets of their own fantasy relationship with Islam and with Muslims. These genres and topoi included martyr stories like the *Passion of Michael the Sabaïte*, hagiographical renditions of the careers of ascetic superstars, dispute texts, and local histories. These texts reveal an abiding concern among Christian authors with the potential of Christians to master their Muslim rulers not through military might or physical force, but through their moral superiority, the power of the numinous truths that resided at the core of their confession, and through the capacity of Christian subjects to strategically evade the coercive force Muslims had at their disposal should they have occasion to use it. Often such evasions were inflected with the supernatural glamour of the "holy man," but it is nevertheless recognizable first and foremost as the nimble penchant of the subaltern trickster to find the cracks and crevices left in the workings of imperial power, and to profitably exploit them.

One such trickster was the anti-Chalcedonian monk-bishop of Alexandria, Isaac. Isaac enjoyed an irenic and even cordial relationship with the local Muslim *amīr*, ʿAbd al-ʿAzīz. Despite this, however, the potential for violence that abides at the heart of all imperial relations was ever present if usually unspoken even between Isaac and the *amīr*. We are told, for example, that once certain malicious Muslims talked the *amīr* into forbidding Isaac, on pain of death, to cross himself when he came to dine at the *amīr*'s table. When he received this command, Isaac simply asked if the *amīr* preferred that he sit at the place across the table from him, to the left, to the right or right in front of him, gesturing with his hand to each position (and in the process making the sign of the cross).[37]

More often, however, the power of Christian ascetics as imagined in such texts is unambiguous and grounded in the affinities between Christian and Muslim religious, moral, and ethical systems to which Muslim texts make such frequent reference. This takes the form, for example, of the Syrian monk Timothy of Kākhushtā's capacity to freeze an adulterous Muslim in the act of riding his horse to fornicate with his mistress. The Muslim, it seems, was ashamed to have the monk see him make his way into the village where his lover lived, and so would make the trip at night. Despite his circumspection, however, the Muslim is transformed into a kind of dry husk in the middle of one of his nightly forays. Timothy has his disciples retrieve the man, and eventually restores him to his previous form. When the Muslim can speak again, he says, "I sinned when I committed fornication and lied before God, thinking that you would not know what is hidden... my father, I swear to God that from now on I shall never again commit this sin, not for as long as I shall live in this world."[38]

In this episode, it would seem that Timothy's power to transform human beings into desiccated shells is matched by a moral authority over the Muslim that derives from the closely kindred nature of the moral and ethical codes of their respective communities. The behavior that Timothy corrects is clearly understood to be sinful not only from the point of view of his own Christian morality, but from that of the Muslim *umma* as well. It is for this reason that Timothy's capacity to arrest and forbid the Muslim though supernatural intervention is legible as a demonstration not simply of the power of Timothy as a wonderworker, but of his power as an moral arbiter whose judgments are binding upon Muslims and Christians alike, whatever the arrangements of political and imperial power under which he resides.

This power as moral arbiter derived from the fact that the Christian and Muslim communities both traced their descent through a lineage of the prophetic figures and each, albeit sometimes grudgingly, recognized the other's belief that its holy texts represented the revealed will and attendant moral commandments of the God of Abraham. Christian apologists, for example, frequently credited Muḥammad with leading his people away from idolatry, comparing him to such Old Testament prophets as Moses and Abraham.[39] The Christian monk abided in the imaginations of early medieval Muslims as an arbiter of ancient monotheist knowledge and, clearly, the moral strictures that followed from this knowledge. Moreover, the monk and the charged space that surrounded him were crucial to Muslim claims to a place within the grand sweep of prophetic history. For Christians living under Muslim rule, this monastic/ascetic space became a crucial site of negotiation concerning the role Christians would continue to play as authoritative moral critics and guides. Perhaps more to the point, this monastic/ascetic space was also an ideal venue in which to reimagine relations between the Muslim empire and its Christian subjects.

In Thomas of Margā's ninth-century collection of hagiographical notices on the careers of prominent Iraqi monks, for example, we encounter an intriguing relationship between one ʿImrān b. Muḥammad al-Azdī, a local Muslim magnate, and two Christian monks, Rabban Cyriacus and Rabban Gabriel.[40] ʿImrān enters Thomas's narrative as a violent and acquisitive local grandee who has fixed his sights on ownership of the monastery of Bēth ʿĀbhē. By the time of his conflict with Rabban Cyriacus over control of Bēth ʿĀbhē, ʿImrān had taken by force a series of provinces in northern Mesopotamia, killing or driving away their former owners. The rolling process of conquest he represents comes to a jarring halt when he declares his intention to add Bēth ʿĀbhē to his possessions, however. Standing before the Muslim, Rabban Cyriacus unleashes a blistering torrent of rebuke, not only forbidding the Muslim control of the monastery and its lands, but cautioning him that the wrath of their common God now hangs perilously over his head.

> Behold I have warned you, and behold I have advised you for good; get yourself away from our monastery and it shall be well with you, lest you go quickly to the house of the dead. And know this also: because of all the blood of the believers which you have poured out, and the wretched people whom you have slain and whose houses you have seized, it is written with an iron style on a *shāmīr* stone in the record chamber of the justice of God (cf. Jeremiah 17:1).[41]

Although "by the sharpness of his tongue he put ʿImrān to shame," Rabban Cyriacus had not yet heard the last of the matter. It took first a miraculous visitation to ʿImrān, (rather in the fashion of Habakkuk's journey to Babylon, as Thomas points out), and then the appearance of a fiery, heavenly army standing guard around the monk (rather like that which accompanied Elijah, as Thomas notes) to finally convince the Muslim to abandon his designs on the monastery.[42] We have seen that for many Muslims, as for Christians like Thomas, monks were figures who bound the present to a towering prophetic past, and who could authoritatively locate contemporary figures within a highly compelling metanarrative of revelation, numinous power, and transcendent truth (much as they had done Muḥammad or the *futūḥ*-era *mujāhidūn*). While we need not imagine that a real-life ʿImrān would be dissuaded from his ambitions by a figure like Rabban Cyriacus, it is very easy to understand why contemporary Christians might fantasize about a figure like Rabban Cyriacus who could end, at least at a closely localized level, the rolling acquisition of power and property that the *futūḥ* represented and which is effectively personified in the figure of ʿImrān. That this process was halted not by military might, but by an essentialized representative of Christian moral authority and priority in relation to God's revealed truths, coincides closely with what we have seen elsewhere of the post-conquest fantasies of Christians living under Muslim rule.

More explicitly, the product of these fantasies is Thomas's story of the pact between Rabban Gabriel and ʿImrān. In that story, Gabriel demonstrates his gift of foreknowledge to ʿImrān, whereby "[ʿImrān] knew and perceived with his soul's understanding that the esteem of the Christians was mighty and exalted before God, for behold their holy men see and know things which are hidden." Soon thereafter, ʿImrān enters the cell of the old monk, falls down before him and is granted a kiss on his head from the old man. Then, sitting at the old man's feet and grasping his legs "as a mark of honor," ʿImrān agrees to a sort of covenant with Gabriel. In return for a promise of forbearance toward and protection of the Christians of his territories, Gabriel offers to reveal to ʿImrān the future of his family. The future Gabriel reveals is a brilliant one; ʿImrān's lineage will rule and conquer all those who stand before them, their fortune like a perpetual Nisān full of bounty and plenty. In return, Gabriel reminds ʿImrān, he must "show love to the Christians, and especially to the monasteries and convents, and to ascetics, and scholars and priests, and deacons."[43]

In the imaginative space that surrounded Rabban Gabriel and Rabban Cyriacus, then, Thomas of Margā dreamed a world in which tyrannical local Muslim officials could be brought to heel by the prophetic power of Christian monks, and in which the drumbeat of Muslim conquest could be stilled by the moral and spiritual authority wielded by Christian ascetics. The key to these fantasies was the recognition accorded to the numinous power of the monks by the Muslims themselves. Whereas we have seen that in the decades and centuries after the *futūḥ*, Muslim authors conjured the Prophet Muḥammad, the early Muslim *mujāhidūn*, and the famously pious caliph ʿUmar II in the gaze of Christian monks as a means of legitimating them and locating them within a grand narrative of revelation and empire, here Christian authors pursued their own narrative ends by conjuring the monk in the gaze of powerful Muslims. That what these powerful Muslim saw in the monk caused them to cower in awe, or petition the mercy of such figures as Timothy of Kākhushtā or Rabban Gabriel, reveals as much about the fantasy life of post-conquest Christian authors as the *diyārāt* literature we briefly surveyed above does about the imperial fantasies of their Muslim rulers. This is particularly so when we recall the role of monastic space in both Muslim and Christian literature as a venue in which authors of either community might conjure essentialized, ideal "Christians" as a means of articulating their fantasies about relations between Muslims and Christians, Islam and Christianity.

One final trope commonly encountered in post-conquest Christian literature will serve to further illustrate this tendency. It will also suggest something of both the fluency of each community with the fantasy life of the other, and the perhaps unexpected but also unsurprising agreement between the two communities concerning the ideal forms that intercommunal relations should take. This trope involves healing miracles performed by Christian monks to the benefit of rich and powerful Muslims. In one sense, this was merely a permutation of an age-old topos in Christian hagiography, one in accordance with which Christian holy men attracted converts through acts of healing. Read with due attention to the imperial context in which post-conquest Christian texts were produced, however, such healing stories are legible in a rather different way. In these texts, monastic space is once again the site of an inversion of the power relations that permeated the social and political world through which real Christians and Muslims moved from day to day. Sometimes, these stories culminate with the decision on the part of the Muslims involved to convert to Christianity. In third/ninth century Iraq, for example, the Muslim governor of Mosul was said to have set out with his ailing son to seek the aid of the monk Rabban Hōrmīzd. On the way, however, the boy died. Despite this, locals advised the governor not to return to Mosul without first visiting Rabban Hōrmīzd. When the Muslim arrived with the body of his son, Rabban Hōrmīzd revived the boy, inspiring the Muslim governor to convert to Christianity.[44] Intriguingly, however, this trope was clearly familiar to Muslim authors, and could be reversed. In a Muslim Ḥanbalī *Ṭabaqāt* text, for example, one religious scholar tells of the time he went to a Christian monastery seeking a medical cure, and ended up inspiring the monastery to accept Islam en masse. This decision had everything to do with the manner of the Muslim's arrival at the monastery: he appeared outside its gates riding a lion like a pony.[45]

Often, however, the more interesting of these healing tales do not result in conversion. In the *Life* of Timothy of Kākhushtā, for example, the caliph Hārūn al-Rashīd's son is healed with the aid of oil blessed by Timothy, and in return he promises a series of concessions to the Christians of his realm that reads like a recitation of the basic rights Christians within the caliphate enjoyed under Islamic law. That is, in this text, the generally quite generous rights and obligations afforded to Christians under Muslim law were to be understood as concessions granted by Hārūn al-Rashīd to a powerful Christian ascetic in return for an act of numinous healing![46] Elsewhere in Timothy's *Life*, we encounter another iteration of this trope, which carries within it what I take to be one of the common and enduring concerns of both Muslim and Christian authors as they narrated their fantasies concerning relations between the dominant and subject communities within the *dār al-Islām*.

In that story, a rich Muslim sets out from his home in Persia with his sick little boy. His destination is Timothy's sanctuary, where he hopes that he will find a cure for his son. On the road, however, things go terribly wrong. The man loses his property and his son to robbers. Then, as if mocking him, Satan tries to convince him that even were he to have brought his little boy to the monk's pillar, the monk would have insisted upon his conversion to Christianity in return for a cure. When he arrives at Timothy's enclosure, however, he finds that the devil has tried to deceive him. The old monk says to him, "[I know] the accursed one whispered to you, advising you to return and saying to you that I would desire you to leave your faith; know, rather, that God compels no one." Their common God has seen the Muslim's faith, Timothy assures him, and it has pleased Him. He then promises the man that he will find his son healthy at home, helping to tend his father's fields. From that time on, the story concludes, the man and his son would visit the old monk once a year, honoring him with presents, and he them with his prayers.[47]

This seems as appropriate an image with which to close as anyone might choose. Tellingly, it is an image that will have been as at home in a Muslim narrative as it is in the Christian *Life* of Timothy of Kākhushtā. Within this image, we find the fantasies of post-*futūḥ* Muslims and Christians fulfilled as completely as any single image could do. For the Christian reader, the monk's proximity to God has manifested itself in the dominant positioning of the Christian with regard to the Muslim, and in the properly reverential attitude taken by the Muslim to that Christian. For the Muslim reader, the Muslim protagonist of this story has had his faith in God, and the validity of the route to God he has chosen, validated in the gaze of a Christian ascetic who closely recalls the other Christian *ruhbān* we have encountered above in a variety of Muslim texts. For readers of both communities, the notion that "God compels no one" will have resonated with familiar ideals of toleration and the necessarily voluntary nature of true faith. But it will also have sat uneasily beside tragic, if occasional, failures of Muslims and Christians alike to enact the ethos it expresses. Despite this, however, and despite whatever misgivings we may have about the myriad problems of power and its abuse in any imperial venture, that the imperial fantasies of Muslims and Christians alike revolved around images of coexistence, tolerance, and even mutual aid suggests something rather reassuring about the character of life in the early medieval *dār al-Islām*.

Notes

Thomas Sizgorich passed away before the editing of this volume was completed. The editor apologizes for any inconvenience caused by inconsistencies in the formatting of this chapter.

1. See Edward W. Said, *Culture and Imperialism* (New York, 1993), 12–14 and *passim*.
2. See, as an example, Bruce Robbins, Mary Louise Pratt, Jonathan Arac, R. Radhakrishnan, and Edward Said, "Edward Said's *Culture and Imperialism*: A Symposium," *Social Text* 40 (1994): 1–24.
3. See Anne McClintock, *Imperial Leather: Race, Gender and Sexuality in the Colonial Contest* (New York, 1995); Mary Louise Pratt, *Imperial Eyes: Travel Writing and Transculturation* (New York, 1992).
4. See Edward Said, *Orientalism* (New York, 1978). For a very useful overview of the immediate reaction to *Orientalism*, see Gyan Prakash, "Orientalism Now," *History and Theory* 34 (1995): 199–212.
5. For the Muslim conquests, see Fred M. Donner, *The Early Islamic Conquests* (Princeton, 1981). For relations between Muslims and non-Muslims after the conquests, see Michael G. Morony, *Iraq after the Muslim Conquest* (Princeton, 1984); Michael G. Morony, "History and Identity in the Syrian Chronicles," in J. J. Van Ginkel, H. L. Murre-Van Den Berg, T. M. Van Lint, eds., *Redefining Christian Identity: Cultural Interaction in the Middle East since the Rise of Islam* (Leuven,

2005), 1–33; Harald Suermann, "Copts and the Islam of the Seventh Century," in Emmanouela Grypeou, Mark N. Swanson, and David Thomas, eds., *The Encounter of Eastern Christianity with Early Islam* (Leiden, 2006), 96–109.

6. See, for example, Fred M. Donner, *Narratives of Islamic Origins: The Beginnings of Islamic Historical Writing* (Princeton: Darwin Press, 1998); Thomas Sizgorich, "Narrative and Community in Islamic Late Antiquity," *Past & Present* 185 (2004): 9–42; Lawrence I. Conrad, "The Conquest of Arwad: A Source Critical Study in the Historiography of the Early Medieval Near East," in Averil Cameron and Lawrence I. Conrad, eds., *The Byzantine and Early Islamic Near East: Problems in the Literary Source Material* (Princeton, 1992), 317–401; Chase F. Robinson, *Empire and Elites after the Muslim Conquest: The Transformation of Northern Mesopotamia* (Cambridge, 2000); Mahmoud Ayoub, "Dhimma in Qur'an and Hadith," in Robert Hoyland, ed., *Muslims and Others in Early Islamic Society* (Aldershot, 2004), 27–35; Albrecht Noth, "Problems of Differentiation between Muslims and Non-Muslims: Re-Reading the "Ordinances of ʿUmar" (*al-Shurūṭ al-ʿumariyya*)," ch. 5 in Hoyland, ed., *Muslims and Others in Early Islamic Society*, originally published as "Abgrenzungsprobleme zwischen Muslimen und Nicht-Muslimen, Die 'Bedingungen ʿUmars (*aš-Šur ūṭ al-ʿumatiyya*)' unter einem anderen Aspekt gelesen," *Jerusalem Studies in Arabic and Islam* 9 (1987): 290–315; M. J. Kister, "'Do Not Assimilate Yourselves…' *Lā tashabbahū…*" *Jerusalem Studies in Arabic and Islam* 12 (1989): 321–53. For the Christian communities of Iraq immediately following Muslim conquests, see Michael G. Morony, *Iraq after the Muslim Conquest* (Princeton, 1984), ch. 12, esp. 343–46.

7. *Adab* is "a genre in which literary elements are interwoven with moral and informative components. In modern Arabic, *adab* is 'literature,' but in the Middle Ages it referred to a much wider concept, a sort of very extensive belles lettres." Joseph Sadan, "An Admirable and Ridiculous Hero: Some Notes on the Bedouin in Medieval Arabic Belles Lettres, on a Chapter of *Adab* by al-Rāghib al-Iṣfahānī, and on a Literary Model in Which Admiration and Mockery Coexist," *Poetics Today* 10 (1989): 471–92, here 471.

8. See Sizgorich, "Narrative and Community."

9. See Sara Sviri, "*Wa-Rahbānīyatan Ibtadaʿūhū*: An Analysis of Traditions Concerning the Origin and Evolution of Christian Monasticism," *Jerusalem Studies in Arabic and Islam* 13 (1989): 195–208; and Ofer Livne-Kafri, "Early Muslim Ascetics and the World of Christian Monasticism," *Jerusalem Studies in Arabic and Islam* 20 (1996): 105–29.

10. On the opposition between these groups, see Nimrod Hurvitz, "Biographies of Mild Asceticism: A Study in Muslim Moral Imagination," *Studia Islamica* 85 (1997): 41–65.

11. Homi Bhabha, *The Location of Culture* (London, 1994 [1998]), 93–101. See also Jeffery Jerome Cohen, "Hybrids, Monsters, Borderlands: The Bodies of Gerald of Wales," in Jeffery Jerome Cohen, ed., *The Postcolonial Middle Ages* (New York, 2000), 85–104, esp. 87–89.

12. See David Brakke, *Athanasius and the Politics of Asceticism* (Oxford, 1995); David Brakke, *Demons and the Making of the Monk: Spiritual Combat in Early Christianity* (Cambridge, Mass., 2006); David Brakke, *Demons and the Making of the Monk: Spiritual Combat in Early Christianity* (Cambridge, Mass., 2006); James Goehring, "Monastic Diversity and Ideological Boundaries in Fourth-Century Egypt," *Journal of Early Christian Studies* 5 (1997): 61–83; David Brakke, "'Outside the Places, Within the Truth': Athanasius of Alexandria and the Localization of the Holy," in David Frankfurter, ed., *Pilgrimage and Holy Space in Late Antique Egypt* (Leiden, 1998), 445–81.
13. Brakke, "Outside the Places, Within the Truth," 445–81 and esp. 465–67.
14. See, for example, Timothy Gregory, *Vox Populi: Popular Opinion and Violence in the Religious Controversies of the Fifth Century A.D.* (Cincinnati, 1979); Susan Ashbrook Harvey, *Asceticism and Society in Crisis: John of Ephesus and the Lives of the Eastern Saints* (Berkeley, 1990); Michael Gaddis, *There Is No Crime for Those Who Have Christ: Religious Violence in the Christian Roman Empire* (Berkeley, 2005).
15. See Goehring, "Monastic Diversity," 61–83.
16. Leslie S. B. MacCoull, "Prophethood, Texts, and Artifacts," *Greek, Roman, and Byzantine Studies* 39, no. 3 (1998): 307–24 at 318.
17. See Fredrik Barth, "Boundaries and Connections," in Anthony Cohen, ed., *Signifying Identities: Anthropological Perspectives on Boundaries and Contested Values* (London, 2001), 17–36.
18. See Sizgorich, "Narrative and Community."
19. *Muḥammad Ibn Sīrat rasūl Allāh*, ed. Ferdinand Wüstenfeld, 3 vols. (Frankfurt am Main, 1961), 115–20. For a brief but thorough survey of the appearances of Baḥīrā in early Muslim texts connected with Muḥammad, see Uri Rubin, *Eye of the Beholder: The Life of Muhammad As Viewed by the Early Muslims—Textual Analysis* (Darwin Press, 1995), 49–52; cf. S. Gero, "The Legend of the Monk Baḥīrā: The Cult of the Cross, and Iconoclasm," in Pierre Canivet and Jean-Paul Rey-Coquais, eds. *La Syrie de Byzance à l'Islam* (Damascus: Institut français de Damas, 1992), 46–58, for a discussion of previous scholarship surrounding the Baḥīrā legend. For non-Muslim Baḥīrā stories, see Robert G. Hoyland, *Seeing Islam as Others Saw It: A Survey and Evaluation of Christian, Jewish and Zoroastrian Writings on Early Islam* (Princeton, 1997) 270–78, 476–79, 505–8, 538.
20. Al-Balādhurī, *Ansāb al-ashrāf*, I, ed. Muḥammad Hamīd Allāh, (Cairo, 1959), 96.
21. Muḥammad b. ʿAbd Allāh al-Azdī al-Baṣrī, *Taʾrīkh futūḥ al-Shām*, ed. ʿAbd al-Munʿim ʿAbd Allāh ʿĀmir (Cairo, 1970), 211.
22. ʿAbd Allāh b. Muḥammad b. ʿUbayd b. Abī al-Dunyā, *al-Riqqat wa-'l-bukāʾ*, ed. Musʿd ʿAbd al-Ḥamīd Muḥammad al-Saʿdanī (Cairo, 1996), 48 (#138).
23. See Nadia Maria El Cheikh, "Muḥammad and Heraclius: A Study in Legitimacy," *Studia Islamica* 89 (1999): 5–21; Lawrence I. Conrad, "Heraclius in Early Islamic

Kerygma," in *The Reign of Heraclius (610–641): Crisis and Confrontation*, ed. Gerrit J. Reinink and Bernard H. Stolte (Leuven, 2002), 113–56.

24. See Muqātil b. Sulaymān, *Tafsīr Muqātil b. Sulaymān*, ed. Aḥmad Farīd, 3 vols. (Beirut, 2003), 3:5–6. See Nadia Maria El Cheikh,. "Sūrat Al-Rūm: A Study of the Exegetical Literature." *Journal of the American Oriental Society* 118, no. 3 (1998): 359. The second/eighth century *tafsīr* of Mujāhid b. Jabr refers to the Roman victory as a victory of the "People of the Book over the People of Idols," although he does not connect the Roman success to the battle of Badr. See Mujāhid b. Jabr, *Tafsīr al-imām Mujāhid b. Jabr*, ed. Muḥammad ʿAbd al-Salām Abū al-Nīl (Cairo, 1989), 538. See also, from the third/ninth century, Hūd b. Muḥakkam al-Hawwārī, *Tafsīr Kitāb Allāh al-ʿazīz*, 4 vols., ed. Bālḥājj bin Saʿid Sharīfī (Beirut, 1990), 3:313.
25. The traditionalists with whom Wahb reports are described as "party of the *ahl al-ʿilm* who had left the *ahl al-Kitāb*." See See Abū Rifāʿa ʿUmāra b. Wathīma b. Mūsā b. al-Furāt al-Fārisī al-Fasawī, *Kitāb bad' al-ḥalq wa-qiṣaṣ al-anbiyā'*, ed. Raif Georges Khoury, *Les légends prophétiques dans l'Islam depuis le* 1e *jusqu'au III*[e] *siècle de l'Hégire* (Wiesbaden, 1978), 299:9–10.
26. See al-Fārisī, *Kitāb bad' al-ḥalq wa-qiṣaṣ al-anbiyā'*, ed. Khoury, 299–300. The Old Testament passage in question is Isa. 21:7. Al- Fārisī's text explains that although Jesus became known as *ṣāḥib al-ḥimār* "the donkey rider" (paired here and elsewhere in the text with Muḥammad as *ṣāḥib al-gamal*—"the camel rider"), he only rode the donkey once, apparently because possession of the donkey conflicted with his ascetic nature. The text explains that Jesus was a wandering ascetic, clothed only in hair, eating only barley, sleeping "wherever the night sheltered him." On resurrection day, the text continues, Jesus will be the head of the ascetics (*nāsikūn*).
27. See El Cheikh, "Muḥammad and Heraclius"; Conrad, "Heraclius in Early Islamic Kerygma."
28. See Nadia Maria El Cheikh, *Byzantium Viewed by the Arabs* (Cambridge, Mass., 2004), 21–138.
29. For this literature, see Hilary Kilpatrick, "Monasteries through Muslim Eyes: The Diyārāt Books," in David Thomas, ed., *Christians at the Heart of Muslim Rule: Church Life and Scholarship in ʿAbbasid Iraq* (Leiden, 2003), 19–37; Hilary Kilpatrick, "Representations of Social Intercourse between Muslims and Non-Muslims in Some Medieval Adab Works," in Jacques Waardenburg, ed., *Muslim Perceptions of Other Religions* (Oxford University Press, 1999) 213–24, esp. 217–19; Gérard Troupeau, "Les Couvents chrétiens dans la literature arabe," in Troupeau, *Etudes sur le christianisme arabe au Moyen Age* (Aldershot, 1995), ch. 20.
30. Kilpatrick, "Monasteries through Muslim Eyes"; Troupeau, "Les Couvents chrétiens."
31. For ʿAmmūriyya, see ʿUbayd Allāh b. ʿAbd Allāh b. Khurradādhbih, *Kitāb al-masālik wa-'l-mamālik*, ed. M. J. De Goeje (Leiden, 1889), 101–2; Abū al-Ḥassan ʿAli b. al-Ḥusayn b. ʿAlī al-Mas'ūdī, *Kitāb al-tanbīh wa-'l-ishrāf*, ed. M. J. De Goeje (reprint, Leiden, 1967), 169–71.

32. Abū l-Faraj al-Iṣbaḥānī, *Kitāb al-diyārāt*, ed. Jalil al-Attyeh (London, 1991), 48–52 = 'Abd al-Raḥmān Naṣr al-Shayzarī, *Rauḍat al-qulūb wa-nuzhat al-muḥibb wa-'l-maḥbūb*, manuscript facsimile, 38–40.
33. For early medieval Muslim raiding culture on the Byzantine frontier, see Michael Bonner, *Aristocratic Violence and Holy War: Studies in the Jihad and the Arab-Byzantine Frontier* (New Haven, Conn., 1996).
34. Abū l-Faraj al-Iṣbaḥānī, *Kitāb al-diyārāt*, ed. Jalil al-Attyeh, 112–14 = Abū l-Faraj al-Iṣbaḥānī, *Kitāb adab al-ghurabā'*, ed. Ṣalāḥ al-Dīn al-Munajjid (Beirut, 1972), 64–68.
35. See Kilpatrick, "Monasteries through Muslim Eyes," 23.
36. See the Latin translation of the Georgian original by P. Peeters, "La Passion de S. Michel le Sabaïte," *Analecta Bollandiana* 48 (1930): 65–98, here 68–70. See also the English translation by Monica J. Blanchard, "The Georgian Version of the Martyrdom of Saint Michael, Monk of Mar Sabas Monastery," *ARAM Periodical* 6 (1994): 149–63, here 150–52. This text is partly traditional Christian martyr story and partly apologetic dispute text. For this genre, in which Christian monks also figure prominently, see Sidney H. Griffith, "The Monk in the Emir's *Majlis*: Reflections on a Popular Genre of Christian Literary Apologetics in Arabic in the Early Islamic Period," in Hava Lazarus-Yefeh, Mark R. Cohen, Sasson Somekh, and Sidney H. Griffith, *The Majlis: Interreligious Encounters in Medieval Islam* (Wiesbaden, 1999), 13–65.
37. The *amīr* was fooled, but his deputies were not. When they informed the *amīr* about the Christian's trick, however, the *amīr* was simply charmed. See Mÿna of Nikiou, *The Life of Isaac of Alexandria*, ed. and French trans. E. Amélineau, *Histoire du patriarche Copte Isaac* (Paris, 1890), 67–71. English trans. David N. Bell, *The Life of Isaac of Alexandria and the Martyrdom of Saint Macrobius* (Kalamazoo: Cistercian Publications, 1988), 72. For 'Abd al-'Azīz's gentle relationship with Isaac's predecessor John, and with Isaac himself, see Sāwirūs b. al-Muqaffa', *History of the Patriarchs of Alexandria*, part 1, ch. 15, ed. and trans. B. Evetts, *Patrologia Orientalis* 5.1 (Paris, 1947) 16–18, 20; For 'Abd al-'Azīz's career of cooperation with Isaac's successor, Simon, see part 1, ch. 16, 27–42.
38. *The Life of Timothy of Kākhushtā*, Saidnaya Version, 23, ed. and trans. John C. Lamoreaux and Cyril Cairala, *Patrologia Orientalis* 48.4 (2000), 558–59.
39. See, for example, "The Apology of Timothy the Patriarch before the Caliph Mahdi," Syriac text ed. and trans. A. Mingana, *Woodbrooke Studies* 2 (1928): 1–162, here, 61f. See also the Arabic version, ed. Hans Putman, *L'Église et L'Islam sous Timothée I (780–823)* (Beirut, 1986), 32–33 (#162–68).
40. Thomas of Margā, *The Book of Governors*, ed. and trans. E. A. Wallis Budge, 2 vols. (London, 1893 [Piscataway, 2003]), 450–57, 656–58 (English), 239–45, 386–88 (Syriac).
41. Thomas of Margā, *Book of Governors*, ed. and trans. Wallis Budge, 451 (English), 240 (Syriac).

42. Thomas of Margā, *Book of Governors,* ed. and trans. Wallis Budge, 451–57 (English), 240–45 (Syriac).
43. Thomas of Margā, *Book of Governors,* ed. and trans. Wallis Budge, 656–58 (English), 386–88 (Syriac).
44. Rabban Mār Simon, *The History of Rabban Hōrmīzd,* XI–XII, trans. E. A. Wallis Budge, *The Histories of Rabban Hōrmīzd the Persian and Rabban Bar-ʿIdtā* (London, 1902 [Piscataway, N.J., 2003]), 101–6.
45. Ibn Abī Yaʿlā, *Ṭabaqāt al-fuqahāʾ al-Ḥanābila,* ed. ʿAlī Muḥammad ʿUmar, 2 vols. (Cairo, 1998), 1:268f.
46. *Life of Timothy of Kākhushtā,* Saidnaya Version, 33.9–33.11, ed. and trans. Lamoreaux and Cairala, 584–87.
47. *Life of Timothy of Kākhushtā,* Saidnaya Version, 43.1–43.6, ed. and trans. Lamoreaux and Cairala, 599–603.

Index